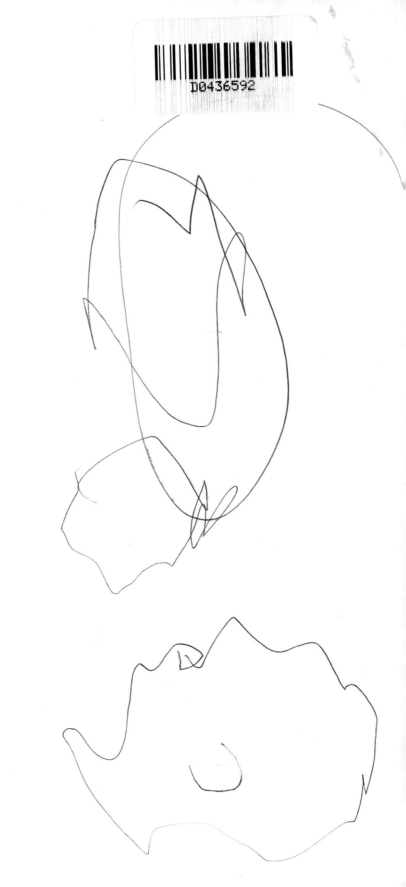

Measuring the Software Process

Measuring the Software Process

Statistical Process Control for Software Process Improvement

William A. Florac
Anita D. Carleton

ADDISON–WESLEY

Boston • San Francisco • New York • Toronto • Montreal
London • Munich • Paris • Madrid
Capetown • Sydney • Tokyo • Singapore • Mexico City

Software Engineering Institute

The SEI Series in Software Engineering

Many of the designations used by manufacturers and sellers to distinguish their products are claimed as trademarks. Where those designations appear in this book and Addison-Wesley was aware of a trademark claim, the designations have been printed in initial capital letters or all capitals.

The authors and publisher have taken care in the preparation of this book, but make no expressed or implied warranty of any kind and assume no responsibility for errors or omissions. No liability is assumed for incidental or consequential damages in connection with or arising out of the use of the information or programs contained herein.

The publisher offers discounts on this book when ordered in quantity for special sales. For more information, please contact:

U.S. Corporate and Government Sales
(800) 382-3419
corpsales@pearsoned.com

Visit AW on the Web at www.awprofessional.com

Special permission to use *Practical Software Measuremnet: Measuring for Process Management and Improvement,* CMU/SEI-97-HB-003, and *Goal-Driven Software Measurement—A Guidebook,* CMU/SEI-96-HB-002, by Carnegie Mellon University, in *Measuring the Software Process: Statistical Process Control for Software Process Improvement,* is granted by the Software Engineering Institute.

PSP and Personal Software Process are service marks of Carnegie Mellon University. Additional copyright information appears on page 250.

Library of Congress Cataloging-in-Publication Data

Florac, William A.
    Measuring the software process : statistical process control for
  software process improvement / William A. Florac, Anita D. Carleton.
      p. cm. -- (The SEI series in software engineering)
    Includes bibliographical references.
    ISBN 0-201-60444-2
    1. Software measurement. 2. Computer software--Quality control-
-Statistical methods. I. Carleton, Anita D. II. Title.
III. Series.
QA76.76.S65F56   1999
005.1'4--dc21
                                   99-20519
                                      CIP

Text printed on recycled and acid-free paper.
ISBN 0201604442
5 6 7 8 9 10 CRW 08 07 06 05
5th Printing August 2005

Contents

Figures

Foreword

A most useful guideline for people who are in trouble is: When you are in a hole, stop digging. Put the shovel down and think! Look at what is going on and try to understand the causes of the trouble. Remember that the software business has had serious problems for a very long time, and it won't get better by itself. While it is usually helpful to launch improvement programs, many such programs soon get bogged down in detail. They either address the wrong problems or they keep beating on the same solutions wondering why things don't improve. This is when you need an objective way to look at the problems. This is the time to get some data.

This book is for two kinds of groups: those who don't think that software work can be measured and those who have started measuring the software process but do not know what to do with the data. In either case, you most likely have two problems. First, you are unable to plan with any precision, and second, you cannot identify the causes of the organization's principal problems. This not only makes it difficult to do good software work; it also limits your ability to make orderly improvements.

Most people understand that data can be very useful. It would never occur to them, for example, to drive a car that did not have a gas gauge. When they get an unusually large electric or water or phone bill, they look at the attached data to understand why the bill is so big. They may then resolve to stop making so many long-distance phone calls on Sunday afternoons, or they might turn down the thermostat at night to conserve fuel.

For some reason, however, it never occurs to most software people to use data to guide their work. Even those professionals who accept the importance of data often have no idea what to measure, or what to do with the data once they have it. In one organization, the CEO was proud of the company tradition of making fact-based decisions. They really did run manufacturing this way, and they had achieved an enviable reputation for quality and productivity. So management not unnaturally decided to apply the same principles to software. Corporate headquarters put out a directive: "Henceforth, all the company's software groups will start measurement programs." When I visited the group, this directive had been in place for several years, and the software people had gathered mountains of data. While these data were all recorded in a giant database, as far as I could tell, nobody had yet used any of the data. They had what I call a write-only database.

This book will help you to address such problems. It describes many useful software measures, and it gives fully worked-out examples of how to use the data you gather. The emphasis is on the use of statistical process control methods to understand process behavior, and to bring stability, predictability, and improvement to software processes. It starts by providing a framework for measuring and analyzing process behavior, and walks you through the reasons to measure, measurement planning, and data collection. It then deals with data analysis and the methods for analyzing the data that you have. Next, it discusses how to use these data to improve your software process. The final book chapter is particularly useful, since it answers many of the questions you will likely be asked as you start to apply statistical process control methods and techniques.

This book is easy to read, and it is small enough to be read in a few hours. While there are a few formulas, none of them are complicated and they are very clearly explained. There are also many completely worked-out examples. The software process "state-of-the-practice" is now at the point where many organizations are considering using statistical process control. If you are in such a group, or expect to be, this book is just what you have been looking for.

Watts S. Humphrey
March 1, 1999
Sarasota, Florida

Preface

This book is about using statistical process control (SPC) and control charts to measure and analyze software processes. It shows how characteristics of software products and processes can be measured and analyzed using statistical process control so that the performance of activities that produce the products can be managed, predicted, controlled, and improved to achieve business and technical goals.

If you are a software manager or practitioner who has responsibilities for product quality or process performance, and if you are ready to define, collect, and use measurements to manage, control, and predict your software processes, then this book is for you. It will put you on the road to using measurement data to control and improve process performance. Not only will the discussions here introduce you to important concepts, but also they will introduce you to tried-and-true process measurement and analysis methods as set forth in a software environment.

On the other hand, if your organization does not yet have basic measurement processes in place, you should make establishing measures for planning and managing projects your first priority. Handbooks such as *Practical Software Measurement: A Foundation for Objective Project Management* [McGarry 1998] and *Goal-Driven Software Measurement* [Park 1996] make excellent starting points, as do the examples and advice found in books by people such as Watts S. Humphrey and Robert B. Grady [Humphrey 1989; Grady 1987, 1992].

This book is an extension and elaboration of the Software Engineering Institute (SEI) guidebook *Practical Software Measurement: Measuring for Process Management and Improvement* [Florac 1997]. The guidebook grew out of a collaborative effort with the authors of *Practical Software Measurement: A Foundation for Objective Project Management* [McGarry 1998]. Both publications were written to encourage and guide software organizations to use measurements to quantitatively manage software projects and processes.

This book is organized into eight chapters. The focus of Chapter 1 is to introduce you to the primary concepts associated with managing, measuring, controlling, and improving software processes. The motivation for using statistical process control is also discussed—that is, utilizing control charts for making process decisions and for predicting process behavior. This chapter begins by characterizing the term *software process,* especially as it is used in SPC applications. Issues of process performance, stability, compliance, capability, and improvement are briefly introduced (and elaborated throughout the book) since these form the basis for improving process performance. A section on measuring process behavior then follows. A framework for measuring process behavior is presented next and serves as the guiding structure for the rest of the book. The remaining chapters follow this framework with more detailed discussions, expanding on the activities associated with using statistical process control techniques for improving the software process.

The focus of Chapter 2 is to discuss the activities associated with measuring the software process. They include identifying process management issues, selecting and defining the measures, and integrating the measurement activities with the organization's processes. The idea here is to understand what you want to measure and why and to select appropriate measures that will provide insight into your issues.

In Chapter 3, we discuss the specifics associated with collecting software process data. The principal tasks include designing methods and obtaining tools for data collection, training staff to execute the data collection procedures, and capturing and recording the data. Additionally, there is a discussion of many of the important tools available to analyze, understand, and explain causal relationships to the process performance data.

In Chapter 4, we embark on the initial discussion of analyzing process behavior with Shewhart's control charts by graphically illustrating the concepts of process variation and stability. The basics of constructing control charts, calculating limits, and detecting anomalous process behavior are given to provide a basis for the ensuing chapters.

Chapter 5 is dedicated to providing the information to construct and calculate limits for the several different control charts applicable to software processes. Examples of the calculations and charts are set in familiar software settings.

Chapter 6 discusses a number of topics that arise when using control charts. Guidelines are offered for how much data is necessary for control charting, recognizing anomalous process behavior patterns, rational subgrouping, aggregation of data, and insufficient data granularity.

Chapter 7 provides insight on what actions to take after you have plotted your data on process behavior charts. The actions involve removing assignable causes of instability, changing the process to make it more capable, or seeking ways to continually improve the process.

The book concludes with Chapter 8. It provides ten steps for getting started using statistical process control, cites the experiences by some of those who have used statistical process control in a software environment, and addresses a number of frequently asked questions.

The appendixes include several of the more commonly used tables for calculation of control chart limits and a special topics section that contains detailed discussions addressing statistical process control fundamentals. For those who wish to learn more about the topics addressed in this book, we have included an extensive list of references following the appendixes.

Everything in this book has its roots in experience—often that of the authors, at times that of others. Much of the experience comes from software settings, while other lessons are adapted from other service- and industrial-oriented environments. Some of the numerical examples are composed rather than factual; in others, the names of organizations providing the data are disguised to maintain confidentiality. We have tried to ensure that the examples represent reasonable extensions of practices that have been demonstrated to be meaningful and successful in software settings.

The focus, then, is on the acquisition of quantitative information and the use of statistical process control methods to help you to reliably identify the problems (and the opportunities) present in the processes you operate. When the methods are properly used, you can confidently use the results to control and predict your process behavior and guide your improvement actions. We recognize that much more can be said about the use of measurements and statistical methods for controlling and improving processes than this book addresses. On the other hand, we have striven to provide the information, ideas, and methods that are sufficient for you to get started using statistical process control to better understand the behavior of your software processes. We trust that it will encourage you and others to begin applying the concepts that it explains and illustrates.

Acknowledgments

This book represents the aggregation of many years' lessons and experiences in undertaking software process improvement initiatives and from implementing software measurement practices. Throughout the years, we have learned a great deal from a great many—what software process improvement entails, what it means to implement a measurement program, what to measure, how to measure, and how to use measurements to manage projects. We are indebted to Watts S. Humphrey for influencing our thinking on software process improvement and quantitative software process management.

These experiences, in turn, have led us to ask more questions. How can we use measurements to control, improve, and, better yet, predict? This questioning brought us to the use of statistical techniques, specifically to the world of statistical process control (SPC). This is where our diagnostic journey began.

We learned about basic statistical process control issues and techniques from Donald J. Wheeler, Douglas C. Montgomery, Thomas Pyzdek, Gerald J. Hahn, and the authors of the Western Electric *Statistical Quality Control Handbook*. We are indebted to them all for presenting SPC concepts in a very understandable and pragmatic way.

We would also like to acknowledge the support and contributions of our colleagues and friends at the SEI and in the software community. First, we are grateful to our friend and colleague Robert E. Park. Bob was our coauthor on *Practical Software Measurement: Measuring for Process Management and Improvement*, the SEI guidebook that served as a starting point for our work. We appreciated Bob's tenacity in researching the "roots" of SPC and his meticulous attention to all of the details for producing the SEI guidebook. Thanks to Bob, our work had a solid foundation from which to go forward. We also appreciate the enthusiastic support and encouragement from Dave Zubrow and Bill Peterson at the SEI. We also are grateful for the insights, discussions, and review comments from our colleagues associated with the Practical Software Measurement Project: Jack McGarry, Dave Card, Pam Geriner, and Betsy Clark. We would also like to thank Julie Barnard, Betsy Clark, Watts S. Humphrey, Dan Nash, Dan Paulish, Mark Paulk, Ed Weller, and Dave Zubrow for reviewing the manuscript and offering many helpful comments. We also want to especially acknowledge Julie Barnard, Calvin Armstrong, Ricardo de la Fuente, Ted Keller, and Tom Peterson involved with the Space Shuttle Onboard Software Project for engaging in a collaboration with us to learn practical applications of SPC. We appreciated their enthusiasm, willingness, and openness in working with their data and with experimenting and learning with us. All of these folks encouraged our work and provided support in many ways for which we are very grateful.

Special thanks go to Peter Gordon, Helen Goldstein, Marty Rabinowitz, and Katherine Pizzuti at Addison Wesley Longman, Inc., and to copyeditor Jean Peck and compositor Rob Mauhar for their help in producing this book. We appreciated their advice and guidance in this process.

Finally, we want to recognize the support and enthusiasm of our respective spouses, Marilyn Florac and Dennis Carleton. Somehow, you knew just when we needed some words of encouragement, some quiet moments, or a cup of hot chocolate. Our deepest thanks for your patience, love, and understanding.

William A. Florac and Anita D. Carleton

1

Managing and Measuring Process Behavior

We can, however, no longer muddle through on intuition; the process is too complex and the products too important.

Watts S. Humphrey 1989

Every organization asks the question, Are we achieving the results we desire? This question is expressed in many ways: Are we meeting our business objectives? Are our customers satisfied with our products and services? Are we earning a fair return on our investment? Can we reduce the cost of producing these products or services? How can we improve the response to our customers' needs or increase the functionality of our products? How can we improve our competitive position? Are we achieving the growth required for survival? For many software organizations, the answers to questions like these are rooted in the relationships that exist within the organization's basic makeup, its overall philosophy, its people, its management, and the facilities and operational processes used by the organization to deliver its products and services.

The understanding and the appreciation of this relationship have not come easily to organizations in the software industry, be they in the defense sector or the commercial sector. After years of software product development characterized by missed schedules, overexpenditures, burnt-out engineers, and poor-quality products, competitive pressure and the increasing demand for more software products, and for more reliable ones, made it imperative to find a better way to produce software products and services. Initially, new technology innovations and improvements (languages, compilers, CASE tools, and so forth) were viewed as the "silver bullet." For the most part, the technology helped, but it did not provide the breakthrough desired.

In the meantime, other industries were also finding it necessary to find a better way to compete and produce quality products due to worldwide competition. They began to adopt the approach advocated by W. Edwards Deming and successfully implemented by many competitive industries in Japan. Deming's approach, greatly influenced by the work of Walter A. Shewhart, deals with the notions of process management and continual improvement. Deming's approach contends that to be competitive, improve quality, and increase productivity, the following actions are required:

- Focus on the processes that generate the products and services to improve quality and productivity. Consider the task of building the product or providing the service as a series of integrated and interconnected processes.
- Ensure that the processes are properly supported.
- Manage poorly behaving processes by fixing the process, not blaming the people.
- Recognize that variation is present in all processes and that existence of variation is an opportunity for improvement. Improvement comes from reducing variation.
- Take variation into account in the decision-making process. Management action uses data from the process to guide decisions.

As you may surmise, the preceding "process-thinking" principles require a unique relationship within the organization, involving its management and management philosophy, its people, and the management of the processes used to produce products and provide services. These principles are embodied in Shewhart's continual improvement cycle [Shewhart 1939], popularized by Deming [Deming 1986], which has been characterized as "Plan, Do, Check (or Study), Act" (PDCA). It is an iterative learning cycle that allows one to continually improve processes by learning, evaluating and working on improvement one step at a time.

These notions of process thinking were adapted to the development of software by Watts S. Humphrey in his book *Managing the Software Process* [Humphrey 1989]. Humphrey related this process thinking to the software development process by constructing a framework of software process maturity levels having the objective of achieving a controlled and measured process as a foundation for continual improvement.

Over the past decade, the concepts, methods, and practices associated with process management and continual improvement have gained wide acceptance in the software community. These concepts, methods, and practices embody a way of thinking, a way of acting, and a way of understanding the data generated by processes that collectively result in improved quality, increased productivity, and competitive products.

The acceptance and the use of this process-thinking approach by much of the software industry have required many of those charged with collecting and analyzing software data to consider ways to measure software processes that are responsive to questions relating to process performance (such as effectiveness, efficiency, timeliness, predictability, improvements, and product quality) in quantitative terms. Traditional software measurement and analysis methods, those that provide status at a point in time and compare against the "plan," are not sufficient for determining past process performance or for predicting process performance.

Other disciplines have addressed this issue by using statistical process control methods, specifically using Shewhart's control charts. Managers and engineers within the manufacturing, chemical, petroleum, food-processing, electronics, and aerospace industries have used control charts for many years. They have come to realize that control charts provide the basis for making process decisions and predicting process behavior.

However, there are those in the software community who look upon the use of control charts as an analysis tool unique to manufacturing or high-quantity, repetitive processes. Since they view the software development process as a highly human-centric, intellectual, design-oriented process, they reason that statistical process control and control charts are not applicable and cannot (or should not) be used to measure software processes. Needless to say, our experience does not support such reasoning and is, in fact, quite the contrary.

We have come to appreciate the value added when control charts are used to provide engineers and managers with quantitative insights into the behavior of their software development processes. In many ways, the control chart is a form of instrumentation—like an oscilloscope, or a temperature probe, or a pressure gauge—providing data to guide decisions and judgment by process-knowledgeable engineers and managers.

We recognize that statistical process control principles and control charts have received little use as of yet in most software organizations. Nevertheless, we refuse to let the current state of software measurement stop us from promoting their use. The benefits of the empirical methods associated with statistical process control (SPC) have been so evident in other development, production, and service activities that it would be foolish to ignore their potential for improving software products and services.

1.1   What Is a Software Process?

The term *process* means different things to different people, so it is important to clearly define what we mean when we use the word, especially in the context of a software development or support environment.

> *A process can be defined as the logical organization of people, materials, energy, equipment, and procedures into work activities designed to produce a specified end result.*
>
> Gabriel A. Pall 1987

Pall's definition of *process* is illustrated in Figure 1.1. It differs from the definitions of *process* and *software process* given in the Capability Maturity Model (CMM) for Software[1] in that it includes people, materials, energy, and equipment within the scope of *process*. Version 1.1 of the CMM, by way of contrast, views a process as a "sequence of steps" performed by people with the aid of tools and equipment to transform raw material into a product [Paulk 1993b, 1995].

---

[1] Capability Maturity Model and CMM are service marks of Carnegie Mellon University.

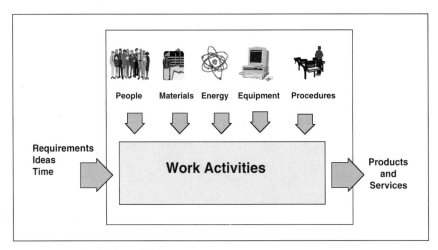

People   Materials   Energy   Equipment   Procedures

Requirements
Ideas
Time

Work Activities

Products
and
Services

FIGURE 1.1   Definition of *Process*

Including people, materials, energy, and tools within the concept of process becomes important when we begin to apply the principles of statistical process control to improve process performance and process capability. Here, we use measures of variability to identify opportunities for improving the quality of products and the capability of processes. In searching for causes of unusual variation, it would be a mistake to exclude people, materials, energy, and tools from the scope of the investigation. This view of process, as enunciated by Pall, has been at the very heart of statistical process control since its founding in the 1920s [Shewhart 1931; Western Electric 1958; Juran 1988].

In keeping with the broad view of process, we use the term *software process* in this book to refer, not just to an organization's overall software process, but to any process or subprocess used by a software project or organization. In fact, a good case can be made that it is only at subprocess levels that true process management and improvement can take place. Thus, readers should view the concept of software process as applying to any identifiable activity that is undertaken to produce or support a software product or service. This includes planning, estimating, designing, coding, testing, inspecting, reviewing, measuring, and controlling, as well as the subtasks and activities that comprise these undertakings.

1.2   What Is Software Process Management?

Software process management is about successfully managing the work processes associated with developing, maintaining, and supporting software products and software-intensive systems. By successful management, we mean that the products and services produced by the processes conform fully to both internal and external customer requirements and that they meet the business objectives of the organization responsible for producing the products.

This concept of process management is founded on the principles of statistical process control. These principles hold that, by establishing and sustaining stable levels of variability, processes will yield predictable results. We can then say that the processes are *under statistical control*. This was first enunciated by Shewhart as follows:

> *A phenomenon will be said to be controlled when, through the use of past experience, we can predict, at least within limits, how the phenomenon may be expected to vary in the future.*
>
> Walter A. Shewhart 1931

Controlled processes are stable processes, and stable processes enable you to predict results. This, in turn, enables you to prepare achievable plans, meet cost estimates and scheduling commitments, and deliver required product functionality and quality with acceptable and reasonable consistency. If a controlled process is not capable of meeting customer requirements or other business objectives, the process must be improved or retargeted.

At the individual level, then, the objective of software process management is to ensure that the processes you operate or supervise are predictable, meet customer needs, and (where appropriate) are continually being improved. From the larger, organizational perspective, the objective of process management is to ensure that the same holds true for every process within the organization.

1.3 The Role of Software Process Management

In this section, we identify four key responsibilities of software process management and show how they relate to measurement of process performance. Our discussion of the activities and issues associated with the responsibilities will be neither all encompassing nor definitive, but it will provide a starting point from which process measurement methods and techniques can be developed with something more substantial than just abstract terms. The four responsibilities that are central to process management are as follows:

1. Define the process.
2. Measure the process.
3. Control the process (ensure that variability is stable so that results are predictable).
4. Improve the process.

These responsibilities are analogous to Shewhart's continual improvement cycle [Shewhart 1939], popularized by Deming [Deming 1986], and characterized as "Plan, Do, Check (or Study), Act" (PDCA). As an iterative learning cycle, it allows you to improve processes by learning, evaluating, and working on improvement in step-by-step fashion and, by continuing with this cycle, to reduce process variation.

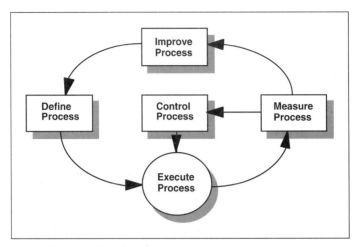

FIGURE 1.2   The Four Key Responsibilities of Process Management

The four key responsibilities of process management are shown as boxes in Figure 1.2. Execution of the process is depicted with a different (circular) shape because execution is not a process management responsibility. Rather, it is an inherent responsibility of project management, whether performed by a software developer or a software maintainer. People responsible for process management may have project management responsibilities as well, and project managers may implicitly assume process management responsibility for processes that they define and use.

A concept of process ownership is implicit in Figure 1.2. Responsibility for this ownership lies with the function of process management. This is especially so whenever processes cross organizational boundaries or involve multiple organizational entities. Process ownership includes responsibilities for process design, for establishing and implementing mechanisms for measuring the process, and for taking corrective action where necessary [Pall 1987].

The following subsections outline the four key responsibilities of process management.

1.3.1   DEFINING THE PROCESS

Defining a software process creates the disciplined and structured environment required for controlling and improving the process. Management's responsibility to define each process inherently includes responsibilities for implementing and sustaining the process. The four key objectives associated with defining, implementing, and sustaining are to

1. Design processes that can meet or support business and technical objectives.

2. Identify and define the issues, models, and measures that relate to the performance of the processes.

3. Provide the infrastructures (the set of methods, people, and practices) that are needed to support software activities.

4. Ensure that the software organization has the ability to execute and sustain the processes (skills, training, tools, facilities, and funds).

1.3.2 MEASURING THE PROCESS

Measurements are the basis for detecting deviations from acceptable performance. They are also the basis for identifying opportunities for process improvement. The three key objectives of process measurement are to

1. Collect data that measure the performance of each process.

2. Analyze the performance of each process.

3. Retain and use the data as follows:

- To assess process stability and capability.
- To interpret the results of observations and analyses.
- To predict future costs and performance.
- To provide baselines and benchmarks.
- To plot trends.
- To identify opportunities for improvement.

1.3.3 CONTROLLING THE PROCESS

Controlling a process means keeping the process within its normal (inherent) performance boundaries—that is, making the process behave consistently. This involves

- Measurement (obtaining information about process performance).
- Detection (analyzing the information to identify variations in the process that are due to assignable causes).
- Correction (taking steps to remove variation due to assignable causes from the process and to remove the results of process drift from the product) [Pall 1987].

To say this another way, the three key actions needed to establish and maintain control of a software process are to

1. Determine whether or not the process is under control (is stable with respect to the inherent variability of measured performance).

2. Identify performance variations that are caused by process anomalies (assignable causes).

3. Eliminate the sources of assignable causes so as to stabilize the process.

Once a process is under control, sustaining activities must be undertaken to forestall the effects of entropy. Without sustaining activities, processes can easily fall victim to the forces of ad hoc change or disuse and deteriorate to out-of-control states. This requires reinforcing the use of defined processes through continuing management oversight, measurement, benchmarking, and process assessments.

1.3.4   IMPROVING THE PROCESS

Even though a process may be defined and under control, it may not be capable of producing products that meet customer needs or organizational objectives. For most organizations, processes must be technologically competitive, adaptable, and timely, and they must produce products that consistently meet customer and business needs. Moreover, resources must be available and capable of performing and supporting the processes. Processes can be improved by making changes that improve their existing capabilities or by replacing existing subprocesses with others that are more effective or efficient. In either case, the three key process improvement objectives of an organization are to

1. Understand the characteristics of existing processes and the factors that affect process capability.
2. Plan, justify, and implement actions that will modify the processes so as to better meet business needs.
3. Assess the impacts and benefits gained, and compare these to the costs of changes made to the processes.

1.4   Issues on the Road to Process Improvement

All processes are designed to produce results. The products and services they deliver and the ways they deliver them have measurable attributes that can be observed to describe the quality, quantity, cost, and timeliness of the results produced. If we know the current values of these attributes, and if a process is not delivering the qualities we desire, we will have reference points to start from when introducing and validating process adjustments and improvements.

So, our first concern on the road to process improvement is to understand the existing performance of the processes we use—to ask, What are they producing now? Knowing how a process is performing will enable us to assess the repeatability of the process and whether or not it is meeting its internal and external needs. Notice that we said "how," not "how well." When we measure process performance, our purpose is not to be judgmental, but simply to get the facts. Once the facts are in hand and we know the current levels and variabilities of the values that are measured, we can proceed to evaluating the information from other perspectives. Our first concern, then, is that of *process performance.*

- **Performance.** What is the process producing now with respect to measurable attributes of quality, quantity, cost, and time?

Measures of process performance quantify and make visible the ability of a process to deliver products with the qualities, timeliness, and costs that customers and businesses require. When measurements of process performance vary erratically and unpredictably over time, the process is not in control. To attain control, we must ensure first that we have a process whose variability is stable, for without stability we cannot predict results. So, another important property associated with any process is that of *process stability*.

- **Stability.** Is the process that we are managing behaving predictably?

How do we know whether a process is stable? We examine process performance through the use of process behavior charts that allow us to determine whether the process is stable (within limits) and hence predictable. If process performance is erratic and unpredictable, we must take action to stabilize that process. Stability of a process depends on support for and faithful operation of the process. Three questions that should concern people responsible for processes are

1. Is the process supported such that it will be stable if operated according to the definition?

2. Is the process, as defined, being executed faithfully?

3. Is the organization fit to execute the process?

Questions of this sort address the issue of *process compliance*.

- **Compliance.** Are the processes sufficiently supported? Are they faithfully executed? Is the organization fit to execute the process?

Having a stable and compliant process does not mean that process performance is satisfactory. The process must also be capable, meaning that variations in the characteristics of the product and in the operational performance of the process, when measured over time, fall within the ranges required for business success. Measures of *process capability* relate the performance of the process to the specifications that the product or process must satisfy.

- **Capability.** Is the process capable of delivering products that meet requirements? Does the performance of the process meet the business needs of the organization?

If a software process is not capable of consistently meeting product requirements and business needs, or if an organization is to satisfy ever-increasing demands for higher quality, robustness, complexity, and market responsiveness while moving to new technologies and improving its competitive position, people in the organization will be faced with the need to continually improve process performance. Understanding the capability of the subprocesses that make up each software process is the first step in making progress toward *process improvement*.

- **Improvement.** What can we do to improve the performance of the process? What would enable us to reduce variability? What would let us move the mean to a more profitable level? How do we know that the changes we have introduced are working?

Resolution of these process improvement issues revolves around measurement and analysis of process performance, which leads to the question of process measurement.

1.5   The Need for Software Process Measurement

Advances in technology are continually increasing the demand for software that is larger, more robust, and more reliable over ever-widening ranges of application. The demands on software management are increasing correspondingly. Software developers and maintainers—managers and technical staff alike—are repeatedly confronted with new technologies, more competitive markets, increased competition for experienced personnel, and demands for faster responsiveness [Card 1995]. At the same time, they continue to be concerned about open-ended requirements, uncontrolled changes, insufficient testing, inadequate training, arbitrary schedules, insufficient funding, and issues related to standards, product reliability, and product suitability.-

Software measurement by itself cannot solve these problems, but it can clarify and focus your understanding of them. Moreover, when done properly, sequential measurements of quality attributes of products and processes can provide an effective foundation for initiating and managing process improvement activities.

The success of any software organization is contingent on being able to make predictions and commitments relative to the products it produces. Effective measurement processes help software groups succeed by enabling them to understand their capabilities so that they can develop achievable plans for producing and delivering products and services. Measurements also enable people to detect trends and to anticipate problems, thus providing better control of costs, reducing risks, improving quality, and ensuring that business objectives are achieved.

Using measurements to manage and improve software processes shows how quality characteristics of software products and processes can be quantified, plotted, and analyzed. In turn, the performance of activities that produce the products can be predicted, controlled, and guided to achieve business and technical goals. In short, measurement methods that identify important events and trends and that effectively separate signals from noise are invaluable in guiding software organizations to informed decisions.

Not surprisingly, when we decide to measure, measurement questions and issues arise: What should be measured? How should the characteristics be measured? What is the data telling us? How is our process behaving? What are the signals that we should be reacting to? How do we know that something is a signal? What should we do when we recognize a signal? These questions and similar ones form the basis for this book. In the chapters that follow, we present the principles and fundamentals of process measurement as applied to software for use by software engineers and managers engaged in managing and improving their software processes.

1.6   Measuring Process Behavior

For measurement activities to be cost-effective, they must be designed and targeted to support the business goals of your organization and provide effective, economical information for decision making. This is not as simple and straightforward as it may sound. One of the dangers in enterprises as complex as software development and support is that there are potentially so many things to measure that we are easily overwhelmed by opportunities [Park 1996].

Experience has taught us that we must identify the critical factors that determine whether or not we will be successful in meeting our goals [Basili 1994]. These critical factors are often associated with issues. Issues, in turn, relate to risks that threaten our ability to meet goals, responsibilities, or commitments. Goals and issues serve to identify and focus the measurements needed to quantify the status and performance of software processes.

To help address business goals, we can usefully view software management functions as falling into three broad classes: *project management*, *process management*, and *product engineering*. These management functions address different concerns, each with its own objectives and issues.

1. **Project management.** The objectives of software project management are to set and meet achievable commitments regarding cost, schedule, quality, and function delivered—as they apply to individual development or maintenance projects. The key management issues are those that appear to jeopardize these commitments. Software project management is interested primarily in creating achievable plans and in tracking the status and progress of its products relative to its plans and commitments.

2. **Process management.** The objectives of process management are to ensure that the processes within the organization are performing as expected, to ensure that defined processes are being followed, and to make improvements to the processes so as to meet business objectives (such as lowering risks associated with commitments and improving the ability to produce quality products).

3. **Product engineering.** The objectives of product engineering are to ensure customer acceptance of and satisfaction with the product. The issues of greatest concern relate primarily to the physical and dynamic attributes of the product—architecture, producibility, reliability, usability, responsiveness, stability, performance, and so forth. Information about these attributes and customer satisfaction is important to assessing the attainment of product engineering goals.

The kinds of data that are needed to achieve these objectives can differ significantly across these three management functions. Moreover, there are many interactions among the functions in most software organizations. In many cases, these interactions lead to conflicting demands that must be managed. In addition, various organizational entities—corporate, division, program, staff, project, and functional groups—often have different goals, together with differing issues, perspectives, and interests, even when sharing the same overall business goals. This frequently leads to differing measurement needs and priorities. But whatever the priorities, the business goals, objectives, strategies, and plans for all organizations are formed around these fundamental objectives:

- Providing competitive products or services in terms of functionality, time to market, quality, and cost.
- Meeting commitments to customers with respect to products and services.

Success in meeting commitments while achieving or exceeding goals for functionality, quality, cost, and time to market implies a need to ensure that commitments are achievable. This, in turn, implies a need to predict outcomes and evaluate risks.

The processes that software organizations use to produce products and services have critical roles in the execution of strategies and plans aimed at these objectives. Organizations that can control their processes are able to predict the characteristics of their products and services, predict their costs and schedules, and improve the effectiveness, efficiency, and profitability of their business and technical operations.

For example, if our business goals are based on function, cost, time to market, and quality, we can identify both project and process issues (concerns) that relate to achieving these goals. Process performance can then be quantified by measuring attributes of products produced by our processes as well as by measuring process attributes directly. Figure 1.3 lists some typical business goals that often concern us and relates these goals to corresponding project and process issues and examples of attributes that can be measured to assess the performance of a process with respect to these issues.

Measurements of attributes like those shown in column 4 of Figure 1.3 are important, not just because they can be used to describe products and processes, but because they can be used to control the processes that produce the products, thus making future process performance predictable. Measurements of product and process attributes can also be used to quantify process performance and guide us in making process improvements. This, in turn, helps keep our operations competitive and profitable.

In addition to product and process attributes like those listed in column 4 of Figure 1.3, there are two properties of the process itself that are important to successfully achieving business goals: *process stability* and *process capability*. These properties are orthogonal to all measures of process and product attributes.

Process stability, as we shall see shortly, lies at the heart of all process management and process improvement efforts. It is what enables us to act as if results are repeatable. Process stability lets us predict future performance and prepare

Business Goals	Project Issues	Process Issues	Measurable Product and Process Attributes
Increase function	Product growth Product stability	Product conformance	Number of requirements Product size Product complexity Rates of change Percent nonconforming
Reduce cost	Budgets Expenditure rates	Efficiency Productivity Rework	Product size Product complexity Effort Number of changes Requirements stability
Reduce time to market	Schedule Progress	Production rate Responsiveness	Elapsed time, normalized for product characteristics
Improve product quality	Product performance Product correctness Product reliability	Predictability Problem recognition Root cause analysis	Number of defects introduced Effectiveness of defect detection activities Mean time to failure (MTTF)

FIGURE 1.3   Business Goals, Project and Process Issues, and Related Measurable Attributes

achievable plans. It also provides a basis for separating signal from noise so that departures from stability can be recognized and become the basis for effective control and improvement actions.

If a process is in statistical control, and if a sufficiently large proportion of the results fall within the specification limits, the process is termed *capable*. Thus, a capable process is a stable process whose performance satisfies customer requirements.

Stability and capability will be described and illustrated in greater detail in Chapters 4 and 7. For now, we simply point out that assessments of process stability and process capability are obtained by measuring attributes of product and process quality and analyzing the variability and central tendency in the measured results. The measures that we use are often the same ones that we use when quantifying business-related issues like those listed in Figure 1.3. We also use the same measures, together with data that characterize the resources used by the processes, to quantify and analyze issues associated with process compliance and process improvement.

Because of the multiplicity of goals, issues, processes, and perspectives within any organization, it makes little sense to attempt to lay out detailed instructions for measuring all conceivable product and process attributes. Instead, this book focuses on the acquisition of quantitative information and the use of statistical process control methods to help you to reliably identify the problems (and the opportunities) present in the processes you operate.

1.7   A Framework for Process Behavior Measurement

The means for improving these processes and products becomes critical. The performance of the processes, the effectiveness of these processes, and the capability of the processes become important considerations as we mature and improve our operations and enterprises. Figure 1.4 outlines a framework for measuring and improving process behavior. Notice that this process behavior measurement framework also serves as the guiding structure for how the following activities are discussed in this book:

- **Clarify business goals.** Understand how your business goals, objectives, strategies, and plans relate to your software processes. Business goals based on functionality, cost, time to market, and quality have both project and process issues that must be addressed to provide competitive products and services to customers and to meet customer commitments.

- **Identify and prioritize issues.** Identify the critical issues that determine whether or not your processes succeed in meeting the goals that you have set forth. Processes that have experienced problems or issues in the past or that are executed for the first time or across various projects or organizational boundaries may serve as prime candidates for study or investigation.

- **Select and define measures.** Select measures that will help you to characterize your processes or products. Create an operational definition for the measure(s) that you have selected. To have an operational definition, you must know what the data represents and how the data is collected. The primary objective of measuring is to control and improve your processes.

- **Collect, verify, and retain data.** Collect data to visualize your process or to investigate assignable causes and potential improvements, and organize and summarize the data for patterns, trends, and relationships. You will most likely need to measure the process of interest over a period of time.

- **Analyze process behavior.** Using appropriate calculations (based on the data), plot the measurement data on the control charts. Assess whether the process is stable. If it is stable, you can assess the capability of the process. If the process is not stable, you will need to identify and remove assignable causes.

- **Evaluate process performance.** After the process performance measurements are analyzed and plotted on control charts (process behavior charts), the results will more than likely point to one of three directions: removing assignable causes, changing the process, or continually improving the process.

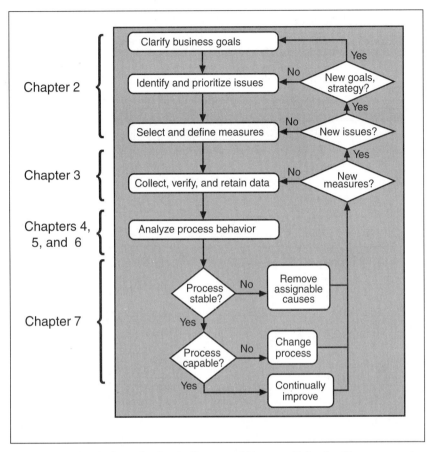

FIGURE 1.4   Book Organization in Context of Process Behavior Measurement Framework

1.8   Summary

Over the past decade, practices associated with process management and continual improvement have gained increased importance in the software community. These concepts, methods, and practices embody a way of thinking, a way of acting, and a way of understanding the data generated by the processes that collectively result in improved quality, increased productivity, and competitive products. The acceptance of this "process-thinking" approach has motivated many to start measuring software processes that are responsive to questions relating to process performance. In that vein, traditional software measurement and analysis methods of measuring "planned versus actual" are not sufficient for measuring process performance or for predicting process performance. So, the time has come, we believe, to marry, if you will, the process thinking with "statistical thinking" [Britz 1997], which embraces three principles:

1. All work occurs in a system of interconnected processes.

2. Variation exists in all processes.

3. Understanding and reducing variation are keys to success.

The first principle stresses a quality management axiom that work should be viewed as a process that can be studied and improved, yielding better products and results. It also stresses the important point that processes do not operate in isolation but are intertwined with the system as a whole. This is consistent with the systems view that suboptimizing parts of a system can have a disastrous consequence on the rest of the system. The second principle—variation exists in all processes—is also an important point to understand. Every process displays variation, but we need to understand how and why measurements vary and the result of measurement interactions. The third principle about understanding and reducing variation is consistent with Deming's and Shewhart's interpretations and is aimed at not only quantifying the variation but also actually doing something about it—improving it.

Other disciplines have addressed these principles by applying statistical process control methods to the improvement of their processes. Specifically, they have used control charts (or process behavior charts) for making process decisions and predicting process behavior. It is time to examine how statistical process control techniques can help to address our software issues.

Improving software processes requires an understanding of the process, executing the process, monitoring the behavior of the process and collecting data on it, analyzing the data to control and improve the process, and taking appropriate action based on the data. This may entail removing assignable causes, stabilizing the variability, and improving the process performance.

A framework for measuring process performance includes the following activities:

- Clarifying business goals.
- Identifying and prioritizing issues.
- Selecting and defining measures.
- Collecting, verifying, and retaining data.
- Analyzing process behavior.
- Evaluating process performance.

By working through this framework, you will be able to understand the concepts and issues that lie behind classical statistical process control (SPC), the steps associated with effectively implementing and using SPC, and real examples with software data that demonstrate how SPC can be applied to software process improvement.

2

Planning for Measurement

Measurement is a sampling process designed to tell us something about the universe in which we live that will enable us to predict the future in terms of the past through the establishment of principles or natural laws.

Walter A. Shewhart 1931

The purpose of this chapter is to examine and discuss the activities that are prerequisite to collecting and analyzing process performance data. The material will cover topics contained in the first three shaded blocks in Figure 2.1.

Measuring the software process commences with planning. Measurement planning progresses in three stages: *identifying* process management issues, *selecting and defining* the corresponding product and process measures, and *integrating* the resulting measurement activities into the organization's existing software processes. Figure 2.2 illustrates the sequence of these stages.

Each stage in Figure 2.2 builds on the one that precedes it. The goals and objectives of your organization will guide you in identifying issues; identifying your issues leads to selecting and defining measures; and selecting and defining measures puts you in position to plan the related measurement activities and integrate them into your software processes.

Sections 2.1 through 2.3 describe the three stages of measurement planning and suggest approaches to each stage.

2.1   Identifying Process Issues

Process management responsibilities can encompass the entire life cycle of a software product. They can also focus on specific aspects of the development or support cycle. In either case, the process or subprocess that is being managed has a purpose or an objective—a raison d'etre that can be traced back to the software organization's business goals.

Experience has shown that it is important to identify the critical factors that determine whether or not your processes succeed in meeting the goals you set.

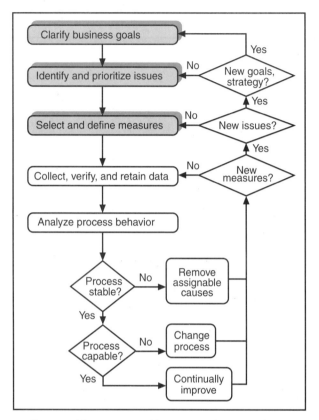

FIGURE 2.1 Process Measurement Framework Guide to Chapter 2

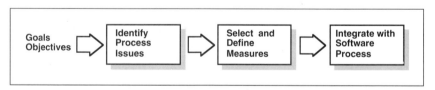

FIGURE 2.2 The Three Principal Activities of Measurement Planning

These critical factors often arise from concerns, problems, or issues that represent levels of risk that threaten your ability to meet your goals, responsibilities, or commitments. They also arise from specifications that must be met to satisfy customer requirements or downstream process needs. We refer to critical factors collectively as "issues." Note that issues are not necessarily problems. Rather, based on your understanding and experience with the processes and the products the processes produce, they describe situations that require attention.

2.1.1 STEPS FOR IDENTIFYING PROCESS ISSUES

The following steps outline a straightforward approach for identifying process issues:

1. **Clarify your business goals or objectives.** You will need to understand how your business goals or objectives relate to your software processes. In most cases, business goals and objectives that are tied to cost, quality, or time can be mapped readily to the appropriate software processes.

2. **Identify the critical processes.** Processes that have experienced problems in the past, are executed across organizational boundaries, use a technology for the first time, or operate under higher work loads than have been used before are all prime candidates for your list of critical processes. Processes that provide inputs or support to downstream processes are candidates as well. The list you identify may vary with the passage of time or with your progress through a development or support cycle.

3. **List the objectives for each critical process.** Listing objectives in terms of process performance will help you identify potential problem areas. The best way to do this is in terms of the attributes of the products or processes that you want to control or improve. You may find that successfully meeting the objectives for a process depends on the performance of upstream processes. If these processes have not been selected for measurement, you may want to consider adding them to the list created in step 2.

4. **List the potential problem areas associated with the processes.** These are concerns or issues that could jeopardize attaining the objectives. Listing potential problem areas requires that you have a good understanding of your processes and how they relate to one another. Process-flow diagrams and listings of the entities associated with them can help significantly here.

5. **Group the list of potential problems into common areas or topics.** This step will help you to identify issues that can be described and quantified by closely related measurements.

2.1.2 THE ROLE OF MENTAL MODELS

One technique for identifying key process issues is to ask questions about the performance of each process and the quality of the products it produces. Your ability to identify critical factors and issues depends on the picture you have in your mind of the tasks, resources, and products required to meet your goals. This picture is often called a *mental model* [Senge 1994]. Sketching or diagramming your mental models for the processes you manage can be very helpful in communicating the issues and measurement possibilities to others, as well as in solidifying your own understanding of the processes. An explicit model of the process under study will visually summarize the relationships among the process tasks.

This often brings to light implicit factors that are otherwise overlooked and that may need to be understood more clearly.

Figure 2.3 illustrates the general shape of many process models. Generic models like this are easily elaborated and adapted to specific situations. To construct a specific process model, you should look for

- Things the process receives (inputs and resources that are used or supplied).
- Things the process produces (outputs, including products, by-products, and effects).
- Things the process consists of (activities, flow paths, and agents—the structure of the process).
- Things that are expended or consumed (consumables).
- Things the process holds or retains (internal artifacts, such as inventory and work in progress).

Each "thing" in the process is an entity, and each entity has attributes that characterize some aspect of the process or its products. Thus, every attribute in a model of a process is a candidate for measurement.

Figure 2.4 shows a simple model for a problem management process. The lines from one box to the next indicate the flow of problem reports. The boxes designate the major tasks that must be carried out to move each problem report

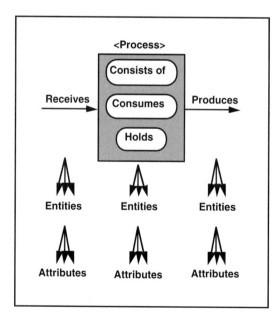

FIGURE 2.3   A Generic Process Model

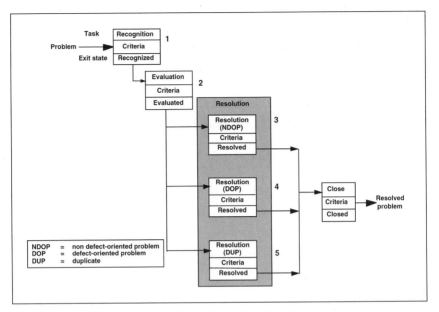

FIGURE 2.4   A Simple Process Model for Defect Tracking

from the "open" state to the "closed" state. Simple models like that of Figure 2.4 are useful not only for identifying process issues that bear watching but also for selecting process attributes for measurement. They are also useful for ensuring that everyone working on process improvement is addressing the same process.

Once you have sketched flowcharts or other pictures that describe a process, step back and examine the process as a whole to see whether you have missed anything. By asking questions such as the following, you may discover additional entities whose properties could be worth measuring:

- What determines product quality? What determines success? What do our customers want?

- What could go wrong? What is not working well? What might signal early warnings?

- Where are the delays? How big is our backlog? Where is backlog occurring?

- What things can we control? What limits our capability? What limits our performance?

As your knowledge of a process increases, or when the process is inherently large and complex, you may find more sophisticated methods useful. For example, structured control-flow diagrams like the one illustrated in Figure 2.5[1] can help you to identify important elements of a process and establish mutually understood frameworks for team-based efforts [Henry 1992].

---

[1] From "Process Definition: Theory and Reality," by Joel Henry and Bob Blasewitz, IEEE Software, November, 1992, ©1992 IEEE.

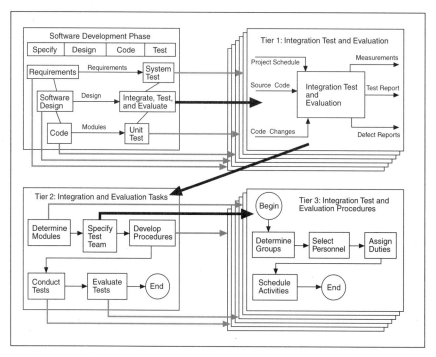

FIGURE 2.5 Example of a Control-Flow Diagram

2.1.3 COMMON PROCESS ISSUES

All processes have at least three, and often four, characteristics in common. In addition to producing a specific product or service, they require expenditures of resources and time to produce the product or service; they are expected to deliver the product on time; and, from time to time, they will produce products with defects or imperfections. Because of these similarities, there are four fundamental issues associated with processes that everyone concerned with process management shares: *product quality* (specifications, tolerances, action limits, and defects), *process time or duration, product delivery,* and *process cost*. These issues tie very closely to the process performance attributes that an organization will want to select for control or improvement. The issues—important to most organizations and common to all software processes—are discussed briefly here. They are readily measured, and understanding the issues provides motivation for all participants in the process.

1. **Product quality (specifications, tolerances, action limits, and defects).**[2]
   Excessive variability and off-target processes cause defects. Defects introduced into a product have multiple effects. They require the effort of

---

[2] Defects occur when products do not meet specifications for designated attributes of product quality. Tolerances are the amount of leeway granted by specifications. Action limits are limits used to control variability in specified attributes of product quality.

skilled personnel to detect, remove, repair, and retest. Defects also increase process cost, time, and complexity. In addition, defects that escape detection and repair before the product is released to a customer reduce user satisfaction with the product. This is just as true for products that go to internal customers as it is for those that go to external customers. Activities that decrease the introduction of defects or increase the early detection of defects are prime targets for measuring the effectiveness of the process.

2. **Process duration.** Process duration is an issue that translates directly to a process attribute. It is the elapsed time from the start of processing until the product is available to the user. The user in this case is not necessarily the customer or "end user" but may be a person or team involved in subsequent process activities. The flow of work through a given process can often be improved by providing better tools, using better technology, making more effective use of time, eliminating unnecessary steps, and improving training.

3. **Product delivery.** Delivery is a process event. At delivery, the timeliness and quantity of a product or service can be measured against expectations or commitments. If a product or service is not on time (late or early), there may be consequences for the customer or user of the product or service. Delivery is directly related to process duration (via lead time and the time required to execute the process) and delivery frequency.

4. **Process cost.** Process cost includes the cost of executing and supporting the process as well as the cost of understanding and managing the factors that drive costs. As in any other activity, the cost of a software process has many elements and is affected by a variety of factors. Examples include the nature of the product, the statement of work, skills and experience of personnel, labor rates, cost of facilities, overhead, and the pacing of the process. The key to managing process cost is to identify the elements of cost that you can control or affect and look for opportunities to reduce or eliminate the costs. Because of the labor-intensive nature of producing and supporting software, effort is frequently the predominant cost driver for software processes. Measuring how and where people spend their time and then relating this to causal factors are important in understanding and controlling the cost of a process [Perry 1994]. This often leads to recognizing the need for better tools, training, and different skill mixes.

2.2   Selecting and Defining Measures

We now turn to the second planning activity, selecting and defining measures, as highlighted in Figure 2.6. Selecting and defining measures are two different but closely related activities. As we will see, it is one thing to select a measure such as the number of reported defects that we might use to characterize a process or

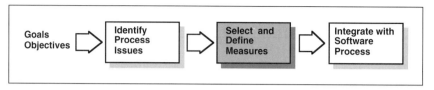

FIGURE 2.6 Measurement Planning Activities—Step 2

product. It is quite another to create an operational definition for a measure once it has been selected.[3]

For example, an operational definition for the number of defects found might include the type of defect, when it occurs, when it is detected, the finding activity, whether the defect is static or dynamic, its criticality, and a description of the processes used to find, classify, and count the occurrences of the defect. To have an operational definition, you must know enough about what the data represent and how they are collected (1) to ensure that different people will implement the measures correctly and consistently and (2) to interpret the data correctly.

The activities of selecting and defining measures are coupled in practice because it is not unusual to have to reconsider a measure due to your organization's inability to apply it easily or consistently once it has been operationally defined. In the pages that follow, we point out several factors to consider when selecting measures. Then, we discuss some important characteristics of operational definitions and suggest methods for making your definitions operational.

As you select and define your measures, keep in mind that you will be seeking to apply them to help you control and improve your processes. The primary vehicles that will help you do this are statistical process control and quality improvement methodology.

2.2.1 SELECTING PROCESS PERFORMANCE MEASURES

What do we mean by process performance measures? Process performance refers to the characteristic values we see when measuring attributes of products and services that come from a process. Process performance can be measured in two ways: (1) by measuring attributes of products that the process produces and (2) by measuring attributes of the process itself. Histories of these values describe how the process has performed in the past. Under the right conditions, the histories give reference points for judging what the process is doing now and might do in the future.

Examples of measurable product attributes include function, size, execution speed, module strength, and profiles of statement types. They also include any quality attributes (such as ease of use and reliability) that would make the product more or less desirable to a user or customer. Examples of process attributes, on the other hand, include the amount of effort expended, the clock time or computer time required to perform a process or task, the sizes and durations of work flows

---

[3] Operational definitions tell people *how* measurements are made, and they do this in sufficient detail that others will get the same results if they follow the same procedures.

and backlogs, the characteristics and quantities of resources used, and the number, types, and sources of defects detected, repaired, or reported.

Product and process measures may well be the same measures. Measurements of product attributes such as McCabe complexity, average module size, and degree of code reuse that are tracked over time and used to investigate trends in process performance are just a few examples.

We may also seek reasons for variations in process performance by measuring attributes of the resources or environments that support the process—for example, the experience and training levels of the software engineers or the amount of computer time or memory available.

In each case, the key to measuring process performance is to choose attributes and measures that are relevant to the particular process and issues under study. We do this by selecting measures that not only reflect the intended purpose of the process but also address the issues being considered.

To measure process performance, we measure as many product quality and process performance attributes as needed, and we do this at several points in time to obtain sequential records of their behavior. It is these sequential records that are the basis for establishing statistical control and, hence, for assessing the stability and capability of the process.

The choices of attributes to measure will change from process to process and from issue to issue. This is where your knowledge of your organization's processes comes into play. We offer the guidelines in Figure 2.7 as a check against your selections.

Criteria for Measures Used to Characterize Process Performance

- The measures should relate closely to the issue under study. These are usually issues of quality, resource consumption, or elapsed time.

- They should have high information content. Pick measures of product or process qualities that are sensitive to as many facets of process results as possible.

- They should pass a reality test. Does the measure really reflect the degree to which the process achieves results that are important?

- They should permit easy and economical collection of data.

- They should permit consistently collected, well-defined data.

- They should show measurable variation. A number that does not change does not provide any information about the process.

- They should, as a set, have diagnostic value and be able to help you identify not only that something unusual has happened but also what might be causing it.

FIGURE 2.7   Guidelines for Selecting Process Performance Measures

Selecting measures can be a hectic and time-consuming activity if you do not have a clear understanding of the factors that can influence your selection. The following procedure can help you develop an understanding of many of these factors so that you can choose measures that shed light on the issues. Keep in mind that the goal is to find measures that provide information relevant to the issues you identified in the initial stage of your planning efforts.

1. Clarify the issue. Make sure that you understand all facets and dimensions of the issue. Put the issue in context as follows:

- By listing the questions that are being asked.
- By listing the questions that need to be answered (even if they are not asked).
- By identifying who is asking and why (to ensure that you understand the perspectives of those using the measurement results).
- By identifying the time elements relative to the issue. (Is the issue periodic, transient, or event-based?)
- By identifying the purpose of the measures relative to the issue. (What does the issue suggest in terms of data analysis and action? Will the data be used to understand, compare, predict, control, assess, or improve some aspect of the process?)

2. Identify the processes encompassed by the issue. You have done some of this already when you identified the critical process issues that concern you. You may now see other processes whose results affect the issue.

3. Review the relationships among the processes to determine which processes need to be measured. Some processes, although encompassed by the issue, may contribute little or no risk or uncertainty relative to the issue. Those processes can often be ignored. Sketches that make explicit the mental models for your processes will be of significant help, both here and in the steps that follow.

4. For each process, select the entities and attributes to be measured and the data elements to be collected. That is, select attributes whose measures will be most influential or dominant in determining product quality or in meeting process objectives. Your knowledge of the process will be a significant factor in selecting entities and attributes that are important. You should try to identify entities and attributes that have direct relationships to process results. If you are interested in process cost, product size, number of defects found, and so forth, measure these attributes directly. If you must rely on indirect relationships to measure process results, have a theory and data to support the validity of a particular cause-and-effect or predictive relationship.

5. Test the potential usefulness of the selected measures. Sketch indicators, especially charts and graphs, that show how you propose to use the measurements you will obtain. Do not be surprised if this leads you to sharper, more focused questions and definitions.

In selecting entities, attributes, and data elements for measurement, it is helpful to frame your selections in the context of a model that describes the process of interest. Visual models are especially helpful. With a concrete (explicit) model of the process as your guide, you can solidify your understanding of the process as well as communicate with others regarding the selection of entities to measure. Good models will help you identify the products and by-products that are produced at all stages of a process.

Some examples of the kinds of entities often found in processes are listed in Figure 2.8. You may want to include some of these elements in your mental models and consider measuring one or more of them when seeking to understand what your processes are doing and why they are doing it.

Figure 2.8 gives an extended (but by no means complete) set of entities to consider when looking for useful product and process measures. Note that characterizations of process performance will usually be based on attributes of entities found in the four rightmost columns. Measures of process compliance, on the other hand, will usually address entities found in the two leftmost columns. (Entities in column 2 can be of interest in both cases.)

Figure 2.9 is similar to Figure 2.8. It gives examples of attributes of process entities that you may want to consider as candidates for measurement when studying process performance.

Measurable Entities in a Software Process				
Things Received or Used	**Activities and Their Elements**	**Things Consumed**	**Things Held or Retained**	**Things Produced**
Products and by-products from other processes	Processes and controllers	Resources • Effort	People	Products • Requirements
Ideas, concepts	• Requirements analysis	• Raw materials	Facilities	• Specifications
Resources	• Designing	• Energy	Tools	• Designs
• People	• Coding	• Money	Materials	• Units
• Facilities	• Testing	• Time	Work in process	• Modules
• Tools	• Configuration control		Data	• Test cases
• Raw materials	• Change control		Knowledge	• Test results
• Energy	• Problem management		Experience	• Tested components
• Money	• Reviewing			• Documentation
• Time	• Inspecting			• Defects
Guidelines and directions	• Integrating			• Defect reports
• Policies	Flow paths			• Change requests
• Procedures	• Product paths			• Data
• Goals	• Resource paths			• Acquired materials
• Constraints	• Data paths			• Other artifacts
• Rules	• Control paths			By-products
• Laws	Buffers and dampers			• Knowledge
• Regulations	• Queues			• Experience
• Training	• Stacks			• Skills
• Instructions	• Bins			• Process improvements
				• Data
				• Good will
				• Satisfied customers

FIGURE 2.8 Examples of Measurable Entities in a Software Process

Measurable Attributes of Software Process Entities			
Things Received or Used	**Activities and Their Elements**	**Things Consumed**	**Things Produced**
Changes ▪ Type ▪ Date ▪ Size ▪ # received Requirements ▪ Requirements stability ▪ # identified ▪ % traced to design ▪ % traced to code Problem reports ▪ Type ▪ Date ▪ Size ▪ Origin ▪ Severity ▪ # received Funds ▪ Money ▪ Budget ▪ Status People ▪ Years of experience ▪ Type of education ▪ % trained in XYZ ▪ Employment codes Facilities and environment ▪ Square feet per employee ▪ Noise level ▪ Lighting ▪ # of staff in cubicles ▪ # of staff sharing an office or cubicle ▪ Investment in tools per employee ▪ Hours of computer usage ▪ % of capacity utilized	Flow paths ▪ Processing time ▪ Throughput rates ▪ Diversions ▪ Delays ▪ Backlogs Length, size ▪ Queues ▪ Buffers ▪ Stacks	Effort ▪ # of development hours ▪ # of rework hours ▪ # of support hours ▪ # of preparation hours ▪ # of meeting hours Time ▪ Start time or date ▪ Ending time or date ▪ Duration of process or task ▪ Wait time Money ▪ Cost to date ▪ Cost variance ▪ Cost of rework	Status of work units ▪ # designed ▪ # coded ▪ # tested Size of work units ▪ # of requirements ▪ # of function points ▪ # of lines of code ▪ # of modules ▪ # of objects ▪ # of bytes in database Output quantity ▪ # of action items ▪ # of approvals ▪ # of defects found Test results ▪ # of test cases passed ▪ % test coverage Program architecture ▪ Fan-in ▪ Fan-out Changes ▪ Type ▪ Date ▪ Size ▪ Effort expended Problems and defects ▪ # of reports ▪ Defect density ▪ Type ▪ Origin ▪ Distribution by type ▪ Distribution by origin ▪ # open ▪ # closed Critical resource utilization ▪ % memory utilized ▪ % cpu capacity utilized ▪ % I/O capacity utilized

FIGURE 2.9 Examples of Measurable Attributes Associated with Software Process Entities

Figures 2.8 and 2.9 are useful as an informal taxonomy or a classification scheme. Their purpose is to guide you as you look for elements and attributes that can provide useful information for managing or improving process performance. In practice, it makes little difference whether or not you have things classified "right" (whatever that means), but it makes a big difference if you have overlooked something important. Reviewing Figures 2.8 and 2.9 may give you some ideas and help avoid oversights.

When using Figures 2.8 and 2.9 as checklists, keep in mind that inputs to one process are almost always outputs of another. Things received or used have to be produced somewhere, and things produced presumably get received and used by some downstream customer or activity. Depending on the process, activity, or task that you are examining, you may find elements in column 1 that belong in column 5 and vice versa. If so, simply put them where you think they belong. The important thing is not where they fit, but that you found something worth measuring.

It is important to note that many measurements that can be used to quantify process performance are the same as those used for project management. The attributes in Figure 2.9, for example, are often important, not just to process management, but to program and project management as well. The document *Practical Software Measurement: A Foundation for Objective Project Management* [McGarry 1998] contains similar lists of things to measure. Many of the measures in that document can be used for managing and improving processes too.

In the final analysis, selecting process measures comes down to understanding the purpose and operation of the process and determining the inherent issues (potential problems and risks) that may prevent the process from meeting its purpose. In most cases, these issues will have an underlying basis in one or more of the common issues described in Section 2.1.3. In these situations, we are frequently led to selecting certain core measures—such as defect counts, cost, and time—to quantify the issues.

Recall that our discussions in Chapter 1 pointed out that measures of product and process quality can be used to achieve process stability and determine process capability. The measures that you select to quantify management issues are often exactly the ones that you use to determine whether a process is stable and capable.

2.2.2 DEFINING PROCESS PERFORMANCE MEASURES

We now turn our attention to the activity of defining process measures.[4] Once you have identified your measures, you must define them; names alone will not suffice. You must be able to tell others exactly how each measure is obtained so that they can collect and interpret the values correctly.

Measurement of software products and processes is not new. Some organizations have been measuring for years. At a minimum, we have all dealt with

---

[4] The discussions here are elaborated in *Goal-Driven Software Measurement—A Guidebook* [Park 1996].

schedules. Many organizations have also recorded effort expenditures, perhaps weekly, if for no other reason than to ensure that employees get paid. Some organizations use these data in conjunction with measures of software artifacts to track and control progress, especially when developing products under contract. Some of these organizations have structured estimating processes that use empirical models to help them translate records from past projects into bids, proposals, and plans for future work.

But, despite all this measurement activity, few in the software industry would call measurement a success story. This is especially true when we attempt to use data that were collected or reported by someone else. Some reasons for our lack of success are as follows:

- **Different users of measurement data have different needs.** Data collected for one purpose may not be suitable for another because the rules used for collecting the data are inconsistent with the ways others want to use the data.

- **Different organizations have different established practices.** In many cases, these practices have sound reasons behind them and should not be changed. Moreover, it may be difficult and often impractical to change the way an organization collects data, just to satisfy an external need.

- **Unambiguous communication of measurement results is inherently difficult.** Even if individuals understand perfectly well how their data are collected, it is not easy for them to communicate adequate descriptions of the operational rules to others. These rules may be complex, and they may never have been stated explicitly.

- **Structured methods for communicating measurement results seldom exist.** What you think you hear is often not what they meant to say. This, in a way, restates the ambiguity point just made but frames it in a way that suggests a potential solution.

To overcome these types of measurement obstacles, we suggest that you embody the notion of *well-defined* measures. For performance measures to be well defined, as required by the guidelines provided by W. Edwards Deming in referring to operational definitions, they must satisfy three criteria:

1. **Communication.** Will the methods used to define measures or describe measured values allow others to know precisely what has been measured and what has been included in and excluded from aggregated results? Moreover, will every user of the data know how the data were collected so that they can interpret the results correctly?

2. **Repeatability.** Would someone else be able to repeat the measurements and get the same results?

3. **Traceability.** Are the origins of the data identified in terms of time, source, sequence, activity, product, status, environment, measurement tools used, and collecting agent?

The traceability requirement is especially important to assessing and improving process performance. Because measures of performance can signal process instabilities, it is important that the context and circumstances of the measurement be recorded. This will help in identifying assignable causes of the instabilities.

For example, suppose that a software problem report is prepared whenever a defect is encountered by a defect-finding activity. To find and fix the defect, programmers and analysts must know as much as possible about the circumstances of the encounter—how, when, and where the defect happened, under what conditions, and so forth. So, it is helpful if this information is recorded on the problem report.

For the same reason, measurements of process performance should always be accompanied by similar contextual information. When the data show process instabilities, the people who evaluate the data will look for incidents or events that are not part of the normal process in order to identify assignable causes. Contextual information, together with data gathered from measures of process compliance, will help them identify these causes.

Donald J. Wheeler and David S. Chambers, in their book *Understanding Statistical Process Control,* discuss the need for contextual information [Wheeler 1992, 112]. They give examples of the kinds of questions that must be answered if performance data are to be interpreted correctly. Here are some of the questions:

- What do the individual values represent? What are these numbers?
- How are the values obtained? Who obtains them? How often? At which location? By what method? With what instrumentation?
- What sources of variation are present in these data?
- How are these data organized into subgroups? Which sources of variation occur *within* the subgroups? Which sources of variation occur *between* the subgroups?
- How should such data behave? Are there natural barriers within the range of observed values?

When you collect product and process measures, you should always be prepared to answer these kinds of questions. The answers will help point you (correctly) to assignable causes.

2.2.3 OPERATIONAL DEFINITIONS

The criteria for well-defined data are used as the basis for creating operational definitions for process measurements. These criteria are closely related. In fact, if you cannot communicate *exactly* what was done to collect a set of data, you are in no position to tell someone else how to do it. Far too many organizations propose measurement definitions without first determining what users of the data will need to know about the measured values in order to use them intelligently. It is no surprise, then, that measurements are often collected inconsistently and at odds with users' needs. When it comes to implementation, rules such as "Count all noncomment, nonblank source statements" and "Count all open problems" are open to far too many interpretations to provide repeatable results.

Although communicating measurement definitions in clear, unambiguous terms requires effort, there is good news as well. When someone can describe exactly what has been collected, it is easy to turn the process around and say, "Please do that again." Moreover, you can give the description to someone else and say, "Please use this as your definition, but with these changes." In short, when we can communicate clearly what we *have* measured, we have little trouble creating repeatable rules for collecting future data.

We suggest the use of structured, checklist-based frameworks to help define, implement, and communicate operational definitions for software measures. The primary issue is that everyone understands *completely* what the measured values represent. Only then can we expect people to collect values consistently and have others interpret and apply the results to reach valid conclusions.

Communicating clear and unambiguous definitions is not easy. Having structured methods for identifying all the rules that are used to make and record measurements can be very helpful in ensuring that important information does not go unmentioned. When designing methods for defining measures, you should keep in mind that things that do not matter to one user are often important to another. Thus, measurement definitions—and structures for recording the definitions—often become larger and more encompassing than the definitions most organizations have traditionally used. This is all the more reason to have a well-organized approach. Definition deals with details, and structured methods help ensure that all details get identified, addressed, and recorded. They also help you deal with people who believe that attention to detail is no longer their responsibility.

2.2.4   EXAMPLES OF OPERATIONAL DEFINITIONS

Frameworks for constructing operational definitions for some frequently used size, effort, schedule, and quality measures have been described in three Software Engineering Institute (SEI) technical reports [Park 1992; Goethert 1992; Florac 1992]. The frameworks are based on checklists, supplemented by forms for summarizing operational information that is not amenable to checklist treatment.

An example of a checklist that has been used to define the counting of problems and defects found during system testing is shown in Figure 2.10. Here, the check marks in the Include and Exclude columns spell out the rules to be followed when deciding whether or not a particular problem, defect, or report is to be included in a given count. Similarly, once a count has been made, the check marks tell you exactly what has been counted and what has not. The Value Count and Array Count columns of the checklist provide structures for requesting specialized counts, either for subsets of the total or for tables (arrays) that cross-tabulate the frequencies of occurrence for sets of results from different attributes.

The central theme in the checklists lies in stating exactly what is included in—and excluded from—reported results. The checklists are supported by supplemental forms that describe how the inclusions and exclusions were (or are to be) accomplished. These practices should be part of an operational definition because they affect the way measured results should be interpreted.

Although the first (and most important) use of definition checklists and supplemental forms is to let users of data know exactly how the data were obtained, the same kinds of descriptions can be used to specify how future measurements are to be made. The latter "let me tell you what to do" approach is the one we

Problem Status	Include	Exclude	Value Count	Array Count
Open	✔		✔	
Recognized				✔
Evaluated				✔
Resolved				✔
Closed	✔		✔	
Problem Type	**Include**	**Exclude**	**Value Count**	**Array Count**
Software defect				
Requirements defect	✔		✔	
Design defect	✔		✔	
Code defect	✔		✔	
Operational document defect	✔		✔	
Test case defect		✔		
Other work product defect		✔		
Other problems				
Hardware problem		✔		
Operating system problem		✔		
User mistake		✔		
Operations mistake		✔		
New requirement/enhancement		✔		
Undetermined				
Not repeatable/cause unknown		✔		
Value not identified		✔		
Uniqueness	**Include**	**Exclude**	**Value Count**	**Array Count**
Original	✔			
Duplicate		✔	✔	
Value not identifed		✔		
Criticality	**Include**	**Exclude**	**Value Count**	**Array Count**
First level (most critical)	✔			✔
Second level	✔			✔
Third level	✔			✔
Fourth level	✔			✔
Fifth level	✔			✔
Value not identified		✔		
Urgency	**Include**	**Exclude**	**Value Count**	**Array Count**
First (most urgent)	✔			
Second	✔			
Third	✔			
Fourth	✔			
Value not identified		✔		

FIGURE 2.10 A Checklist-Based Definition for Counting Defects

Finding Activity	Include	Exclude	Value Count	Array Count
Synthesis of				
Design		✔		
Code		✔		
Test procedure		✔		
User publications		✔		
Inspections of				
Requirements		✔		
Preliminary design		✔		
Detailed design		✔		
Code		✔		
Operational documentation		✔		
Test procedures		✔		
Formal reviews of				
Plans		✔		
Requirements		✔		
Preliminary design		✔		
Critical design		✔		
Test readiness		✔		
Formal qualification		✔		
Testing				
Planning		✔		
Module (CSU)		✔		
Component (CSC)		✔		
Configuration item (CSCI)		✔		
Integrate and test		✔		
Independent verif. and valid.		✔		
System	✔			
Test and evaluate		✔		
Acceptance		✔		
Customer support				
Production/deployment		✔		
Installation		✔		
Operation		✔		
Undetermined				
Value not identified		✔		
Finding Mode	Include	Exclude	Value Count	Array Count
Static (nonoperational)	✔			
Dynamic (operational)	✔			
Value not identified		✔		

FIGURE 2.10   A Checklist-Based Definition for Counting Defects (Continued)

usually see in software organizations, but without visible structures for ensuring that the measurement instructions will be interpreted and executed consistently by all who collect the data.

Formats for checklists like the one in Figure 2.10 should be tailored to the particular problem-tracking process that is used within your organization. Since these processes and the terms that they employ vary from organization to organization, you should make sure that the checklists you use to define problem and defect counting fit your needs. This is true for your other measures as well.

2.2.5 CREATING YOUR OWN DEFINITION FRAMEWORKS

There are, of course, many measures for which checklists and descriptive forms do not yet exist. When you propose measures that have no current checklists, you should develop similar (or equivalent) vehicles for communicating the rules and procedures that you want used to capture and record your data. Checklists are useful, especially when inclusion and exclusion decisions affect results.

Whatever frameworks you choose, your structured methods must tell the people who collect the data exactly what is to be included in (and excluded from) the values they report to you. Where it makes a difference—and it usually does— they must also describe how the measurements will be carried out. An appropriate definition framework ensures that any variation in the method for measuring that could affect either the values themselves or the way they should be interpreted gets described.

When constructing checklists and supporting forms for defining software measures, you will find that the best way to ensure full coverage and achieve consensus is to focus, not on telling people what they should do, but rather on identifying what you and others need to know to use the data correctly. Not only will this minimize controversy and confrontation, but also, once you have a structure that communicates all relevant information about a measurement's result, it is easy to use that structure to tell others how to collect the data you want.

2.3 Integrating Measures with the Software Process

The third stage in measurement planning, as highlighted in Figure 2.11, is to integrate your defined measures with your software processes. In this section, we discuss the three steps that comprise this stage: *analysis, diagnosis,* and *action.* Analysis involves identifying the measures that your organization collects now and how they are being used. Diagnosis means evaluating the extent to which these measures can be used to meet your newly identified needs and determining where additional work is needed. Action is directed at translating the results of *analysis* and *diagnosis* into action plans for collecting and using the additional data you seek. These steps are described in the subsections that follow.

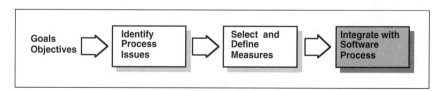

FIGURE 2.11 Measurement Planning Activities—Step 3

2.3.1   ANALYSIS OF EXISTING MEASUREMENT ACTIVITIES

Analysis establishes the baseline for the work that follows. Knowing what measures your organization collects now and how people are using them gives you a starting point for implementing the measures you have defined. If your organization is like most, you will not be starting from scratch. Some measurement activities will already be in place, and you should use these as springboards if you can. Revolutionary approaches often meet strong resistance. Where possible, it makes sense to build on things that are currently in use, strengthening them in the process and refocusing them where necessary. When analyzing your existing measures and measurement practices, you should ask questions such as these:

- What data elements are required for my measures?
- Which ones are collected now?
- How are they collected?
- Which processes provide the data?
- How are the data elements stored and reported?

Often, you will find that there are more potential data sources than were apparent at first glance. The mental models that you create for your processes can help you locate these sources. For example, several sources often exist for data about defects and problems. The situation shown in Figure 2.12 is typical of many organizations [Florac 1992]. Here, people who build products (product synthesis) write problem reports; teams that inspect products (as in peer reviews) prepare inspection reports; participants in formal milestone reviews produce action items; test groups produce test reports; and customer support groups document customer problems. All of these reports are followed by analyses and corrective actions, and the results and status are usually recorded somewhere, often in one or more databases. You should find and examine these databases to see what they can give you.

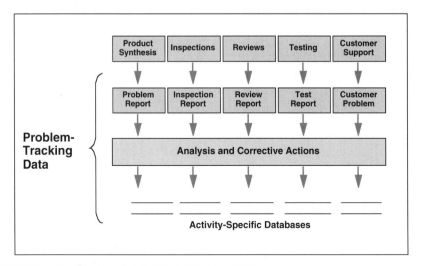

FIGURE 2.12   Sources for Problem-Tracking Data

2.3.2 DIAGNOSIS OF EXISTING MEASURES

Diagnosis means evaluating the data elements that your organization is collecting now, determining how well they meet the needs of your goal-driven measures, and proposing appropriate actions for (1) using the data, (2) adapting the data to your needs, (3) adapting your needs to the data, and (4) obtaining what is missing.

Where analysis is fact finding, diagnosis is evaluative and judgmental. When diagnosing, you are identifying alternatives and setting the stage for finding solutions. You are asking questions such as these:

- What existing measures and processes can be used to satisfy our data requirements?
- What elements of our measurement definitions or practices must be changed or modified?
- What new or additional processes are needed?

2.3.3 ACTION TO INTEGRATE MEASUREMENTS

Action means translating the results of your analyses and diagnoses into implementable steps. It is concerned with finding solutions and making the solutions happen, and it includes identifying tasks, assigning responsibilities and resources, and following through to make sure that the actions happen.

Action starts with identifying the elements that you will build on or address in your measurement plans. Here are several things you will want to do before writing your plans:

1. Identify the sources of data within your existing software process(es).
2. Define the methods that will be used to collect and report the data.
3. Identify (and specify) the tools that will be required to collect, report, and store the data.
4. Determine your requirements for points in time and frequencies of measurement.
5. Document your data collection procedures in detail:
   - Identify responsible persons and organizations.
   - Determine where, how, and when to collect and report.
   - Create sketches for the data collection records you will use.
6. Determine who will use the data.
7. Define how the data will be analyzed and reported.
8. Prepare a data definition and collection process guide.

You should also analyze your data storage and access requirements. This includes identifying or determining the following:

- Your historical retention needs.
- Who will collect, store, maintain, and access the data.

- The organizational levels to be served. (Serving more than one organizational level often translates into a need for more than one database.)
- The granularity of the data. (Will the data be retained as initially recorded or aggregated in some way?)
- The procedures to be used for dynamically editing and verifying data as the data elements are entered into the database.
- The number of people with access to the data.
- The need for recording the definitions associated with the data so that users can tie the data to the descriptive information that is needed to use the data correctly.

In addition, you should pay close attention to issues of data privacy wherever you encounter them. This is especially important for data that could be used (or perceived to be used) to evaluate the performance of individuals or teams. Much anecdotal evidence exists to suggest that the surest way to make measurement fail is to have people suspect that the measures might be used against them.

2.3.4   TASKS FOR DEFINING YOUR MEASUREMENT PROCESSES

When you are preparing to write your measurement plans, it helps to have a checklist such as the one in Figure 2.13 to ensure that nothing gets overlooked. This checklist can be transformed easily into a display for summarizing your status with respect to defining the measurement process you intend to implement, as illustrated

---

How to Prepare a Measurement Action Plan

- Define the data elements.
- Define the scales to be used for measuring and recording observed values for each data element.
- Define the frequencies of collection and the points in the process where measurements will be made.
- Define the timelines required for moving measurement results from the points of collection to databases or users.
- Create forms and procedures for collecting and recording the data.
- Define how the data are to be stored and how they will be accessed. Identify who is responsible for designing the database and for entering, retaining, and overseeing the data.
- Determine who will collect and access the data. Assign responsibilities for these actions.
- Define how the data will be analyzed and reported.
- Identify the supporting tools that must be developed or acquired to help you automate and administer the process.
- Prepare a process guide for collecting the data.

FIGURE 2.13   Checklist for Preparing a Measurement Action Plan

in Figure 2.14. Here, codes have been used to show the status of each task. Actions to complete the unfinished tasks are things that you will want to address as you prepare your plan.

2.3.5 ACTION PLANS

Once you know what you have to start with (analysis), how well your present measures meet your business needs (diagnosis), and the actions that you will want to take to meet the remaining needs (action), you are ready to prepare plans for implementing the actions you have identified. Your next step is to write the plans. These plans should translate your objectives into operational actions. They should make the measurement objectives clear; describe the goals and scope of the efforts and their relationships to other functional activities; spell out the tasks, responsibilities, and resources needed; provide for progress tracking and risk management; and establish frameworks and resources for sustained successful operation and evolution.

Keep in mind that there is no need to wrap all your measurement activities into a single, monolithic plan. You are not trying to establish an empire—you just want to get and use the data you need. Several small plans may be easier to implement and sustain than a single, all-encompassing endeavor. As time passes, your

	Data Element						
Planning Tasks	**1**	**2**	**3**	**4**	**5**	**6**	**7**
Data elements defined	Y	N	60%	Not doc'd.	Y?	•	•
Data collection frequencies and points in the software process defined	50%	N	60%	Not doc'd.	•	•	•
Timelines defined for getting measurement results to databases and users	N	N	30%	Not doc'd.	•	•	•
Data collection forms defined	N	N	N	N	•		
Data collection procedures defined	N	N	•	•			
Data storage, database design, and data retention responsibilities defined	N	N	•	•			
Who will collect and who will access the data identified	N	N	•	•			
Analysis processes defined	N	N					
Reporting processes defined	N	N					
Supporting tools identified and made available	N	N					
Process guide for data definition and collection prepared	Y						

FIGURE 2.14 Status of Action-Planning Activities

needs will change. With a modular planning strategy, you will find it easier to update, augment, or replace your plans when the need arises.

2.4 Summary

Planning is critical to the execution of any process, and the measurement process is no exception. Measuring the software process begins with planning. Measurement planning involves identifying process management issues, selecting and defining the product and process measures, and integrating the resulting measurement activities into the organization's existing software processes.

An approach for identifying process issues entails the following steps:

1. Clarifying business goals or objectives and understanding how they relate to your software processes.
2. Identifying the critical processes.
3. Listing the objectives for each critical process.
4. Listing the potential problem areas associated with the processes.
5. Grouping the list of potential problems into common areas or topics.

There are a number of issues that are important to most organizations and common to all software processes. These include product quality, process time or duration, product delivery, and product cost. These issues tie closely to process performance attributes that an organization will want to select for control or improvement.

Once issues have been identified, measures can be selected and defined. Selecting measures requires more than simply stating an issue. For instance, you will want to ask the following questions:

- What processes have effects on the issue?
- What products are affected by the issue?
- What product entities and attributes should be measured?
- What process entities and attributes should be measured?
- What resource entities and attributes should be measured?
- How will the measurements be used?
- How will the measurements be analyzed?
- Who will use the measurement results?

One high-maturity software organization developed the idea of a "Metric Evaluation Table" [Paulk 1999] to help them determine what measures to select and the information value the measures would provide. Figure 2.15 shows an example of such a table.

Topic	Evaluation Consideration
Indicator of Process Performance	Is the measure a good indicator of how well the process is performing? Example: an indicator of efficiency or effectiveness.
Controllable	Can the values for this measure be predictably changed by changing the process or how the process is implemented?
Objective	Can the measurement be consistently reproduced by different people?
Timely	Can data be collected and analyzed such that you can predict and/or control process performance?
Readily Available	Is the data relatively easy and cost-effective to obtain?
Represents Customer's View of Quality	Is the measure one that the customer thinks is an important indicator of process and/or product quality? Example: an indicator of reliability.
Customer-Required	Is the measure one that the customer requires be reported?
Represents End-User View of Quality	Is the measure one that the end user thinks is an important indicator of process and/or product quality? Example: an indicator of usability.
Represents Senior Management's View of Quality	Is the measure one that senior management thinks is an important indicator of process and/or product quality?
Organization-Required	Is the measure one that the organization requires be reported? That is, is it one of the common, standard measures defined for the organization?
Represents Project Manager's View of Quality	Is the measure one that the project manager thinks is an important indicator of process and/or product quality? Example: an indicator of progress.

FIGURE 2.15 Example of Factors to Consider for Measurement Evaluation

In any case, the key to measuring process performance is to choose attributes and measures that are representative of the particular process and issues that are to be studied. Then, once measures have been selected, you must define them in such a way that you can tell others exactly how each measure is obtained so that they can collect and interpret values correctly. This is where operational definitions come into play. To have an operational definition, you must know enough about what the data represent and how they are collected (1) to ensure that different people will implement the measures correctly and consistently and (2) to interpret the data correctly.

The next step is to integrate your defined measures with your software processes. The three steps that comprise this stage include analysis, diagnosis, and action. Analysis involves identifying the measures that your organization collects now and how they are being used. Diagnosis means evaluating the extent to which these measures can be used to meet your newly identified needs and determining where additional work is needed. Action is directed at translating the results of analysis and diagnosis into action plans for collecting and using the additional data you seek.

Now we are ready to execute the process—we are ready to start collecting the data.

3

Collecting the Data

An element of chance enters into every measurement; hence every set of measurements is inherently a sample of certain more or less unknown conditions. Even in the few instances where we believe that the objective reality under measurement is a constant, the measurements of this constant are influenced by chance or unknown causes. Hence, the set of measurements of any quantity, even though the quantity itself be a constant, is a sample of a possible infinite set of measurements which we might make of this same quantity under essentially the same conditions.

From this viewpoint, measurement is a sampling process designed to tell us something about the universe in which we live that will enable us to predict the future in terms of the past through the establishment of principles or natural laws.

Walter A. Shewhart 1931

In Chapter 2, we discussed the notion that measuring the software process commences with planning and that measurement planning progresses in three stages: identifying process management issues, selecting and defining the corresponding product and process measures, and integrating the resulting measurement activities into the organization's existing software processes. In this chapter, we turn our attention to collecting and retaining process management data. The shaded area in Figure 3.1 indicates the positioning of these activities with respect to the process measurement framework.

3.1   Principal Tasks

The operational activities of measurement begin with collecting data. The procedures that you define for collecting and retaining data need to be integrated into your software processes and made operational. This means putting the right people, sensors, tools, and practices into the processes in the right places. It also means capturing and storing the data for subsequent use in analysis and process improvement.

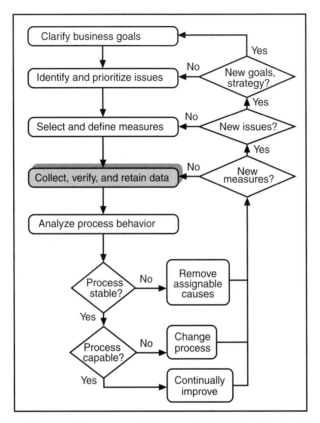

FIGURE 3.1   Process Measurement Framework Guide to Chapter 3

The principal tasks associated with collecting and retaining data for process management are as follows:

- Designing the methods and obtaining the tools that will be used to support data collection and retention.
- Obtaining and training the staff that will execute the data collection procedures.
- Capturing and recording the data for each process that is targeted for measurement.
- Using defined forms and formats to supply the collected data to the individuals and groups who perform analyses.
- Monitoring the execution (compliance) and performance of the activities for collecting and retaining data.

The following sections discuss these tasks in more detail.

3.2   The Specifics of Collecting Software Process Data

Once you have selected and defined your measures and planned your implementation actions, you are ready to begin collecting data. Collecting data is more than just making measurements. It consists of implementing your plans, ensuring that they work, and sustaining the measurement activities that result. These actions will be facilitated if you document in detail your procedures for collecting, recording, and reporting data. Documenting your procedures involves

- Identifying the responsible persons and organizations.
- Specifying where, when, and how measurements will be made.
- Defining the procedures to be used for recording and reporting results.
- Providing standard "fill-in-the-blank" forms to simplify manual recording of the data.

The complexity of your data collection processes will increase as additional organizations or software processes become involved. Each organization or process may use a different tool or method to obtain the "same" data. If you wish to compare or aggregate the data you collect, you must ensure that the methods different people use to collect the data are, in fact, collecting exactly the same kinds of data. That is, your different tools and procedures should be counting, extracting, or otherwise processing data in ways that produce equivalent results. The concept of well-defined data that was defined in Chapter 2 comes into play here. When it is possible to do so, providing standard tools such as code counters and work-breakdown structures will make achieving consistency and common understandings easier.

The fact that data will subsequently be analyzed can impose requirements on data collection in ways that may not be obvious. For example, measures of process performance that are used to assess process stability and capability require that special attention be paid to four important issues:

1. **Time sequence.** The order in which observations are made contains crucial information for estimating the inherent variability in a process. Moreover, knowledge of the sequence and of its relationships to time and process-related events is what enables you to identify the point where assignable causes of variation entered a process. This helps greatly in identifying the causes and preventing recurrences. You should ensure that any measurements collected for estimating, controlling, or improving process performance are accompanied by records of the sequence of observations. Where feasible, it helps also to relate the sequence to time and to any events or milestones that might affect measured values.

2. **Context data.** Analyzing control charts requires information about the context in which the data were produced in order to properly interpret the record of performance that is plotted on the charts. Thus, as pointed out in

Chapter 2, process performance data should always be accompanied by information that permits questions like the following to be answered [Wheeler 1992]:

- What do the individual values represent? What are these numbers?
- How were the values obtained? Who obtained them? When or how often?
- What sources of variation are present in the data?

Your data collection process must include practices that ensure that context data are captured when reporting product and process measurements.

3. **Rounding of data values.** Your collection processes must ensure that the scales for measuring and recording data are of appropriate granularity and that recorded values are not rounded inappropriately. Either condition can cause control charts to generate out-of-control signals even when the process is in a state of statistical control. A brief illustration of the types of problems that insufficiently precise measurement scales can cause is provided in Chapter 6 of this book. Additional examples and guidelines related to this subject can be found under the topic of "Inadequate Measurement Units" in Wheeler's books [Wheeler 1989, 1992, 1995].

4. **Measurement stability.** When you institute new measures or revise existing measures, your data collection procedures may have to be changed as well. This can result in destabilizing the measurement process. Testing and evaluating new or changed data collection processes with pilot runs can help shake out problems with the procedures and avoid collecting and retaining inappropriate data.

Having a data collection guide that fully describes your data definitions and collection processes will shorten the amount of time required to stabilize your measurement results. It will also improve the quality of the data you collect.

Collecting data is a process. Like any other process, it must be monitored to ensure not only that the data are being collected but also that they are timely, complete, ungarbled, authentic, accurate, and otherwise of good quality. In short, if the results are to be reliable, the collecting process must be stable and under control. This implies that the performance of the measurement process itself should also be measured.

The Personal Software Process (PSP)[1] [Humphrey 1995] serves as an example of obtaining consistent data on individual process performance. The PSP incorporates a self-learning strategy that uses data from the software engineer's own performance to motivate improvement [Hayes 1997]. Figure 3.2 shows that each level of the PSP builds on the capabilities developed and on the historical data gathered in the previous level. Engineers learn to use the PSP by writing ten programs and preparing five written reports. Typically, the engineers choose a programming

---

[1] Personal Software Process and PSP are service marks of Carnegie Mellon University.

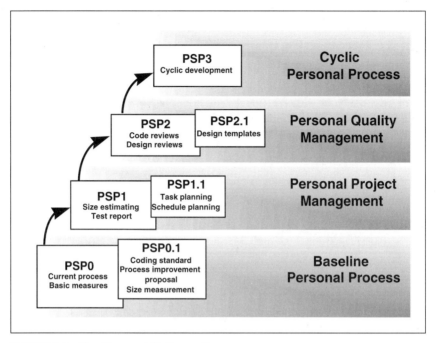

FIGURE 3.2 The Personal Software Process

language and design method in which they are proficient. When the engineers are developing their programs, they collect data on their process that they then summarize, analyze, and feed back to their own process during a postmortem phase. Because of a short feedback cycle, the engineers realize the effect of the PSP and use their own performance data to gauge their improvements.

Figure 3.3 shows the derived measures[2,3,4] with accompanying definitions available in the PSP. Development time, defects, and size are the three primary measures used in this process. Some seventy pieces of data are then collected for each of the ten programming assignments. This data is used by the engineers to assess progress and to determine and guide improvement actions. This serves as one example of how data can be obtained from a defined process designed to motivate personal process improvement. (See Chapter 7 for an example of process improvement using the PSP.)

---

[2] An error or mistake made by a software engineer becomes a *defect* when it goes undetected during design or implementation. If it is corrected before the end of the phase in which it was injected, then typically there is no defect. If it is found at the phase-end review or during compile, test, or after test, then a defect is recorded.

[3] The standard definition of *COQ* includes appraisal cost, failure cost, and prevention cost. In the PSP, only appraisal costs and failure costs are included.

[4] Design *review rates* are based on new and changed LOC. For planning purposes, engineers use estimated new and changed LOC to arrive at planned review rates.

Measure	Definition
Interruption Time	Elapsed time for small interruptions from project work such as a phone call.
Delta Time	Elapsed time in minutes from start to stop less interruptions: stop – start – interruptions.
Planned Time in Phase	Estimated time to be spent in a phase for a project.
Actual Time in Phase	Sum of delta time for a phase of a project.
Total Time in Phase	Total time spent in all phases of a project. Both planned and actual are time in phase are recorded.
To-Date Time in Phase	Sum of actual time in phase of all completed projects.
To-Date Total Time in Phase	Total time spent in all phases of all projects. Only actual to-date total time in phase is recorded.
To-Date % Time in Phase	100 * to-date time in phase for a phase ÷ to-date total time in phase.
Compile Time	Time from start of first compile until first clean compile.
Test Time	Time from start of initial test until test completion.
Defect	Any element of a program design or implementation that must be changed to correct program.
Defect Type	Each defect is classified to a defect type standard (eg: function, interface, document, etc.).
Fix Time	Time to find and fix a defect.
LOC	Logical line of code as defined in engineer's counting and coding standard.
LOC/Hour	Total new and changed LOC developed ÷ total development hours.
Estimating Accuracy	Degree to which estimate matches result. Calculated for time and size. % error = 100 * (actual – estimate)/estimate.
Test Defects/KLOC	Test defects removed per new and changed KLOC. 1,000 * (defects removed in test)/actual new and changed LOC.
Compile Defects/KLOC	Compile defects removed per new and changed KLOC. 1,000 * (defects removed in compile)/actual new and changed LOC.
Total Defects/KLOC	Total defects removed per new and changed KLOC. 1,000 * (total defects removed)/actual new and changed LOC.
Yield	Percent of total defects removed before first compile. 100 * (defects found before first compile)/(defects injected before first compile).
Appraisal Time	Time spent in design and code reviews.
Failure Time	Time spent in compile and test.
Cost of Quality (COQ)	Cost of quality = appraisal time + failure time.
COQ Appraisal/Failure Ratio (A/FR)	A/FR = appraisal time/failure time.
Review Rate	Review rate is lines of code reviewed per hour: 60 * new and changed LOC/review minutes.

FIGURE 3.3   PSP Measures and Definitions

3.3   Reviewing and Assessing Collected Data

Before you begin analyzing measurement data, there are certain criteria that the reported values must satisfy if your analyses are to have any merit or credibility. These criteria—*verity, synchronicity, consistency,* and *validity*—are discussed briefly here. It is important to determine whether or not the reported values satisfy the criteria, and to do this very early in the measurement process. You will also avoid unnecessary rework and improve the reliability of analyses if you keep these criteria in mind when selecting and defining data elements to be measured and the processes you will use for collecting, recording, and retaining measurement results.

3.3.1   CRITERION 1: VERITY

Verified data are data that have been examined to assure that they have been collected according to specifications and contain no errors. Typically, the examination ascertains that the reported values have the following characteristics:

- **Are of the correct type (numeric, alphanumeric).** Often, some data elements can be predetermined to be numeric only. Other data elements may be limited to the use of certain characters or symbols. The examination for verity ascertains that collected and reported data are consistent with such specifications.

- **Are in the correct format.** Nearly all data elements will have specified formats. Dates, monetary values, counts, product names, process names, product IDs, job codes, tools, and priorities are typical examples of data that will have specified formats. In these cases, the values that are reported must be verified to be in the expected formats.

- **Are within specified ranges.** Many kinds of collected data can be examined for valid ranges of values. Valid ranges can be lists of acceptable names or numerical ranges of acceptable dates or values. Impossible values should be investigated and corrected before they contaminate a database.

- **Are complete.** Measurement data must contain the essential data elements and the associated definitions and contextual information that are needed to understand and interpret the data values. For example, each reported value should be identified in terms of the entity measured, time of occurrence, time of collection, collector, definition, and measurement tools used.

- **Are arithmetically correct.** If the collected data contain values that result from arithmetic operations, the examination should verify that the arithmetic operations have been performed correctly.

3.3.2 CRITERION 2: SYNCHRONICITY

You can think of measurements as being synchronous when the values for two or more attributes are related with respect to the time of their occurrence. The notion of synchronized measurements is particularly important when measuring attributes of a process or when using attributes of products and resources to describe the performance of a process.

Measures that are based on arbitrary time frames are particularly susceptible to problems with synchronicity. For example, productivity rates that are computed by comparing outputs to inputs over a period of time can easily be misleading if the resources actually expended are not appropriately matched to the products produced or the period measured. If the time to execute the process is not considered, lags within a process may mean that output statistics do not correspond to input statistics. That is, there is not a valid cause-and-effect relationship. The ratios of outputs to inputs that get used for productivity measures may then have little significance.

3.3.3 CRITERION 3: CONSISTENCY

Consistency is difficult to determine since it implies that the examiner is sufficiently knowledgeable of previously reported data to be able to make this determination. Nevertheless, it is important that outlandish or improbable data elements be investigated and their correctness verified if erroneous analyses are to be avoided. This may involve contacting the source of the data to confirm the correctness of the reported values. It may also involve understanding and recording the circumstances associated with the occurrence of the value so that others can judge later whether or not the data should be used in an analysis.

Inconsistencies in the way measurements get defined or collected can lead to flawed analyses. Examples include the following:

- Values associated with accounting months that become intermixed or confused with values that apply to calendar months.
- Effort expenditures reported in terms of calendar months that contain differing numbers of working days.
- Work-breakdown structures, measurement definitions, and process definitions that change from project to project.
- Changes to personnel or job descriptions that cause reclassifications of effort categories or tasks performed.

No value should be entered into a database until it is confirmed that its definition is consistent with other recorded values of the same type. Self-consistency is essentially an "apples-to-apples" issue. If the ground rules for measurements shift with time or from project to project, it will be very difficult to compare one measured value to another. This, in turn, will make it difficult to attach significance to observed changes or trends in measured results. When data you are recording are inconsistent with data that exist, you should ensure that the two types are kept distinct and that the definitions for each are recorded.

3.3.4   CRITERION 4: VALIDITY

At the most basic level, you must be able to demonstrate that the values used to describe an attribute truly describe the attribute of interest. For this to be true, the measurements must be well defined. In particular, the rules for measuring must be stated explicitly, and this must be done in ways such that there are no questions as to what the rules are. Any decisions left to local interpretation or to the judgment of data collectors must, at worst, lead to only immaterial differences in measured values. These points are discussed fully in Chapter 2.

Requiring that measured values match their definitions does not mean that every project must use exactly the same definitions, but it does mean that the definitions must be stated and recorded explicitly and then communicated explicitly to all who collect or use the measurement results. Without adequate and consistent definitions at all points in the measurement process, no data can be considered to validly represent what they purport to represent.

We are also concerned with validity in another sense—the validity of a prediction system, estimating process, or planning model. Here, validity can be judged only in the context of the purpose for which the measurement results are used. Although validity of this kind may be suggested by theory, it can be tested only by empirical means, such as through comparisons of predicted results with subsequently observed values. When differences occur, you must determine the extent to which the model that is being used differs from the observed process and the extent to which the observed process differs from the expected (future) process. Shewhart's control charts can be of great help here since they help guide judgments about the reasonableness of extrapolating observed performance to future scenarios. In particular, if a process is not stable, there is little basis for assuming that tomorrow's results will be like those of the observed process. In fact, many people would say that you have not one process then, but several. In that case, no extrapolation is likely to be statistically supportable.

Two things are worth noting here. First, predictive validity cannot be determined solely by looking at the data. Claims of predictability always require empirical verification (does the predicting method have a record of success?) [Wheeler 1995]. Second, predictive validity can be affected strongly by the specific definitions used for a measure. This is especially true when decisions of inclusion and exclusion are to be made. For example, how one counts code, what code is counted, what staff hours are counted, and what problems or defects are counted can have marked effects on the abilities of models that use these data as a basis for predicting future outcomes. Checking for predictive validity must include careful checking of both the static and operational portions of measurement definitions to ensure that the rules followed are fit for the purposes intended. This must then be followed up by testing the predictive system to see whether or not the results it predicts are borne out by subsequent experience.

3.4 Retaining Data

Retaining data inherently involves creating and using one or more databases to organize and save the data for later use. Depending on the nature of your measurement activities, this may be a reasonably simple task or a very complex and technically demanding one. In either case, it is important to give serious consideration to the data retention system that will be employed. For example, while hard-copy forms may suffice for some data collection purposes, experience has shown that paper forms are often inadequate for retaining and aggregating measured results.

A personal computer database system and a full-functioned spreadsheet program may be sufficient for retaining and analyzing data for many processes. However, the size and complexity of the retention system will increase significantly if there is a need to support multiple projects or multiple organizations or if you are using the measurement results for multiple purposes. The length of time you must retain the data can also influence your choice of a database system. For example, data for process management will often be retained and used well beyond the duration of individual projects.

3.4.1 DATABASE MANAGEMENT ISSUES

A project management database, if it exists, may well serve as the basis for retaining process measurements for process management. This is something to be considered seriously before undertaking to develop a separate process management database, as there are often many overlaps between data collected for managing projects and data collected for managing processes. There are a number of important considerations for planning, creating, and managing a process measurement database system:

1. Capture and retain definitions and context descriptions, not just direct measurement data.
2. Tie measured values to measurement definitions, rules, practices, and tools used.
3. Tie measured values to the entities and attributes measured.
4. Tie measured values to the contexts and environments in which they were collected (product, environment, and process descriptors; process and project status; time and place measured; method of measurement; and so forth).
5. Accommodate process tailoring (by recording descriptions of process specializations, tailorings, and other differences among processes).
6. Accommodate evolving measurement definitions and process descriptions.
7. Address linking to, accessing, and coordinating with other databases, such as those used for time and cost reporting, cost estimating, configuration management, quality assurance, personnel, and so forth.

8. Avoid storing indirect measures (such as defect densities and rates of change) that can be computed by users from directly measured results. There are three reasons for this advice:

- Storing computed values introduces redundancies in databases that are difficult to keep synchronized. When the underlying data change, indirect measures may not get recomputed.

- If only the results of computations are stored, essential information easily becomes lost.

- Other people may want to compute alternative indirect measures or compute them differently, so the underlying values will need to be retained anyway.

Once you have settled the database planning issues, you should document your operational procedures in detail. This includes identifying

- Who will enter and maintain the data.

- Who can access the data.

- Levels of access. For example, you may not want certain financial data to be available to everyone who has access to staff-hour time records.

- Where the data will be retained.

- The tools you will use, including the editing and retrieval mechanisms.

3.4.2 ADDITIONAL DATABASE MANAGEMENT ISSUES

Some additional database management issues to consider are listed next. None of these issues are unique to software process management. However, we provide the list here to serve as a checklist and a reminder that the methods you use to retain and access data play a significant role in the success of any measurement activity.

- **Operation of the database.** What are the primary responsibilities for operating a database? What tools and practices exist for preventing simultaneous editing? What tools and practices exist for preventing contamination and corruption of previously verified data? What tools and training are available to support browsing, searching, retrieval, and display? What are the backup provisions and practices? Is there sufficient funding to meet the requirements of users? What training is available for database operators?

- **Access to data.** Who is permitted to enter or change data? Who is permitted to access data? Who grants authority to access or change data? Who enforces access and change authority? Who provides the verification of the data? What tools and practices will be used to support controlled access?

- **Data retention.** Where? How long? In what format and media? What are the backup practices (frequency and off-site storage)? Who is responsible?

- **Archiving.** Where? How long? In what format and media? What are the backup practices (frequency and off-site storage)? Who is responsible? Is there sufficient funding?

- **Privacy of personnel and personal performance data.** Is there a need to isolate protected data from public data? Who grants authority to access protected data? Who enforces access rules? What tools and practices will be used to protect privacy?

- **Protection of proprietary data.** Who designates proprietary data? How is proprietary data identified? What tools and practices are used to protect proprietary information? Who can authorize access to or use of proprietary data? What are the ground rules for authorizing access?

- **Security (provisions for handling classified information).** Is there a need for security procedures? Is multilevel security a requirement? What tools and practices will be used to protect security?

- **System design.** Who is responsible for hardware and software selection? What is the nature of the database design (structure) and of communications among databases? Who provides system maintenance, evolution, and operational support? Is there sufficient funding? What training is available?

3.5   Tools for Understanding Your Data

As you collect data to visualize your process or to investigate assignable causes and potential improvements, you will often face the need to sort through and understand the information you obtain. This involves organizing and summarizing your data and looking for patterns, trends, and relationships. Tools such as scatter diagrams, run charts, cause-and-effect diagrams, histograms, bar charts, and Pareto charts can all help you. These tools are described briefly here and illustrated in greater detail in the subsections that follow.

- *Scatter diagrams* (sometimes called *scatter plots*) display empirically observed relationships between two process characteristics. A pattern in the plotted points may suggest that the two factors are associated, perhaps with a cause-and-effect relationship. When the conditions warrant—that is, when there is a constant system of chance causes—scatter diagrams are natural precursors to regression analyses that reveal more precise information about interrelationships in the data.

- *Run charts* are a specialized, time-sequenced form of scatter diagram that can be used to examine data quickly and informally for trends or other patterns that occur over time. They look much like control charts, but without the control limits and centerline.

- *Cause-and-effect diagrams* (also known as *Ishikawa charts*) allow you to probe for, map, and prioritize a set of factors that are thought to affect a particular process, problem, or outcome. They are especially helpful in eliciting and organizing information from people who work within a process and know what might be causing it to perform the way it does.

- *Histograms* are displays of empirically observed distributions. They show the frequencies of events that have occurred over a given set of observations and period of time. Histograms can be used to characterize the observed values of almost any product or process attribute. Examples include module size, defect repair time, time between failures, defects found per test or inspection, and daily backlogs. Histograms can be helpful for revealing differences that have taken place across processes, projects, or times.

- *Bar charts* are similar in many ways to histograms, but they need not be based on measures of continuous variables or frequency counts.

- *Pareto charts* are a special form of histogram or bar chart. They help focus investigations and solution finding by ranking problems, causes, or actions in terms of their amounts, frequencies of occurrence, or economic consequences.

The subsections that follow give brief descriptions of these analytical tools and techniques. More complete illustrations, albeit in nonsoftware settings, can be found in several references [Ishikawa 1986; Brassard 1988, 1989; Montgomery 1996]. The Venn diagram in Figure 3.4 shows where the tools described next fit relative to the fact-finding and analysis activities that lead to identifying root causes and potential solutions [Brassard 1988, 1989].

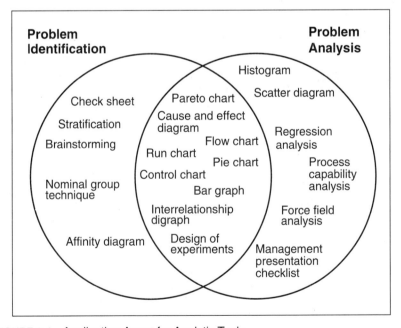

FIGURE 3.4 Application Areas for Analytic Tools

3.5.1   SCATTER DIAGRAMS

A scatter diagram, like the one in Figure 3.5, is a plot of observed values that shows how one variable has behaved relative to another. Scatter diagrams are often used as a first step in the exploration of data, especially as part of a search for cause-and-effect relationships. Sometimes, there is an assumption that one variable is "dependent" and that the other is "independent," but this does not have to be the case.

Scatter diagrams are used to address questions such as these: Does company A's product work better than company B's? Does the length of training have anything to do with the number of defects an engineer injects? Are there any obvious trends in the data? When a scatter diagram suggests that a relationship may exist between two variables, its use is often followed by more formal statistical methods such as exploratory data analysis or regression analysis.

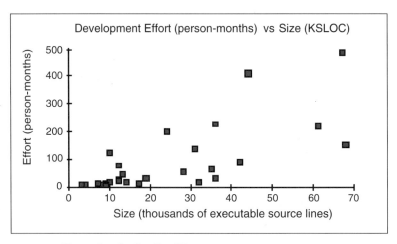

FIGURE 3.5   Example of a Scatter Diagram

Scatter diagrams (sometimes called *scatter plots*) are limited in that they usually deal with only two variables at a time. This constraint exists because the results are displayed on sheets of paper or CRT screens, both of which are two-dimensional media. When you have reason to investigate more than two dimensions at a time, you will likely want to use more formal (statistical) methods that facilitate multivariate analyses. Here, though, the pitfalls are many, and it is easy for amateurs to go astray. We strongly suggest that you solicit the assistance of a competent statistician. Furthermore, we urge you to do this before the data are collected. Good statisticians know things that will help you get data in ways that will help you reach valid conclusions economically.

3.5.2   RUN CHARTS

A run chart is a plot of individual values arranged in a time sequence. Example charts are given in Figures 3.6 through 3.9. Run charts can be used to monitor a

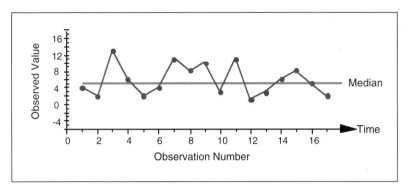

FIGURE 3.6 Example of a Run Chart with Level Performance

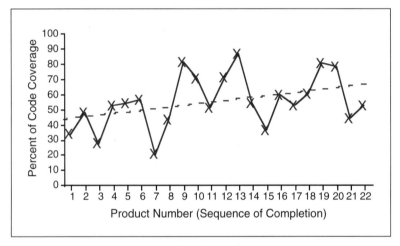

FIGURE 3.7 Example of a Run Chart with a Rising Trend

process to see whether trends are apparent or whether the behavior of the process is changing in other ways. Observed values of production throughput, product size, team size, number of defects found, backlogs, and cumulative or daily resource consumption are all candidates for run charts. Run charts can visually display the behavior of any interval- or ratio-scale variable.

One danger in using a run chart is the tendency to see every variation in the plotted values as being important. The control charts discussed and illustrated in Chapters 4, 5, and 6—with their control limits, run tests, and formal tests for unusual patterns—were developed specifically to counter this tendency. In one sense, run charts are nothing other than precursors to control charts. Although interpreting run charts can be risky without a formal methodology, it is often possible to relate sudden shifts in plotted values or trends to specific events. When these relationships exist, it is helpful to annotate the run chart to indicate the events.

Run charts, like Pareto charts and histograms, refer to events that occurred in a particular time period. Thus, they should show the time period covered, the

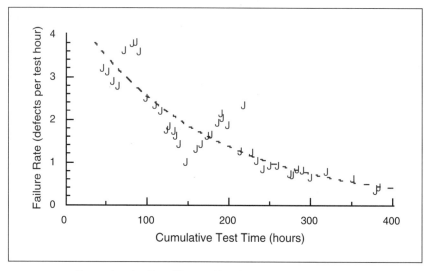

FIGURE 3.8   Example of a Run Chart with a Falling Trend

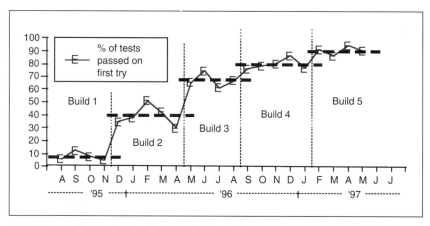

FIGURE 3.9   Example of a Sequential Run Chart

frequency of measurement (if appropriate), and the unit of measurement used. Centerlines such as medians of means (averages) are sometimes shown, but this can induce misinterpretation when the process that produced the data is not under statistical control.

3.5.3   CAUSE-AND-EFFECT DIAGRAMS

A cause-and-effect diagram is a graphical display that is used to probe for and show relationships between a problem (the effect) and its possible causes. Cause-and-effect diagrams are often called *Ishikawa charts,* after the man who originated them in 1943 [Ishikawa 1986]. They are also called *fishbone charts* because of their visual similarity to the skeleton of a fish.

When cause-and-effect diagrams are used to explore the behavior of a process, it is best if the diagrams are assembled by people who actually work in the process. When it comes to pinpointing problems and searching for root causes, there is no substitute for firsthand knowledge.

It is also wise to have people expert in different parts of the process participate. Diagrams drawn by one or two people are apt to be ineffective because they lack a sufficiently broad base of observational experience. For this reason, cause-and-effect diagrams are often drawn during brainstorming sessions that include people with differing viewpoints. Although cause-and-effect diagrams are (initially) subjective, they can be based on (and annotated to show) factual information such as measured values and dates of occurrences.

Cause-and-effect (CE) diagrams can be divided into three types [Ishikawa 1986]:

1. **Dispersion analysis type.** The dispersion analysis type of CE diagram is constructed by repeatedly asking the question, Why does this dispersion (or scatter) occur? Its strong point is that it helps organize and relate factors that cause variability in products and other process outcomes. Its weak points are that the form of the resulting diagram is dependent on the views of the people making it and that small causes may not get isolated or observed.

2. **Production process classification type.** The production process classification type of CE diagram is constructed by stepping mentally through the production process. This may be done in one of two ways: (1) by making the steps in the process the major ribs of a fishbone diagram or (2) by superimposing boxes on the backbone so that each box is a step in the production process. When the process steps are displayed along the backbone as illustrated in Figure 3.10), the causes are depicted on lines

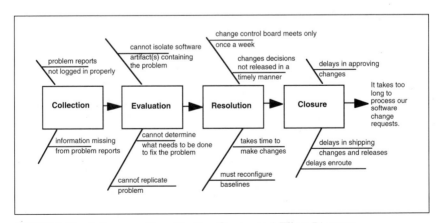

FIGURE 3.10   A Process Classification Cause-and-Effect Diagram

(ribs) that feed into either a box or one of the backbone segments that connects sequential boxes. The strength of this type of diagram is that it is easy to assemble and understand. The weaknesses are that similar causes often appear in more than one place and that problems resulting from combinations of more than one factor are difficult to illustrate.

3. Cause enumeration type. The cause enumeration type of CE diagram is generated by listing all possible causes and then organizing the causes to show their relationships to the aspect of product or process quality that is being examined [Ishikawa 1986]. Figure 3.11 shows a simple example. This type of cause-and-effect diagram can also be produced in brainstorming sessions where principal categories such as manpower, materials (inputs), methods, and machinery (tools) are used to prompt probing questions that uncover possible causes. The completed diagram may end up looking much like one produced by the dispersion analysis process, but it may not. The thought processes used to generate cause enumeration charts are (and should be) more free-form and less constrained than for dispersion analysis charts. The strength of the cause enumeration chart is that enumerating large numbers of likely causes reduces the probability of overlooking a major problem area. When done well, this tends to give a more complete picture than a chart produced by dispersion analysis. The weakness is that it may be hard to relate the twigs of the tree to the end result, which can make the diagram difficult to draw and to interpret.

Whatever method you use for producing cause-and-effect diagrams, be on the lookout for diagrams with many major ribs and few twigs. This almost always indicates either that the understanding of the process was shallow or that the diagram is too generalized. Use care also when a diagram lists only five or six causes. This kind of diagram is usually inadequately penetrating, even though its form may be correct.

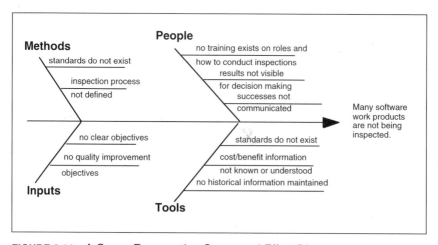

FIGURE 3.11   A Cause Enumeration Cause-and-Effect Diagram

3.5.4 HISTOGRAMS

A histogram takes measurement data and displays the distribution of the observed values. Histograms are created by grouping the results of measurement into "cells" and then counting the number in each cell. The cells are nonoverlapping, equal-width intervals along some continuous scale. The heights of the bars in histograms are proportional to the number of occurrences within each cell, as illustrated in Figure 3.12.

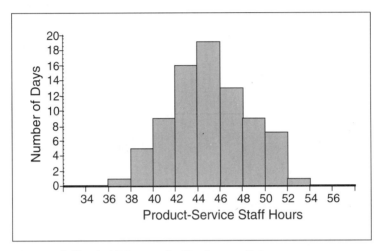

FIGURE 3.12 A Simple Histogram for Continuous Data

Histograms display frequency counts in ways that make it easy to compare distributions and see central tendencies and dispersions. As we will see in Chapters 5 and 7, histograms are useful for investigating and summarizing the performance of a process with respect to the specification limits that the process or its products must satisfy.

Histograms can be helpful troubleshooting aids. Comparisons between histograms from different subprocesses, operators, vendors, or periods of time often provide insights that point to potential causes, trends, or needs for stratification. For example, twin peaks may indicate that the data have come from two different sources, each with its own distinct characteristics. If so, control charting and other interpretive or predictive applications would not be appropriate until the data have been stratified according to source.

3.5.5 BAR CHARTS

A bar chart, like a histogram, is used to investigate the shape of a data set. Figure 3.13 is an example. Bar charts are similar in many respects to histograms but are defined on sets of discrete values. Thus, they can display any numerical value, not just counts or relative frequencies. So, bar charts can be used to display data such as the total size, cost, or elapsed time associated with individual entities or with sets of products or process steps.

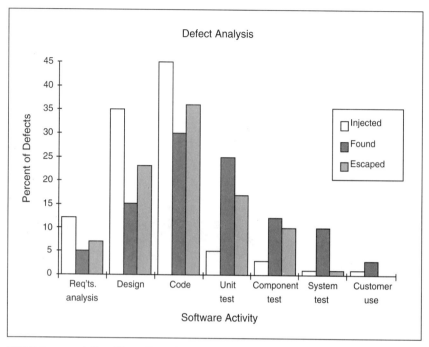

FIGURE 3.13 A Bar Chart That Compares Three Discrete Distributions

Because bar charts are defined on discrete scales, cell width is irrelevant, and there are always gaps between cells. You are free to use bars of any width you like. Bars of different widths, though, should be used only as one of several possible ways to distinguish between different data sets (coloring, shading, staggering, or labeling are usually preferable).

The concepts of average and standard deviation have no meaning for the independent variable in bar charts that are defined on discrete scales whose values are not equally spaced on the real number line. Medians, modes, and ranges, however, can be used with ordinal scales, even though the distance between cells has no meaning.

3.5.6 PARETO CHARTS

Pareto analysis is a process for ranking causes, alternatives, or outcomes to help determine which should be pursued as high-priority actions or opportunities for improvement. It is a useful technique for separating the "vital few" from the "trivial many" [Juran 1988]. A Pareto chart can be used at various stages in a quality improvement program to help select the steps to take next. Pareto charts can also be used to address questions such as these: On which types of defect should we concentrate our efforts? What parts of the process are the biggest contributors to the problem we are examining?

In their simplest forms, Pareto charts are essentially frequency counts or amounts displayed in descending order, as illustrated in Figure 3.14. In more sophisticated analyses, Pareto charts may rank causal factors or potential actions in decreasing order of their estimated economic costs or consequences.

Pareto charts may seem simple, and they are. Nevertheless, the benefits that this kind of visual display has over a table of numbers should not be underrated. As those who have succeeded in quality improvement can attest, much of the battle lies in getting everyone in a group—employees and managers alike—to share a common view of the problems faced and the actions needed.[5] Pareto charts help to create this common view.

As simple as Pareto charts are, there are some points that should not be overlooked. In particular, the frequencies or other values plotted on a Pareto chart almost always have a time period associated with them. This time period should be made explicit so that viewers of the chart can attach correct interpretations to the rankings that are displayed.

One effective use of Pareto charts is to compare the before and after states related to improvement actions. This can give a quick visual appreciation of the effectiveness and progress (or lack thereof) related to actions that have been taken. Formal methods exist for testing whether or not differences between successive Pareto charts may be due solely to chance so that inappropriate conclusions will not be drawn [Kenett 1991].

One caution: If the processes that produced the data are not stable, Pareto charts easily lead to erroneous conclusions and improper actions. This is especially true when the chart shows frequencies of occurrence for different types of problems, some of which may have assignable causes. Assignable causes mean uncontrolled

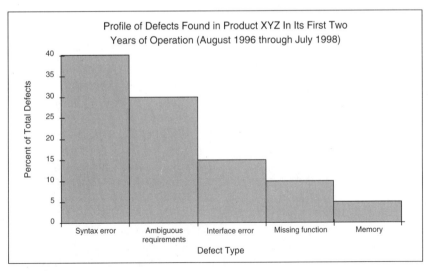

FIGURE 3.14 Example of a Pareto Chart

---

[5] For example, that it is easier and more consequential to reduce a tall bar by half than to reduce a short bar to zero.

variation, and these causes come and go. Frequencies associated with assignable causes have little meaning since there is no single distribution that underlies them. When a process is not in statistical control, the Pareto chart can easily look radically different from month to month, even when no action is taken.

3.6 Summary

In this chapter, we focused our attention to collecting and retaining process management data. The operational activities of measurement begin with collecting data. The procedures that you define for collecting and retaining data need to be integrated into your software processes and made operational. This means putting the right people, sensors, tools, and practices into the processes in the right places. It also means capturing and storing the data for subsequent use in analysis and process improvement.

The principal tasks associated with collecting and retaining data for process management are as follows:

- Designing the methods and obtaining the tools that will be used to support data collection and retention.
- Obtaining and training the staff that will execute the data collection procedures.
- Capturing and recording the data for each process that is targeted for measurement.
- Using defined forms and formats to supply the collected data to the individuals and groups who perform analyses.
- Monitoring the execution (compliance) and performance of the activities for collecting and retaining data.

Collecting data is more than just making measurements. It involves identifying the responsible persons and organizations; specifying where, when, and how measurements will be made; defining the procedures to be used for recording and reporting results; and providing standard "fill-in-the-blank" forms to simplify manual recording of the data.

Retaining data inherently involves creating and using one or more databases to organize and save the data for later use. Depending on the nature of your measurement activities, this may be a reasonably simple task or a very complex and technically demanding one. In either case, it is important to give serious consideration to the data retention system that will be employed.

And finally, as you collect data to visualize your process or to investigate assignable causes and potential improvements, you will often face the need to organize and summarize your data and look for patterns, trends, and relationships. Tools such as scatter diagrams, run charts, cause-and-effect diagrams, histograms, bar charts, and Pareto charts can assist you with these analyses.

4

Analyzing Process Behavior

A phenomenon will be said to be controlled when, through the use of past experience, we can predict, at least within limits, how the phenomenon may be expected to vary in the future. Here it is understood that prediction within limits means that we can state, at least approximately, the probability that the observed phenomenon will fall within the given limits.

Walter A. Shewhart 1931

In this chapter, as well as Chapters 5 and 6, we will address the principles that are the basis for quantifying and analyzing process behavior as shown in Figure 4.1. The discussion in this chapter leads to the introduction of Shewhart's control charts as an operational definition of process behavior in terms of process performance, stability, and predictability. Chapter 5 is dedicated to providing the information to construct and calculate limits for the several different control charts applicable to software processes. Chapter 6 discusses a number of topics that arise when using control charts.

Control charts are techniques for quantifying process behavior.[1] Control charts and associated methods of statistical quality control are most effective when they are used within the broader context of the goals you have established and the activities you perform to achieve those goals. The preceding chapters have set this context. The focus of this chapter is on the fundamental issues that underlie effective use of control charts for guiding process measurement and improvement actions.

There is more to preparing and using control charts than selecting a chart type, plotting data, and calculating control limits. In the next several chapters, we will try to alert you to the significant factors that should be considered. In addition, if you wish to benefit from others experienced in statistical process control and control charts, you should consult one of the many texts available on the subject. The books of Donald J. Wheeler, Thomas Pyzdek, and Douglas C. Montgomery are particularly good at describing how to use control charts, albeit in the more traditional context of industrial processes [Wheeler 1992, 1993, 1995, 1998; Pyzdek

---

[1] In the ensuing chapters, we will use the term *process behavior charts* interchangeably with *control charts* to remind the reader that the purpose of the charts is to understand the process behavior in terms of process improvement, not just control.

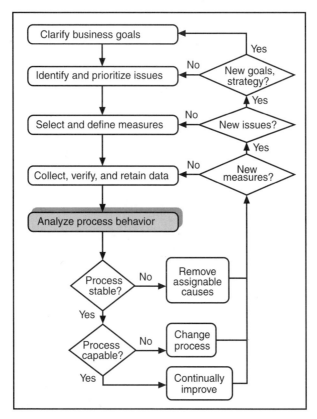

FIGURE 4.1 Process Measurement Framework Guide to Chapters 4, 5, and 6

1990, 1992; Montgomery 1996]. Nevertheless, these references are well grounded in theory, and their real focus is on understanding and applying basic principles and avoiding pitfalls. They do not require an educational background steeped in statistics or advanced mathematics.

4.1 Separating Signals from Noise

ANALYZING PROCESS DATA

Data are generally collected as bases for action. No matter what the data or how the values are presented, you must always use some method of analysis to extract and interpret the information that lies in the data. Making sense of data is a process in itself, as illustrated schematically in Figure 4.2.

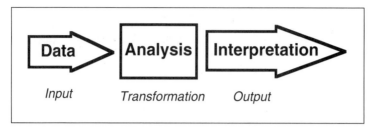

FIGURE 4.2 Interpretation of Data Requires Analysis

Variation exists in all data and consists of both noise (random variation) and signal (nonrandom variation). The values that are reported must be filtered somehow to separate the signals from the noise that accompanies them. This filtration may be based (subjectively) upon a person's experience and his or her presuppositions and assumptions, or it may be based on a more formalized approach. Without formal and standardized approaches for analyzing data, you may have difficulty interpreting and using your measurement results.

When you interpret and act on measurement results, you are presuming that the measurements represent reality. Unless legitimate signals can be distinguished from the noise that accompanies them, the actions that you take may be totally unwarranted. Acting on noise as if it were signal serves only to amplify instabilities and increase the variability in process results. To use data safely, you must have simple and effective methods not only for detecting signals that are surrounded by noise but also for recognizing and dealing with normal process variations when no signals are present.

The reason for analyzing process data is to draw inferences that can be used to guide decisions and actions. Drawing inferences—that is, conclusions and predictions—from data depends not only on using appropriate analytical methods and tools but also on understanding the underlying nature of the data and the appropriateness of assumptions about the conditions and environments in which the data were obtained.

There are two ways to obtain statistical inferences: (1) from *enumerative* studies and (2) from *analytic* studies [Deming 1975]. The aim of an enumerative study is descriptive—to determine "how many" as opposed to "why so many." The aim of an analytic study is to predict or improve the behavior of the process in the future.

The differences between the two are important and affect the kinds of inferences that can be drawn from measurement results. Techniques and methods of inference that are applicable to enumerative studies lead to faulty design and inference for analytic problems. The differences between enumerative and analytic studies are discussed in some detail in Appendix B. The implications of the differences deserve considerable reflection before you begin interpreting and acting on the results of any analysis. We simply reiterate that most analyses of process issues are analytic studies and that the methods in this chapter are aimed at guiding valid interpretations in these kinds of studies.

4.1.2 PROCESS PERFORMANCE VARIATION

All characteristics of processes and products display variation when measured over time. We offer the following excerpt from Shewhart's book *Economic Control of Quality of Manufactured Product* to illustrate this principle:

> *Write the letter "a" on a piece of paper. Now make another a just like the first one; then another and another until you have a series of a's, a, a, a,... You try to make all the a's alike but you don't; you can't. You are willing to accept this as an empirically established fact. But what of it? Let us see just what this means in respect to control. Why can we not do a simple thing like making all the a's exactly alike? Your answer leads to a generalization which all of us are perhaps willing to accept. It is that there are many causes of variability among the a's: The paper was not smooth, the lead in the pencil was not uniform, and the unavoidable variability in your external surroundings reacted upon you to introduce variation in the a's. But are these the only causes of variability in the a's? Probably not.*
>
> *We accept our human limitations and say that likely there are many other factors. If we could but name all the reasons why we cannot make the little a's alike, we would most assuredly have a better understanding of a certain part of nature than we now have. Of course, this conception of what it means to be able to do what we want to do is not new; it does not belong exclusively to any one field of human thought; it is commonly accepted.*
>
> *The point to be made in this simple illustration is that we are limited in doing what we want to do; that to do what we set out to do, even in so simple a thing as making a's that are alike, requires almost infinite knowledge compared with that which we now possess. It follows, therefore, since we are thus willing to accept as axiomatic that we cannot do what we want to do and cannot hope to understand why we cannot, that we must also accept as axiomatic that a controlled quality will not be a constant quality. Instead, a controlled quality must be a **variable** quality. This is the first characteristic.*
>
> *But let us go back to the results of the experiment on the a's and we shall find out something more about control. Your a's are different from my a's; there is something about your a's that makes them yours and something about my a's that makes them mine.*
>
> *True, not all of your a's are alike. Neither are all of my a's alike. Each group of a's varies within a certain range and yet each group is distinguishable from the others. This distinguishable and, as it were, constant variability **within limits** is the second characteristic of control.*
>
> Walter A. Shewhart 1931

Shewhart goes on to categorize sources of variation as follows:

- Variation due to phenomena that are natural and inherent to the process and whose results are common to all measurements of a given attribute.

- Variations that have assignable causes that could have been prevented.

In equation form, the concept is

[total variation] = [common cause variation] + [assignable cause variation]

Common cause variation is variation in process performance due to normal or inherent interaction among the process components (people, machines, material, environment, and methods). Common cause variation of process performance is characterized by a stable and consistent pattern of measured values over time, as illustrated in Figure 4.3.[2] Variation in process performance due to common cause is thus random but will vary within predictable bounds. When a process is stable, the random variations in measured values that we see all come from a *constant system of chance causes.* We can think of a constant system of chance causes as causes that create common cause variation or "noise." The variation in process performance is predictable, and unexpected results are extremely rare. The key word here is *predictable,* which is synonymous with *in control.*

The processes that we use in business and industry, however, are rarely in control. As Shewhart points out,

> *...in the majority of cases there are unknown causes of variability in the quality of a product which do not belong to a constant system. This fact was discovered very early in the development of control methods, and these causes were called assignable.*
>
> Walter A. Shewhart 1931

Variations in process performance due to assignable causes have marked impacts on product characteristics and other measures of process performance.[3] These impacts create significant changes in the patterns of variation, as illustrated in Figure 4.4.[4] Assignable cause variations arise from events that are not part of

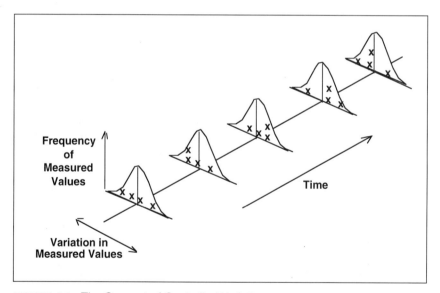

FIGURE 4.3 The Concept of Controlled Variation

---

[2] Figure adapted from *Understanding Statistical Process Control,* 2nd ed., by Donald J. Wheeler and David S. Chambers, © 1992 SPC Press, Inc., Knoxville, Tenn.

[3] Assignable causes are sometimes called *special causes,* a term introduced by W. Edwards Deming.

[4] Figure adapted from *Understanding Statistical Process Control,* 2nd ed., by Donald J. Wheeler and David S. Chambers, © 1992 SPC Press, Inc., Knoxville, Tenn.

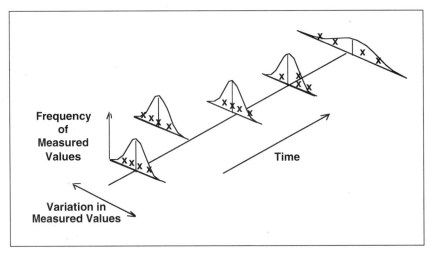

FIGURE 4.4   The Concept of Uncontrolled or Assignable Cause Variation

the normal process. They represent sudden or persistent abnormal changes to one or more of the process components. These changes can be in things such as inputs to the process, the environment, the process steps themselves, or the way in which the process steps are executed. Examples of assignable causes of variation include shifts in the quality of raw materials, inadequately trained people, changes to work environments, tool failures, altered methods, failures to follow the process, and so forth.

When all assignable causes have been removed and prevented from recurring in the future so that only a single, constant system of chance causes remains, we have a stable and predictable process. Stability of a process with respect to any given attribute is determined by measuring the attribute and tracking the results over time. If one or more measurements fall outside the range of chance variation or if systematic patterns are apparent, the process may not be stable. We must then look for the causes of deviation and remove any that we find if we want to achieve a stable and predictable state of operation.

4.2   Evaluating Process Stability

We turn now to the topic of process stability and look at some of the methods that can be used to quantify and evaluate process performance.

4.2.1   THE IMPORTANCE OF STABILITY

When a control chart indicates no special cause present, the process is said to be in statistical control, or stable. The average and limits of variation are predictable with a high degree of belief, over the immediate future. Quality and quantity are predictable. Costs are predictable. "Just in time" begins to take on meaning.

W. Edwards Deming 1993

As we pointed out earlier, process stability is central to any organization's ability to produce products according to plan. It is also central to improving processes and to producing better and more competitive products. The facts are these:

- Without stability and the associated knowledge of what a process can do, we have no way to distinguish signals in measured values from the random noise that accompanies them. Measurements then easily lead to inappropriate actions.

- Without a history of stable performance, uncontrolled excursions can occur at any time. We then have no rational basis for extrapolating observed performance to future situations, and all plans that we make are at risk.

- Without knowing what the stable level of performance is, we have no basis for recognizing assignable causes that signal improvement opportunities.

- Without stability, we have no repeatable process to use as a baseline for process improvement. In fact, some would say that we have, not one process, but many—all different. Effects of improvement actions may then be indistinguishable from other assignable causes.

Therefore, to use product and process measures for predicting future results or as bases for process improvement (two instances of analytic studies), we must first ensure that the process behavior is stable.

4.2.2   STABILITY CONCEPTS AND PRINCIPLES

In a stable process, the sources of variability are due solely to *common causes.* All variations in a stable process are caused by inherent factors that are part of the process itself. Variations due to *assignable causes,* such as those caused by operator errors, environmental changes, deviations from the process, and changing characteristics in raw materials and resources, have been either removed from the process and prevented from reentering (if detrimental) or incorporated as a permanent part of the process (if beneficial).

A stable process is one that is in statistical control. That is, the underlying distributions of its measurable characteristics or process performance are consistent over time. Consider the earlier representation of a stable process (Figure 4.3), illustrated again here in Figure 4.5.[5] Each X in the figure represents a measured value of a given characteristic of a process or product. In this example, randomly selected samples of four units (a *subgroup* of size $n = 4$) of a product were measured at five points in time. The locations of the Xs represent the actual measured

---

[5] Figure adapted from *Understanding Statistical Process Control,* 2nd ed., by Donald J. Wheeler and David S. Chambers, © 1992 SPC Press, Inc., Knoxville, Tenn.

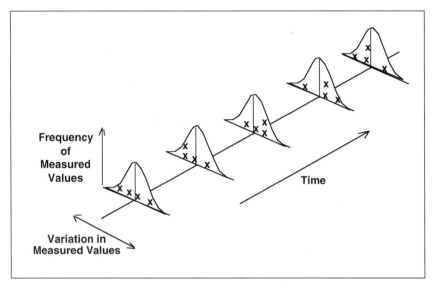

FIGURE 4.5 An Idealized Process in Statistical Control

values of each unit within each subgroup. Different values were observed for each unit at each sampling point due to inherent process variability (common cause variation). The curves in Figure 4.5 represent the distribution of the underlying variability of the measures of each product unit. Each curve has the same central tendency and dispersion. Because the process is stable, the same curve represents the distribution or variability of the product characteristic at each sample point. Continued operation of the process will remain stable as long as the distribution of future measured values of the product are consistent with the central tendency and dispersion of the previous measurements.

4.2.3 TESTING FOR STABILITY

To test a process for stability, (1) we need to know how variable the values are within the subgroup (samples) at each measurement point, and (2) we need to compare this to the variability that we observe from one subgroup to another. More specifically, we need to determine whether the variation over time is consistent with the variation that occurs within the subgroup. We also need to detect possible drifts or shifts in the central tendency of the measured values.

One technique that is often used to establish operational limits for acceptable variation is statistical process control (SPC). SPC and its associated control charts were developed by Walter A. Shewhart in the 1920s to gain control of production costs and quality. Shewhart's techniques were used extensively in World War II and again in more recent years by W. Edwards Deming and others as a basis for improving product quality, both in Japan and in many U.S. companies. As a result of the successes of SPC in industrial settings, the techniques have been adopted for use in many other business areas.

Shewhart's control charts provide a simple and effective means for conducting these tests. They are the statistical tools of choice to use when determining whether or not a process is stable [Wheeler 1992, 1993, 1995].

> *...the method of attack is to establish limits of variability...such that when [a value] is found outside of these limits, looking for an assignable cause is worthwhile.*
>
> Walter A. Shewhart 1931

Look again at Figure 4.5 to see how this idealized view of a stable process is reflected on a control chart. Since we have defined this to be a stable process, the variability of the product characteristic at each sampling point or *subgroup* is due solely to common cause variation. Therefore, each sample can be considered a *homogeneous subgroup*. We can then evaluate changes in central tendency by computing the *average* of the four measurements within each subgroup and plotting the results on a time scale. This lets us view the performance of the process in a time (or sequence) dimension.

The upper portion of Figure 4.6[6] shows the results for the values illustrated in Figure 4.5. This is called an *X-bar* or *average chart*. The changes in the averages show the observed variation in central tendency from one subgroup to the next. Similarly, the *range* of the values within each subgroup can be calculated and plotted, as shown in the lower portion of Figure 4.6. This is called an *R chart*. R charts show the observed dispersion in process performance across subgroups.[7] Control limits for X-bar and R charts can then be calculated from the range data and subgroup averages. Calculating control limits is illustrated later in Chapter 5.

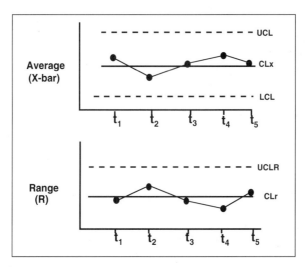

FIGURE 4.6   X-bar and R Charts for a Process That Is in Control

---

[6] Figure adapted from *Understanding Statistical Process Control*, 2nd ed., by Donald J. Wheeler and David S. Chambers, © 1992 SPC Press, Inc., Knoxville, Tenn.

[7] Another form of chart called an *S chart* can also be used for this purpose, but the computations are somewhat more involved.

With control charts like the ones in Figure 4.6, we have a picture that tells us how the process has behaved with respect to a particular product or process characteristic over the period that was examined. The R chart tells us that the range of each subgroup—the difference between the smallest and the largest value in that subgroup—did not exceed the limits of subgroup range variation (UCLR). At the same time, the X-bar chart shows that none of the subgroup average values fell outside the upper or lower variation control limits (UCL and LCL) for subgroups of size 4. Finally, neither chart suggests any systematic or nonrandom patterns in the measured values over the period studied.

In short, plotting this set of data on X-bar and R control charts gives no "out-of-control" indications. This should be no surprise since we stipulated at the outset that the process was in control. By using control charts, we have merely illustrated graphically the empirical conditions that must be satisfied for a process to be considered stable.

Figure 4.7,[8] on the other hand, shows a process that is out of control. By plotting the measured values on averages and range (X-bar and R) control charts as in Figure 4.8,[9] we see that the X-bar chart shows the average of the second subgroup to be above the upper control limit. This, by itself, is sufficient to suggest that the process is not in control. The subgroup range also exceeds its upper control limit at t_5. This is another indication that one or more assignable causes may have affected the process and that the process is out of control and unpredictable.

To some, SPC is a way of thinking, with tools attached. Its aim is to improve processes through causal analysis. SPC differs from other, more traditional

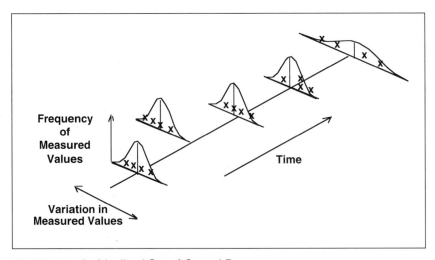

FIGURE 4.7   An Idealized Out-of-Control Process

[8, 9] Figures adapted from *Understanding Statistical Process Control,* 2nd ed., by Donald J. Wheeler and David S. Chambers, © 1992 SPC Press, Inc., Knoxville, Tenn.

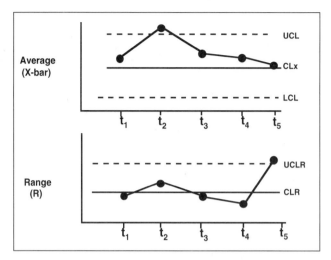

FIGURE 4.8   X-bar and R Charts for an Out-of-Control Process

approaches—such as problem management, zero defects, and repairing and re-working products after they have been produced—in that it provides more constructive help in reducing the causes of defects and improving quality. The principal thesis of this book is that the techniques of SPC can be applied to software processes just as they have been to industrial processes, both to establish process stability and predictability and to serve as a basis for process improvement.

For example, Figure 4.9 shows a control chart for the number of reported but unresolved problems backlogged over the first 30 weeks of system testing. The chart indicates that the problem resolution process is stable and that it is averaging about 20 backlogged problems—the centerline (CL), equals 20.04—with an average change in backlog of 4.35 problems from week to week. The upper control limit (UCL) for backlogged problems is about 32, and the lower control limit (LCL) is about 8. If future backlogs were to exceed these limits or show other forms of nonrandom behavior, it would be likely that the process has become unstable. The causes should then be investigated. For instance, if the upper limit is exceeded at any point, this could be a signal that there are problems in the problem resolution process. Perhaps a particularly thorny defect is consuming resources, thus causing problems to pile up. If so, corrective action must be taken if the process is to be returned to its original (characteristic) behavior.

We must be careful not to misinterpret the limits on the individual observations and moving ranges that are shown in the control chart. These limits are estimates for the *limits of the process,* based on measurements of the process performance. The process limits together with the centerlines are sometimes referred to as the "voice of the process."

The performance indicated by the voice of the process is not necessarily the performance that needs to be provided to meet the customer's requirements. If the variability and location of the measured results are such that the process, albeit stable, does not meet the customer's requirements or specifications—for example,

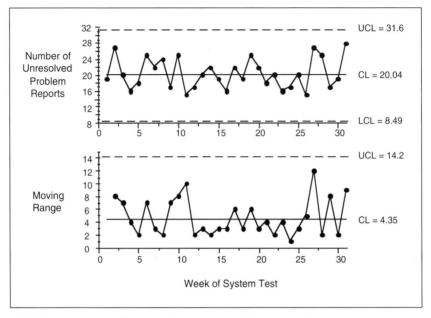

FIGURE 4.9   Control Chart for the Backlog of Unresolved Problems

it produces too many nonconforming products—the process must be improved. This means reducing the process performance variability, moving the average, or both. We will illustrate these alternatives in Chapter 7 when we address the issue of process capability.

4.3   Control Chart Basics

4.3.1   THE STRUCTURE OF CONTROL CHARTS

To begin, all classical control charts have a centerline and control limits on both sides of the centerline. Both the centerline and the limits represent estimates that are calculated from a set of observations collected while the process is running. The centerline and control limits cannot be assigned arbitrarily since they are intended to reveal what the process can actually do (its current level of performance), not what you or anyone else wants it to do.

The values plotted on a control chart can be values obtained from any statistic that has been defined on the sequence of individual measurements.[10] Subgroup averages, subgroup ranges, moving averages, moving ranges, and individual values themselves are all examples of statistics that can be plotted in time sequence and used as a basis for control charts.

---

[10] A statistic is a single-valued function of observable random variables that is itself an observable random variable and that contains no unknown parameters [Mood 1974].

The basic layout of control charts is illustrated in Figure 4.10. The centerline is usually the observed process average, although sometimes other measures of central tendency such as the median or midrange are used. The control limits on either side of the centerline are derived from one of several possible measures of process variability—ranges within subgroups being probably the most common.[11] The traditional (Shewhart) control limits are ±3 sigma, where sigma is the (estimated) standard deviation of the statistic plotted on the chart.[12] When a control limit lies beyond the range of possible outcomes, such as a negative value for product size, number of defects, or subgroup range, that control limit is usually omitted.

Both Shewhart and Wheeler make strong cases for always using 3-sigma limits for control charts [Shewhart 1931, 1939; Wheeler 1992, 1995]. Using 3-sigma limits avoids the need to make assumptions about the distribution of the underlying natural variation. Moreover, experience over many years of control charting has shown 3-sigma limits to be economical in the sense that they are adequately sensitive to unusual variations while leading to very few (costly) false alarms— regardless of the underlying distribution. Appendix B contains a more detailed discussion of 3-sigma limits, the central limit theorem, and the role of the normal distribution.

One of the most important principles (and skills) associated with control charting involves using knowledge of the process to select subgroups that contain, insofar as possible, only common cause variation. This is called *rational*

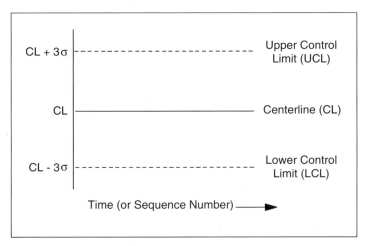

FIGURE 4.10 *Control Chart Structure*

---

[11] Whatever the measure used for establishing estimated control limits, you should always try to ensure that the estimates are based solely on the effects of common cause variation. Any special-cause variations that creep in will make the limits too wide.

[12] On X-bar charts, sigma will be the standard deviation for individual values divided by $\sqrt{n}$, where n is the number of observations in each subgroup. Thus,

$$sigma_{\bar{x}} = \frac{sigma_x}{\sqrt{n}}$$

subgrouping. The purpose of rational subgrouping is to permit the computation of estimates for standard deviations (values for sigma[13]) that are uncontaminated by assignable cause variations. This both narrows the control limits and provides the highest possible reliability for detecting unusual variations (signals) between subgroups with a minimum of false alarms.

Wheeler also shows how easy it is to estimate sigma incorrectly if you don't have a firm grasp on the concepts of rational sampling and rational subgrouping [Wheeler 1992]. For instance, people not well versed in control charting often use the standard deviation across all observed values as their estimate for sigma. This erroneous procedure lumps assignable cause variation together with common cause variation and almost always leads to control limits that are far too wide to be effective.

Since the values you plot on control charts are statistics, they can be any function of the measured properties of a product or process that you wish (or have reason to expect) to vary due to common causes over time. These data can be obtained by measuring attributes such as team size, elapsed time between milestones or events, staff hours expended per task, productivity, personnel turnover, tardiness, tool usage, backlog, number of defective units found, number of defects found per 1,000 units, and so forth.

In software environments, as in many other white-collar activities, measurements often occur only as individual values. You may not have opportunities to draw samples of size $n > 1$ in ways where the inherent variation within each sample can reasonably be assumed to be homogeneous. This is particularly true when measures are separated by a prolonged period. As we shall see shortly, this often leads us away from X-bar and R charts and toward a preference for using individuals and moving range (XmR) charts for examining the time-sequenced behavior of process data. We will illustrate the procedures for constructing and interpreting XmR charts in Chapter 5.

4.3.2   THE DISTINCTION BETWEEN VARIABLES DATA AND ATTRIBUTES DATA

When measurements are used to guide process management and improvement, they are traditionally viewed as falling into one of two classes: *variables data* or *attributes data*. Control limits for attributes data are often computed in ways quite different from control limits for variables data. Unless you have a clear understanding of the distinctions between the two kinds of data, you can easily fall victim to inappropriate control-charting methods.

---

[13] Statisticians use the lowercase Greek letter σ (sigma) to designate the standard deviation of a random variable. Since σ cannot be observed directly, the best we can do is to estimate its value from the measurements we make. As we shall see shortly, there are several ways to do this. Strictly speaking, the symbol for a computed estimate (a statistic) should be different from the symbol used for the parameter itself. The most commonly used symbol today for an estimated standard deviation is $\hat{\sigma}$. When working with control charts, however, the tradition is to use the simpler notation, even though this can be confusing.

Variables data (sometimes called *measurement data*) are usually measurements of continuous phenomena. Familiar examples from physical environments include measurements of length, weight, height, volume, voltage, horsepower, torque, efficiency, speed, and viscosity. In software settings, elapsed time, effort expended, years of experience, memory utilization, CPU utilization, and cost of rework would all be considered examples of variables data.

Attributes data, on the other hand, have a different origin and serve a different purpose. They occur when information is recorded only about whether an item conforms or fails to conform to a specified criterion or set of criteria. Attributes data almost always originate as counts—the number of defects found, the number of defective items found, the number of source statements of a given type, the number of lines of comments in a module of n lines, the number of people with certain skills or experience on a project or team, the percent of projects using formal code inspections, and so forth.

Because attributes data arise from counts and continuous phenomena yield variables data, several authors (some of our favorites included) have fallen into the trap of equating variables data to continuous phenomena and attributes data to counts. Nothing could be further from the truth. There are many situations where counts get used as measures of size instead of frequency, and these counts should clearly be treated as variables data. Examples include counts of the total number of requirements, total lines of code, total bubbles in a data-flow diagram, McCabe complexities, customer sites, change requests received, backlogged items, and total people in an organization or assigned to a project. When we count things like these, we are counting all the entities in a population, not just the occurrences of entities with specific attributes. Counts of entities that represent the size of a total population should almost always be treated as variables data, even though they are instances of discrete counts.

The key to classifying data as attributes data or variables data, then, depends not so much on whether the data are discrete or continuous, but on how they are collected and used. For example, the total number of defects found, although a count based on attributes, is often used as a measure of the amount of rework and retesting to be performed. When it is used this way, most people would view a total count of defects as a measure of size and treat it as variables data, especially when it comes to choosing models for analysis and methods for computing control limits. Similarly, the number of working days in a month might properly be viewed as attributes data (if used as a numerator to compute the proportion of a month that is available for working) or as variables data (if used as a denominator to normalize some other measure of activity or frequency of occurrence).

In short, the method of analysis that you choose for any data you collect will depend on the questions you are asking, the data distribution model that you have in mind, and the assumptions that you are willing to make with respect to the nature of the data. We will illustrate these issues at several points in the discussions that follow.

4.3.3   DETECTING INSTABILITIES AND OUT-OF-CONTROL SITUATIONS

To test for instabilities in processes, we examine control charts for instances and patterns that signal nonrandom behavior. Values falling outside the control limits and unusual patterns within the running record suggest that assignable causes exist.

Several tests are available for detecting unusual patterns and nonrandom behavior. The Western Electric *Handbook* cites four that are effective [Western Electric 1958; Wheeler 1992, 1995]. Figure 4.11 illustrates the following four tests:

- Test 1: A single point falls outside the 3-sigma control limits.
- Test 2: At least two out of three successive values fall on the same side of, and more than two sigma units away from, the centerline.
- Test 3: At least four out of five successive values fall on the same side of, and more than one sigma unit away from, the centerline.
- Test 4: At least eight successive values fall on the same side of the centerline.

Tests 2, 3, and 4 are called *run tests* and are based on the presumptions that the distribution of the inherent, natural variation is symmetric about the mean, that the data are plotted in time sequence, and that successive observed values are statistically independent. The symmetry requirement means that the tests are designed primarily for use with X-bar and individuals charts. Strictly speaking, they are not applicable to R charts, S charts, or moving range charts. However, as the Western Electric *Handbook* shows, you will not go far astray if you use tests 2, 3, and 4 for R charts that are based on samples of size $n = 4$ or 5. For samples of size $n = 2$,

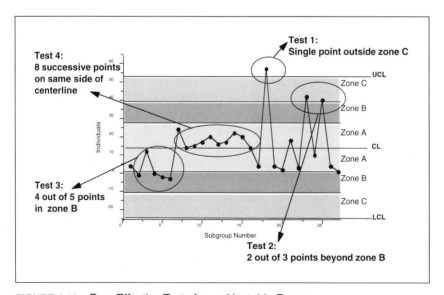

FIGURE 4.11   Four Effective Tests for an Unstable Process

however, the use of tests 2, 3, and 4 should not be used to test instability on an R chart due to the decidedly nonsymmetric nature of the range distribution. If you want to use these kinds of tests with small samples on R charts, check the modified rules described in the Western Electric *Handbook* [Western Electric 1958, 182].

When you use the four tests, process instability is indicated whenever one or more of the conditions exist. The effect of using all four tests together, compared to using test 1 alone, is to reduce the average number of points between false alarms in a controlled process from 370 to 91.25 [Champ 1987].[14] Thus, the increased sensitivity that you get for detecting assignable causes comes at the cost of a fourfold increase in false alarms.

As Wheeler points out, the four tests are a conservative and practical subset of the much larger body of run tests that have been used from time to time in industrial settings [Wheeler 1992, 1995]. Descriptions of more of these run tests and assessments of their properties can be found in several references [Montgomery 1996; Hoyer 1996; Western Electric 1958; Champ 1987]. Each additional run test increases your chances of detecting an out-of-control condition. Unfortunately, it also increases your chances of getting a false alarm. In statistics, as in life, there is no free lunch.

In addition to the run tests just discussed, a number of control chart patterns are recognized as symptomatic of process instability. A subset of these patterns— those prone to occur in software processes—are discussed in Chapter 6.[15]

It is important to understand that any decision to use a test or pattern should, in principle, be made *before* looking at the data. Waiting until after you see the data to decide which patterns to treat as unusual may have the effect of increasing the potential for false alarms, perhaps substantially. The temptation to violate this guideline is strong, as the human mind has a marvelous ability to perceive patterns after the fact. An "I'll know it when I see it" attitude can be very useful when interpreting patterns to deduce what may have caused an unusual event, but it falls easily into the trap of circular reasoning if used to single out a previously undefined pattern as a signal of an unusual event.

Some organizations, though, have very good reasons for identifying specific patterns that are likely to signal something going wrong. For example, you may know that when an assignable cause of type X occurs, a pattern of type Y often follows. If few other causes produce patterns of type Y and if it is possible for assignable causes of type X to creep into the process, it makes sense to be on the lookout for patterns of type Y and to use their appearance as a signal for action. It would be wise, however, to chart the effectiveness of your detection rule in order to determine the frequency with which it leads to false alarms. Your guidelines for using the rule can then be tailored accordingly.

---

[14] The reference value of 370 was derived by assuming that the inherent variation is normally distributed. The number is different for other distributions.

[15] More detailed discussions and illustrations of patterns and what they may tell you can be found in the Western Electric *Handbook* [Western Electric 1958].

4.3.4 THE STABILITY INVESTIGATION PROCESS

Figure 4.12 shows the steps involved in investigating the stability of a process. It provides a context for discussing the use of product or process measurements to evaluate process stability. The steps in Figure 4.12 are as follows:

1. Select the process to be evaluated for stability.

2. Identify the product or process characteristics that describe process performance.

3. Select the appropriate types of control chart.

4. Measure product and/or process characteristics over a period of time. The number of measurements and the period will be a function of the process and will depend on the type of control chart used.

5. Use appropriate calculations, applied to the measurement data, to establish the centerlines and limits of variation for normal process performance. The specific calculations will vary depending on the type of control chart used.

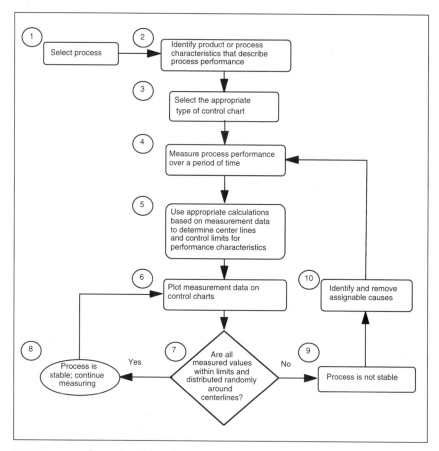

FIGURE 4.12 Steps for Using Control Charts to Evaluate Process Stability

6. Plot the measurement data obtained from step 4 on the control charts.

7. Compare the values plotted in step 6 to the centerline values and limits established in step 5.

8. If all plotted values are distributed randomly above and below the center-lines and within the control limits, conclude that the process has been stable at least for the period or events covered by the measurements. Continue measuring and plotting the data to ensure that the process remains stable.

9. If any plotted value exceeds the limits or if the pattern of values exhibits other nonrandom behavior, conclude that the process is not stable. The reasons for such observations must be investigated. If an assignable cause is found and the result is detrimental, the process must be repaired so that it cannot happen again. If the result is beneficial, try to make the cause part of the process.

10. Once all assignable causes have been removed, the control limits should be recalculated. This may mean that you will need additional observations to determine reliable limits for the process as corrected.

If, by following the preceding steps, you find that the process appears to be in control and if you have grounds for believing that the process will continue to operate in the future as it has in the past, the limits found in step 5 may be used to predict future process behavior. On the other hand, if you find that the process is not stable, the limits derived in step 5 are not valid for predicting process behavior; they merely pass judgment on the past performance of the process. Once the assignable causes have been corrected, the procedure for determining limits must start again at step 4.

Even when out-of-control data are included in the values used to compute the control limits at step 5, effective (rational) subgrouping will ensure that the limits are almost always sufficiently tight to identify lack of control. Using all the data as one large group to compute an estimate for sigma is almost always wrong because it presumes that the process is in control (that a single, stable distribution exists). Limits computed from the full data set can easily be much too wide because they are contaminated by assignable cause variations. The purpose of rational subgrouping is to minimize the effects of assignable cause contamination. We will discuss rational subgrouping in more detail in Chapter 6.

The use of stability criteria to assess the predictability of process performance places this topic squarely in the setting of an analytic study. All the cautions and caveats that are discussed in Appendix B apply. Nevertheless, demonstrating that a process has historically behaved in a controlled and stable way provides the most reasonable basis possible for extrapolating to the future. Just think of the alternative: If you knew that your process was unstable, how much faith would you place in your ability to predict its future performance?

4.4 Summary

Analyzing process data involves separating signals from noise. Unless signals can be distinguished from the noise that accompanies them, the actions that you take may be totally unwarranted. Also, acting on noise as if it were a signal serves only to amplify the instabilities.

When we analyze process behavior, we are engaging in an analytic study where the purpose of the study is to take action on the process (or cause system) that produced the data, not on the materials from which the data came. The aim of an analytic study is to predict or improve the behavior of the process in the future. Shewhart's control charts serve as effective tools to analyze process behavior.

Since all characteristics of processes and products display variation over time, it is important to be able to distinguish between common cause variation and assignable cause variation. Shewhart defines *common cause variation* to be phenomena that are natural and inherent to the process and whose results are common to all measurements of a given attribute and *assignable cause variation* to be variation in process performance due to events that are not part of the normal process. They represent (signal) sudden or persistent abnormal changes to one or more of the process components that often result in process instability.

Control charts are used to measure process variation and evaluate process stability. First, the analysis process for study should be selected and the process or product characteristics to be studied identified. Second, the appropriate control charts should be selected. Remember that this will depend on the questions you are asking, the data distribution model that you have in mind, and the assumptions that you are willing to make with respect to the nature of the data (variables or attributes data). The control chart is constructed based on 3-sigma limits. The type of data representing the process performance, either variables or attributes, will play a large role in determining which type of control chart will best represent the variability in your process.

When a process is stable, the variation in process performance is predictable, and unexpected results are extremely rare. We test for stability by using control charts to establish the limits of variation of process performance. When the limits are exceeded or the performance behaves in a nonrandom fashion, we likely have assignable causes responsible for the process instability. By demonstrating the process has behaved in a stable manner, there is a basis for predicting future behavior.

5

Process Behavior Charts for Software Processes

The control chart is the process talking to us.
Irving Burr, 1953

In this chapter, we continue the discussion on analyzing process behavior using the control chart principles covered in Chapter 4. The material will cover several different types of control charts particularly relevant to software processes:

- Average (X-bar) and range (R) charts
- Average (X-bar) and standard deviation (S) charts
- Individuals and moving range (XmR) charts
- Individuals and median moving range charts
- Moving average and moving range (MAMR) charts
- c charts
- u charts
- Z charts

In Chapter 4 we explained the distinction between variables or discrete data and attributes data. In this chapter we build upon that distinction to explain and illustrate the control charts just listed. The procedures and formulas for calculating control chart limits for each type of chart are covered in detail, and examples are given of each type of chart using a software process setting.

5.1 Control Charts for Variables or Discrete Data

In this section, our discussion focuses on using control charts to analyze process behavior using *variables* or *discrete data*. These data usually consist of observations of continuous phenomena or of counts that describe size or status.

5.1.1 X-BAR AND R CHARTS

Charts for averages (X-bar charts) and range (R) charts are used to portray process behavior when you have the option of collecting multiple measurements within a short period of time under basically the same conditions. When the data are collected under basically the same conditions, measurements of product or process characteristics are grouped into self-consistent sets (subgroups) that can reasonably be expected to contain only common cause variation. The results of the groupings are used to calculate process control limits, which, in turn, are used to examine stability and control the process.

X-bar charts answer the questions, What is the central tendency of the process? How much variation has occurred from subgroup to subgroup over time? The corresponding R charts indicate the variation (dispersion) within the subgroups. By using the stability detection rules discussed in Chapter 4, we can determine whether the subgroup averages (plotted on the X-bar chart) have been affected by assignable causes and if the subgroup ranges (dispersion) have been affected by assignable causes. Charts for averages and ranges are used together to identify points where a process has gone out of control.

The procedure for calculating control limits for X-bar and R charts is as follows:

1. Compute the average $\overline{X}$ and range R for each subgroup of size n, for each of the k subgroups:

$$\overline{X}_k = \frac{X_1 + X_2 + \dots + X_n}{n}$$

$$R_k = \left| X_{MAX} - X_{MIN} \right|$$

2. Compute the grand average $\overline{\overline{X}}$ by averaging each of the k subgroup averages:

$$\overline{\overline{X}} = \frac{\overline{X}_1 + \overline{X}_2 + \dots + \overline{X}_k}{k}$$

3. Compute the average range $\overline{R}$ by averaging each of the k subgroup ranges:

$$\overline{R} = \frac{R_1 + R_2 + \dots + R_k}{k}$$

The equations for determining the centerline (CL) and the upper and lower limits (UCL and LCL) for the X-bar and R control charts are given in Figure 5.1.[1] The terms A_2, D_3, and D_4 are conventional symbols for factors that have been tabulated by statisticians for converting averages of subgroup ranges into unbiased estimates for 3-sigma limits. An abbreviated table of these factors is in Figure 5.2. More extensive tables are available in Appendix A. Also, see almost any book on statistical process control [Duncan 1974; Wadsworth 1986; Ott 1990; Wheeler 1992, 1995; Grant 1996; Montgomery 1996].

---

[1] Figure adapted from *Understanding Statistical Process Control*, 2nd ed., by Donald J. Wheeler and David S. Chambers, © 1992 SPC Press, Inc., Knoxville, Tenn.

Average (X - bar) Chart Limits:

$\text{UCL}_{\bar{X}} = \bar{\bar{X}} + A_2 \bar{R} =$ grand average $+ A_2$ times average range

$\text{CL}_{\bar{X}} = \bar{\bar{X}} =$ grand average

$\text{LCL}_{\bar{X}} = \bar{\bar{X}} - A_2 \bar{R} =$ grand average $- A_2$ times average range

Range (R) Chart Limits:

$\text{UCL}_{\bar{R}} = D_4 \bar{R} = D_4$ times average range

$\text{CL}_{\bar{R}} = \bar{R} =$ average range

$\text{LCL}_{\bar{R}} = D_3 \bar{R} = D_3$ times average range

FIGURE 5.1 Equations for Calculating Control Limits for X-bar and R Charts

n	d_2	A_2	D_3	D_4
2	1.128	1.880	—	3.268
3	1.693	1.023	—	2.574
4	2.059	0.729	—	2.282
5	2.326	0.577	—	2.114
6	2.534	0.483	—	2.004
7	2.704	0.419	0.076	1.924
8	2.847	0.373	0.136	1.864
9	2.970	0.337	0.184	1.816
10	3.078	0.308	0.223	1.777

FIGURE 5.2 Constants for Computing Control Limits for X-bar and R Charts

The following example illustrates the calculation of the X-bar and range control limits and the resulting control charts.

Example 5.1: **X-bar and R Charts**

Mr Smith, a software manager at Homogeonics, Inc., is responsible for developing the follow-on release to an existing product. He is also responsible for providing support service to users of the existing product. The development schedule for the new product is based on the assumption that product-support service will require about 40 staff hours per day until the new product is released. Because of the intermittent behavior and potential complexity of service requests, everyone on the development team must be available to provide support service at any given time. Mr. Smith is concerned that the daily effort to support service requests stays within the range assumed by the plan, for if the effort exceeds the plan for a sustained period, the development schedule will be in jeopardy, and alternative plans will be needed.

The record for product-support staff hours expended per day by the technical staff for the past 16 weeks is shown in Figure 5.3. To examine the variability in the data, Mr. Smith grouped the values by week, computed the average daily hours for each week (each week is a subgroup), and used the results to compute control limits for the weekly averages and ranges. He then plotted the weekly averages, ranges, and limits on control charts to see whether there were any signs of unstable conditions.

The computations he used were as follows; the results are in Figure 5.4:

grand average $\overline{\overline{X}} = 45.06$ staff hours

average range $\overline{R} = 7.33$ staff hours

subgroup size $n = 5$

From the table in Figure 5.2,

$$A_2 = 0.577, D_3 = 0, D_4 = 2.114$$

From the equations in Figure 5.1,

$$\text{UCL}_{\overline{X}} = \overline{\overline{X}} + A_2\overline{R} = 45.06 + 0.577(7.33) = 49.28$$

$$\text{CL}_{\overline{X}} = \overline{\overline{X}} = 45.06$$

$$\text{LCL}_{\overline{X}} = \overline{\overline{X}} - A_2\overline{R} = 45.06 - 0.577(7.33) = 40.83$$

$$\text{UCL}_{\overline{R}} = D_4\overline{R} = 2.144(7.33) = 15.495$$

$$\text{CL}_{\overline{R}} = \overline{R} = 7.33$$

$$\text{LCL}_{\overline{R}} = D_3\overline{R} = \text{undefined (does not exist for } n = 5)$$

Week	Mon	Tues	Wed	Thur	Fri	Average	Range
1	50.5	43.5	45.5	39.8	42.9	44.44	10.7
2	44.3	44.9	42.9	39.8	39.3	42.24	5.6
3	48.8	51.0	44.3	43.0	51.3	47.68	8.3
4	46.3	45.2	48.1	45.7	44.1	45.88	4.0
5	40.6	45.7	51.9	47.3	46.4	46.38	11.3
6	44.4	49.0	47.9	45.5	44.8	46.32	4.6
7	46.0	41.1	44.1	41.8	47.9	44.18	6.8
8	44.9	43.4	49.0	45.5	47.4	46.04	5.6
9	50.0	49.0	42.6	41.7	38.5	44.36	11.5
10	44.5	46.5	41.7	42.6	41.7	43.40	4.8
11	43.8	41.8	45.5	44.5	38.6	42.84	6.9
12	43.2	43.8	44.8	43.5	40.9	43.24	3.9
13	50.0	43.4	48.3	46.4	43.4	46.30	6.6
14	52.3	45.2	42.2	44.8	42.8	45.46	10.1
15	50.0	46.2	47.4	42.2	47.0	46.56	7.8
16	47.3	49.7	48.0	42.0	41.0	45.60	8.7
Grand Averages						45.06	7.33

FIGURE 5.3   Hours of Product-Support Effort for a 16-Week Period

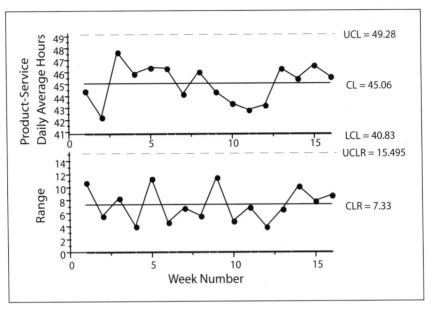

FIGURE 5.4 X-bar and R Charts for Daily Product-Service Effort

The weekly averages and ranges plotted in Figure 5.4 are well within the control limits, thus meeting the primary requirement for statistical control (Shewhart's Criterion I). To test for other signs of instability, the manager also looked for patterns of runs in the data, as discussed in Chapter 4. The additional tests he used were as follows:

- Test 2: At least two out of three successive values fall on the same side of, and more than two sigma units away from, the centerline.

- Test 3: At least four out of five successive values fall on the same side of, and more than one sigma unit away from, the centerline.

- Test 4: At least eight successive values fall on the same side of the centerline.

To perform these tests, he needed an estimate for $\text{sigma}_{\bar{x}}$, the standard deviation of a subgroup average. This estimate is given by

$$\text{sigma}_{\bar{x}} = \frac{A_2 \bar{R}}{3}$$

which, for the example, gives

$$\text{sigma}_{\bar{x}} = \frac{0.577(7.33)}{3} = 1.41 \text{ product-service hours}$$

Mr. Smith used this information to plot lines at 1-sigma intervals on the chart for average daily product-service hours. Figure 5.5 shows the result. With the added guidelines, he could see that none of the patterns described in tests 2 through 4 were present. He concluded, therefore, that the staff hour expenditures for product

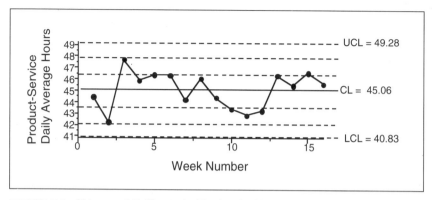

FIGURE 5.5 X-bar and R Charts for Testing for Patterns in Weekly Product-Service Data

service are consistent with a stable process and that the average daily value is approximately five hours per day above the planned value. Since no instances of assignable cause variation are apparent, he knows he will need to change the product-service process (or the quality of the product) if he wants to reduce the variation or center it about his planning target.

5.1.2 SELECTING SUBGROUPS AND RATIONAL SUBGROUPING

It is appropriate at this point to use Example 5.1 to briefly discuss the notion of rational subgrouping. Mr. Smith, the software manager, grouped the daily effort values by week, essentially using a subgroup of five values ($n = 5$), each value representing the daily effort expended on service work. In doing so, Mr. Smith made a judgment about the process that met an initial requirement for rational subgrouping—homogeneity of the subgroups. This judgment, based on his knowledge of the process, was that the effort was expended under essentially the same conditions from day to day and that the differences between values was due to common cause variation. In selecting subgroups in this way, he is implying that he is not interested in variation from day to day and that any differences noted are due to "noise" or common cause variation in the process. He is also implying that it is reasonable to expect few to none assignable causes on a day-to-day basis. On the other hand, the organization of subgroups is such that the variation in average daily effort from week to week will answer the question of primary interest. This meets a second requirement of rational subgrouping. So, here we see the notion of rational subgrouping at work. A judgment is made relative to the organization of the data based on knowledge of the process and on the need to answer the question of interest. Had Mr. Smith been interested in effort variation from day to day, a different organization of the data would be appropriate. (The example illustrating XmR charts in a following section explores this case.) You will find an expanded discussion of rational sampling and rational subgrouping in Chapter 6.

5.1.3 X-BAR AND S CHARTS

The procedure in Section 5.1.1 uses the observed ranges within subgroups as the basis for estimating the standard deviation of the process variation. The efficiency of this method falls off rapidly as the size (n) of the subgroups increases beyond $n = 10$ or 12. For this reason, most experts advise that range charts be used only when there are 10 or less observations in each subgroup. For subgroups of size $n = 10$ or less, the procedure in Section 5.1.1 works very well. For subgroups larger than 10, S charts based on averages of the standard deviation within subgroups give tighter control limits. In the past, range charts were preferred for small ($n < 10$) subgroups because finding the range was less difficult than computing root sum squares. Of course, with the advent of handheld calculators, the personal computer, and the availability of specialized software that computes and plots control charts, this has become less of an issue.

The steps for computing S chart control limits parallel those in Section 5.1.1. However, the factors A_2, D_3, and D_4 are replaced with alternative factors that are consistent with the use of the quadratic estimator for sigma (S). The formulas for the sigma (S) estimator and the average ($\overline{S}$) are given in Figure 5.6.

The equations for computing the control limits for S charts are given in Figure 5.7. Table A.3 in the appendix provides the values for the factors A_3, B_3, and B_4 for subgroup sizes of $n = 2$ to 15 along with the equations for computing the factors for $n > 15$. As the size of the subgroup increases, it becomes increasing difficult to ensure homogeneity of the subgroup. Larger subgroups may require additional data collection costs. On the other hand, larger subgroups result in control charts with tighter control limits and increased sensitivity to assigned causes. For control chart reliability, selection of the subgroup size should be dictated first by the homogeneity of the subgroup and second by the subgroup size.

The following example illustrates the procedure for constructing S charts.

Standard Deviation for Subgroup of Size _n_:

$$S = \sqrt{\frac{\sum_{i=1}^{i=n}\left(X_i - \overline{X}\right)^2}{n - 1}}$$

Average Standard Deviation for _k_ Subgroups:

$$\overline{S} = \frac{\sum_{i=1}^{i=k} S_i}{k}$$

FIGURE 5.6 Formulas for Standard Deviation and Average Standard Deviation

---

Average (X - bar) Chart Limits:

$UCL_{\bar{X}} = \bar{\bar{X}} + A_3\bar{S}$ = grand average + A_3 times average standard deviation

$CL_{\bar{X}} = \bar{\bar{X}}$ = grand average

$LCL_{\bar{X}} = \bar{\bar{X}} - A_3\bar{S}$ = grand average - A_3 times average standard deviation

S Chart Limits:

$UCL_{\bar{S}} = B_4\bar{S} = B_4$ times average standard deviation

$CL_{\bar{S}} = \bar{S}$ = average standard deviation

$LCL_{\bar{S}} = B_3\bar{S} = B_3$ times average standard deviation

---

FIGURE 5.7 Equations for Calculating Control Limits for S Charts

---

Example 5.2: **X-bar and S Charts**

Ms. Jones, a member of the software engineering process group at Homogeonics, Inc., is responsible for analyzing the software inspection process and developing process improvements to increase the inspection effectiveness. With the belief that software inspectors could be more effective with smaller, rather than larger, code inspection packages, she undertook a study of the inspection review time for the past four releases of a major product produced by Homogeonics. She hoped to correlate the inspection review rate with the size of the inspection package and the escaped error rate of the inspection process. Before she used data to make any cause-and-effect correlations, she wanted to determine whether the rate at which the code was reviewed was consistent and under control over the past four releases. Fortunately, Homogeonics had captured and retained data usable for this determination. Among other data, the Homogeonics database identified the number of source lines of code reviewed for each inspection and identified the code review time spent inspecting. Since each inspection package varied in size, Ms. Jones normalized the data by dividing the number of source lines of code (SLOC) by the hours spent reviewing the code. This operation provided an SLOC per review-hour ratio for each inspection.

Ms. Jones' assessment of the inspection process led her to judge that the inspection data for each release were more likely to be homogeneous and based on essentially the same process conditions rather than the data between releases. She made this judgment because of the elapsed time between releases and the difference in release content. She decided to establish subgroups consisting of the inspection data from each release and to compare the variation of inspection review rates between releases. Because the subgroups are larger than 10 observations, she chose to use X-bar and S charts to plot the variation between releases. Figure 5.8 shows the data for each release, as well as the average code inspection review rate for each release (Avg./Insp.) and the standard deviation (S) for each release (subgroup). The values for S were determined by using the formula in Figure 5.6. (The arithmetic details of determining S for release 1 in Figure 5.8 are in Appendix C.1.)

Inspection #	Release 1	Release 2	Release 3	Release 4
1	171.6	100.0	27.5	18.1
2	40.5	45.9	27.6	27.1
3	98.0	28.7	39.5	65.4
4	48.9	60.0	37.7	27.5
5	145.7	79.4	79.9	26.5
6	92.1	63.2	37.1	26.9
7	47.0	26.7	32.2	76.0
8	86.8	39.7	11.0	14.3
9	92.5	79.2	20.9	15.2
10	26.0	27.7	26.0	72.2
11	77.6	58.3	56.8	9.2
12	129.2	13.4	46.9	33.1
13	73.8	129.5	17.4	20.5
14	24.0	22.1	41.4	33.5
15	46.9	18.5	32.2	25.3
Avg./Insp.	80.0	52.8	35.6	32.7
S	43.6	33.2	16.9	21.1

FIGURE 5.8 Code Inspection Review Rates (SLOC/Review Hour) for Four Releases of a Homogeonics Product

The control limits for the data displayed in Figure 5.8 are found as follows:

grand average $\overline{\overline{X}} = 50.29$

average standard deviation $\overline{S} = 28.72$

group size $n = 15$

From Table A.3 in the appendix,

$$A_3 = 0.789, \qquad B_3 = 0.428, \qquad B_4 = 1.572$$

From the equations in Figure 5.7,

$$UCL_{\overline{X}} = \overline{\overline{X}} + A_3\overline{S} = 50.29 + 0.789(28.72) = 72.94$$

$$CL_{\overline{X}} = \overline{\overline{X}} = 50.29$$

$$LCL_{\overline{X}} = \overline{\overline{X}} - A_3\overline{S} = 50.29 - 0.789(28.72) = 27.65$$

$$UCL_{\overline{S}} = B_4\overline{S} = 1.572(28.72) = 45.15$$

$$CL_{\overline{S}} = \overline{S} = 28.72$$

$$LCL_{\overline{S}} = B_3\overline{S} = 0.428(28.72) = 12.29$$

The control chart results are in Figure 5.9. The charts reveal that the variation in the code inspection review rate among releases is not entirely due to common

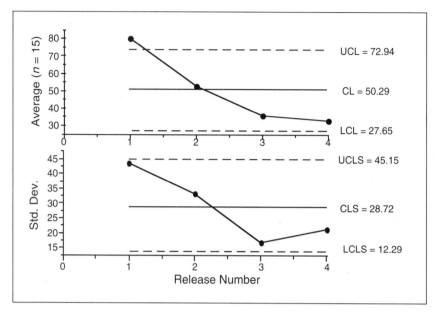

FIGURE 5.9 X-bar and S Charts for Average Code Inspection Review Rate (SLOC/Review Hour) Between Product Releases

causes but rather is a result of a gradual process change of some sort between release 1 and release 4. Ms. Jones now had the task of determining the reason for the assignable cause, which, hopefully, would allow her to proceed with her cause-and-effect analysis of the process effectiveness. Since she made an assumption that each of the release inspection processes was stable, it would be appropriate for her to verify this assumption as one of the first steps toward determining the reason for the assignable cause. (See Appendix C.1 for display of control charts showing stability of the four releases.)

5.1.4 INDIVIDUALS AND MOVING RANGE (XMR) CHARTS FOR CONTINUOUS DATA

When measurements are spaced widely in time or when each measurement is used by itself to evaluate or control a process, a time-sequenced plot of individual values, rather than averages, may be all that is possible. The subgroup size n is then 1, and the formulas based on subgroup ranges that are used for plotting limits for X-bar and R charts no longer apply, so another way is needed to calculate control limits. Here, the principle of rational subgrouping comes into play, and we use the short-term variation between adjacent observed values to estimate the natural (inherent) variation of the process. This leads to a pair of charts—one for the individual values and another for the successive two-point moving ranges. This combination of charts for individual observations and moving ranges is called an *XmR chart,* where X and *mR* symbolize the individual values and moving range, respectively.[2]

The idea behind XmR charts is that, when subgroups can easily include non-random components, we minimize the influence that nonrandom effects have upon estimates for sigma by keeping the subgroups as small as possible. The smallest possible subgroup size is 1. There is no way to estimate sigma from a single measurement, so we do the next best thing—we attribute the changes that occur between successive values to the inherent variability in the process. The absolute values of these changes are called *two-point moving ranges.* When k sequential measurements are available, we will have $k - 1$ moving ranges.

Factors exist that enable us to calculate 3-sigma limits for both individual values and the average moving range. The equations in Figure 5.10 apply.

The subgroup size for two-point ranges is $n = 2$, so the value for D_4 obtained from Figure 5.11 is $D_4 = 3.268$. The value for d_2 is obtained similarly from a table of dispersion adjustment factors (also called *bias correction factors*) that converts average ranges to estimates for sigma.[3,4] Table A in the appendix contains values

---

k sequential measurements provide $k - 1 = r$ (two-point) moving range values

$$i\text{th moving range } = mR_i = |X_{i+1} - X_i|, \text{ where integer } i \text{ is } 1 \le i \le k - 1$$

$$\text{Individuals average moving range } = \overline{mR} = \frac{1}{r}\sum_{i=1}^{i=r} mR_i$$

$$\text{Upper Natural Process Limit } = UNPL_X = \overline{X} + \frac{3\overline{mR}}{d_2} = \overline{X} + 2.660\overline{mR}$$

$$\text{Centerline } = CL_X = \overline{X} = \frac{1}{k}\sum_{i=1}^{i=k} X_i$$

$$\text{Lower Natural Process Limit } = LNPL_X = \overline{X} - \frac{3\overline{mR}}{d_2} = \overline{X} - 2.660\overline{mR}$$

FIGURE 5.10   Equations for Calculating Control Limits for XmR Charts

---

[2] The Western Electric *Statistical Quality Control Handbook* gives these examples for the principal kinds of data for which XmR charts are applicable [Western Electric 1958]:

- Accounting figures of all kinds, including shipments, efficiencies, absences, losses, inspection ratios, maintenance costs, accident reports, records of tests, and so forth.
- Production data such as temperatures, pressures, voltages, humidity, conductivity, furnace heat, gas consumption, the results of chemical analysis, and so forth.

[3] The values for d_2 are computed by H. L. Harter [Harter 1960]. They can be found tabulated for a wider range of n values in the appendix and in most references that provide instruction in control-charting methods.

[4] Strictly speaking, the values tabulated for d_2 assume that the ranges have been averaged for a fairly large number of subgroups—say, 20 or more. When only a few subgroups are available, the values for d_2 are somewhat too small, and limits computed by applying d_2 to the average range will be too wide. If this is of concern to you, you may wish to consult the table of corrected values $\hat{d}_2$ tabulated by A. J. Duncan [Duncan 1974, 950] or refer to Wheeler's work [Wheeler 1995, 417]. In most applications of control charts, however, it suffices to use estimates for sigma that are based on d_2.

for a number of bias correction factors for subgroup sizes of $n = 2$ to 100. An abbreviated form of this table, also shown in Figure 5.11, shows that $d_2 = 1.128$ for $n = 2$.

The 3-sigma distance associated with these individual values is given by the following formula:

$$3\,sigma_X = \frac{3\,\overline{mR}}{d_2} = 2.660\,\overline{mR}$$

So, we can estimate $sigma_X$ as follows:

$$sigma_X = \frac{\overline{mR}}{.d_2}$$

Although the impracticality of grouping may be one reason for charting individual values, there are other reasons that can motivate you to plot individual values voluntarily. For example, the Western Electric *Handbook* lists five types of conditions that may be detected more readily with individuals charts than with X-bar and R charts [Western Electric 1958]:

1. Cycles (regular repetitions of patterns).

2. Trends (continuous movement up or down).

3. Mixtures (presence of more than one distribution).

4. Grouping or bunching (measurements clustering in spots).

5. Relations between the general pattern of grouping and a specification.

XmR charts can also occur as a natural evolution of simple run charts, once sufficient points become available to compute reasonably reliable control limits.

Care should always be exercised when interpreting patterns on a moving range chart. All moving ranges are correlated to some degree, and this correlation can induce patterns of runs or cycles. Wheeler advises not to apply assignable cause tests 2, 3, and 4 to the moving range chart [Wheeler 1992].

n	d_2	A_2	D_3	D_4
2	1.128	1.880	—	3.268
3	1.693	1.023	—	2.574
4	2.059	0.729	—	2.282
5	2.326	0.577	—	2.114
6	2.534	0.483	—	2.004
7	2.704	0.419	0.076	1.924
8	2.847	0.373	0.136	1.864
9	2.970	0.337	0.184	1.816
10	3.078	0.308	0.223	1.777

FIGURE 5.11 Abbreviated Table of Dispersion and Bias Factors for Range Data

Example 5.3:	**XmR Charts for Continuous Data**

Mr. Smith, the software manager at Homogeonics, Inc., is interested in evaluating the day-to-day variation of effort spent on servicing the existing product. He suspects that different factors may influence activity levels on different days of the week and that there may be differences from week to week. Because day-to-day variation lies at the heart of his question, XmR charts that plot the data in the order in which they are obtained then become the appropriate charts to use. The 80 data points in Figure 5.12 provide a sequence that we can use to construct the individuals and moving range charts.

Day	Effort X_i	X_{i+1}	mR	Day	Effort X_i	X_{i+1}	mR
1	50.5	43.5	7.0	41	50	49	1.0
2	43.5	45.5	2.0	42	49	42.6	6.4
3	45.5	39.8	5.7	43	42.6	41.7	0.9
4	39.8	42.9	3.1	44	41.7	38.5	3.2
5	42.9	44.3	1.4	45	38.5	44.5	6.0
6	44.3	44.9	0.6	46	44.5	46.5	2.0
7	44.9	42.9	2.0	47	46.5	41.7	4.8
8	42.9	39.8	3.1	48	41.7	42.6	0.9
9	39.8	39.3	0.5	49	42.6	41.7	0.9
10	39.3	48.8	9.5	50	41.7	43.8	2.1
11	48.8	51	2.2	51	43.8	41.8	2.0
12	51	44.3	6.7	52	41.8	45.5	3.7
13	44.3	43	1.3	53	45.5	44.5	1.0
14	43	51.3	8.3	54	44.5	38.6	5.9
15	51.3	46.3	5.0	55	38.6	43.2	4.6
16	46.3	45.2	1.1	56	43.2	43.8	0.6
17	45.2	48.1	2.9	57	43.8	44.8	1.0
18	48.1	45.7	2.4	58	44.8	43.5	1.3
19	45.7	44.1	1.6	59	43.5	40.9	2.6
20	44.1	40.6	3.5	60	40.9	50	9.1
21	40.6	45.7	5.1	61	50	43.4	6.6
22	45.7	51.9	6.2	62	43.4	48.3	4.9
23	51.9	47.3	4.6	63	48.3	46.4	1.9
24	47.3	46.4	0.9	64	46.4	43.4	3.0
25	46.4	44.4	2.0	65	43.4	52.3	8.9
26	44.4	49	4.6	66	52.3	45.2	7.1
27	49	47.9	1.1	67	45.2	42.2	3.0
28	47.9	45.5	2.4	68	42.2	44.8	2.6
29	45.5	44.8	0.7	69	44.8	42.8	2.0
30	44.8	46	1.2	70	42.8	50	7.2
31	46	41.1	4.9	71	50	46.2	3.8
32	41.1	44.1	3.0	72	46.2	47.4	1.2
33	44.1	41.8	2.3	73	47.4	42.2	5.2
34	41.8	47.9	6.1	74	42.2	47	4.8
35	47.9	44.9	3.0	75	47	47.3	0.3
36	44.9	43.4	1.5	76	47.3	49.7	2.4
37	43.4	49	5.6	77	49.7	48	1.7
38	49	45.5	3.5	78	48	42	6.0
39	45.5	47.4	1.9	79	42	41	1.0
40	47.4	50	2.6	80	41		
				Averages	45.06		3.38

FIGURE 5.12   Daily Product-Support Effort with *mR* Calculations

From the data in Figure 5.12, we find the average staff hours per day ($\overline{X}$) and the average two-point moving range ($\overline{mR}$) to be

$$\overline{X} = 45.06, \quad m\overline{R} = 3.38$$

The computations then proceed as follows:

Centerline (average of individual values) = $\text{CL}_X = \overline{X} = 45.06$

Upper Natural Process Limit = $\text{UNPL}_X = \overline{X} + 2.660\,\overline{mR} = 54.04$

Lower Natural Process Limit = $\text{LNPL}_X = \overline{X} - 2.660\,\overline{mR} = 36.08$

Centerline or average moving range = $\text{CL}_R = \overline{mR} = 3.38$

Upper Control Limit for moving range = $\text{UCL}_R = D_4\,\overline{mR} = 3.268\,\overline{mR} = 11.03$

Sigma for individual values = $\text{sigma}_X = \dfrac{\overline{mR}}{d_2} = \dfrac{3.38}{1.128} = 2.996$

The results of these calculations are plotted with the data on the control charts in Figure 5.13. There are no out-of-limit points and no patterns that suggest unusual behavior. The process appears to be in statistical control from the perspective of individual values, just as it did when weekly averages were plotted on X-bar and R charts.[5]

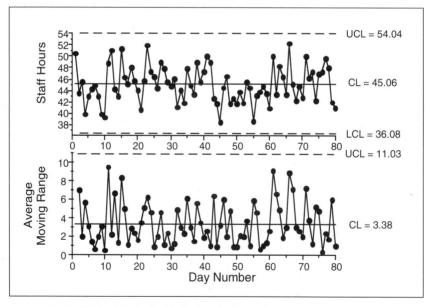

FIGURE 5.13 XmR Charts for Daily Product Service

---

[5] The fact that group averages were in control was no guarantee that the individual values would be in control.

Since nothing unusual is apparent in Figure 5.13, we can use the data to illustrate the concept of natural process limits. That discussion takes place shortly.

5.1.5   INDIVIDUALS AND MOVING RANGE (XMR) CHARTS FOR DISCRETE DATA

Variables data are not always measured on continuous scales. Sometimes, they take on only discrete values, such as when counts of objects are used to describe the size of an entity or the status of an activity. If the discrete measurements range over at least five distinct values, the data can usually be treated as if they were continuous. The usual X-bar, R, and XmR charts then apply. The following example illustrates this point.

Example 5.4:   XmR Charts for Discrete Data

Each week, a system test organization reports the number of critical problems that remain unresolved. The number of unresolved problems (URPs) is compared to the planned number, the average number unresolved since testing began, and the average number of unresolved problems in the previous weeks of the current quarter. At the conclusion of week 31, the weekly report contains the data shown in Figure 5.14.

The system test manager is concerned that something may have happened to the problem resolution process in week 31 and that the schedule for completing testing may now be threatened by something that is causing a surge in the backlog of unresolved problems. However, he is not totally convinced that the most recent value (28) is a signal that something is amiss. To help determine whether or not the current week's value may be simply the result of normal random variation, the history of unresolved problem reports for the current year has been obtained and tabulated. This history is shown in Figure 5.15.

This tabulation shows that, on two previous occasions, the number of unresolved problems approached the value of 28 in the latest week, but this does not fully resolve the issue for the system test manager. Because the problem resolution process had seemed to be stable over the first two quarters, he decided to construct a control chart to see whether it might point to any problems with the

System Test Report for Week 31							
Number of Unresolved Problems (URPs)	Planned # of URPs	Deviation from Planned Value	Average URPs Prior to Current Week	Deviation from Grand Average	Average URPs This Quarter	Deviation from Quarter Average
28	19	+47.4%	20.13	+39.07%	20.50	+36.6%

FIGURE 5.14   Report of Unresolved Problems

History of In-Process Inventory of Unresolved Problem Reports												
Week	1	2	3	4	5	6	7	8	9	10	11	12
First quarter	19	27	20	16	18	25	22	24	17	25	15	17
Second quarter	20	22	19	16	22	19	25	22	18	20	16	17
Third quarter	20	15	27	25	17	19	28					

FIGURE 5.15   Weekly History of Unresolved Problem Reports

process. Since only one data point was obtained each week and since week-to-week variation is the issue that concerns him, the most rational subgrouping for examining the inherent variability in the backlog data is the two-point moving range. XmR charts are then the appropriate tools for examining the issue.

The approach the test manager elected to take was to use the data from the first two quarters (24 weeks) to create the control chart. He then extended the chart by plotting the current quarter's data and holding the control limits constant. His computations, based on data from the first 24 weeks of testing, are shown in the equations that follow. As with XmR charts for continuous data, the average of the moving ranges was used to estimate the standard deviation of the inherent variation. The factors D_4 and d_2 that correspond to $n = 2$ (the subgroup size for two-point moving ranges) were obtained from the table in Figure 5.11. These factors are 3.268 and 1.128, respectively.

From the data in Figure 5.15 for the first 24 weeks,

$$\overline{X} = 20.04, \ \overline{mR} = 4.35$$

The computations then proceed as follows:

Centerline (average of individual values) $= \text{CL}_X = \overline{X} = 20.04$

Upper Natural Process Limit $= \text{UNPL}_X = \overline{X} + 2.660\,\overline{mR} = 31.6$

Lower Natural Process Limit $= \text{LNPL}_X = \overline{X} - 2.660\,\overline{mR} = 8.49$

Centerline or average moving range $= \text{CL}_R = \overline{mR} = 4.35$

Upper control limit for moving range $= \text{UCL}_R = D_4\,\overline{mR} = 3.268\,\overline{mR} = 14.2$

The completed XmR charts for the backlog of critical problem reports, with the points for the third quarter added, are shown in Figure 5.16. These charts show no sign that anything unusual has happened (using all four tests for instability described earlier). Thus, the process appears to be stable, and the occurrence of 28 unresolved problems in week 31 is not a significant signal that the process has changed. Occasional random backlogs of size 28 (or even more) fall within the limits of natural variability that represent the voice of the process. The manager concluded that it would be unwise to take precipitous action to rectify the backlog reported in week 31.

The charts in Figure 5.16 show no signs of instability. The control limits reflect what the process is likely to do as long as it continues to operate consistently

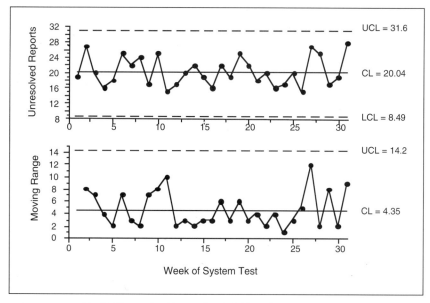

FIGURE 5.16   XmR Charts for Unresolved Critical Problem Reports

and its inputs remain as consistent as they have in the past. If the manager wants to reduce either the average backlog or the amount of variation, the process itself will have to be changed.

5.1.6   FREQUENCY HISTOGRAMS AND THE NATURAL PROCESS LIMITS CONCEPT

The results of measurements are often used to construct histograms that summarize the historical performance of a process. In the following example, the data from Homogeonics, Inc., have been grouped to obtain the frequency counts depicted by the vertical bars of the histogram. The centerline and control limits from the XmR charts have been added to the histogram to help characterize the data.

Example 5.5:   **Frequency Histograms and Natural Process Limits**

One caution: Empirical distributions of the sort shown in Figure 5.17 can be misleading if the process that produced the data is not in statistical control. Histograms obtained from sequences of measurements invariably get interpreted as predictive of future performance. But it is impossible to say what a histogram of an out-of-control process represents. This means that a control chart for individual observations should always be examined before presenting a histogram of process results to anyone. Many erroneous conclusions have been drawn, even by veteran statisticians, because the fundamental assumption of a constant system of chance causes was not tested.

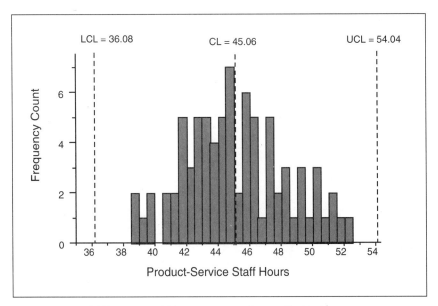

FIGURE 5.17 A Histogram of Measurements from a Stable Process

In this example, however, our investigations showed no signs of out-of-control behavior, so we may be justified in interpreting the Homogeonics data as having come from a single, constant system of chance causes.[6] Fluctuating or shifting distributions and mixtures of distributions, had they been present in significant size, could easily have produced unusual values or patterns. No histogram or control chart would then have predictive merit. It is only when control charts suggest that a process is stable, and we can assure that nothing related to the process will change, that we have a reasonable basis for using histograms like Figure 5.17 to characterize expectations of future performance. In Chapter 7, we will illustrate how histograms like this may be used to determine process capability.

When you have a stable process, the limits associated with a control chart or histogram for individual values describe what the process is able to do, as long as it continues to operate as it has in the past. These limits are called *natural process limits* because they represent the degree of variation inherent in the process once all assignable causes have been removed and prevented from recurring. Natural process limits always describe the variability associated with individual measurements, not the variability of the subgroup averages used to construct X-bar charts.

---

[6] We say "may be" because it would help to know something about the characteristics and frequencies of incoming requests and the repeatability of the process that assigns people to service the requests.

5.1.7 INDIVIDUALS AND MEDIAN MOVING RANGE CHARTS

Rather than use the average moving range to compute the limits for an XmR chart, the median moving range sometimes is used as an alternative. The median moving range is frequently more sensitive to assigned causes when the moving range contains several very large values relative to the rest of the moving range values. Sometimes, the several high range values are such that they unduly inflate the average moving range and cause the upper and lower limits to expand. Using the median moving range to compute the limits under such circumstances often will reveal assigned causes that otherwise would be missed.

Using the median range to compute the control chart limits requires a different set of constant factors and also requires that the median moving range $m\tilde{R}$ be determined rather than the average range. Determination of the median moving range $m\tilde{R}$ requires that the moving range values first be sorted in ascending order. If the number of k observations is odd, the median is found in the order position $[(k-1)/2] + 1$. If k is even, the median is the average of the values in the $k/2$ and $k/2 + 1$ positions. The equations for using the moving range median to estimate control limits are given in Figure 5.18.

$$
\begin{array}{l}
\text{For moving range of } n = 2, \\[2mm]
\text{UNPL}_X = \overline{X} + \dfrac{3m\tilde{R}}{d_4} = \overline{X} + 3.145m\tilde{R} \\[3mm]
\text{CL}_X = \overline{X} \\[3mm]
\text{LNPL}_X = \overline{X} - \dfrac{3m\tilde{R}}{d_4} = \overline{X} - 3.145m\tilde{R} \\[3mm]
\text{UCL}_{\tilde{R}} = D_6\tilde{R} = 3.865m\tilde{R} \\[3mm]
\text{CL}_{\tilde{R}} = m\tilde{R} = 8.5
\end{array}
$$

FIGURE 5.18   Equations for XmR Control Chart Limits Using the Median Range

The following example illustrates the use of the XmR chart using the median range.

Example 5.6:   Individuals and Median Moving Range Charts

Mr. James, the product service manager of Medic Data, Inc., has just received a monthly report indicating that the average number of unresolved customer problems for the just completed month was 13.5 problems per day. Mr. James noted that this was about 50% higher than typically reported over the past quarter. The control chart used to track the process performance accompanied the report and is shown in Figure 5.19.

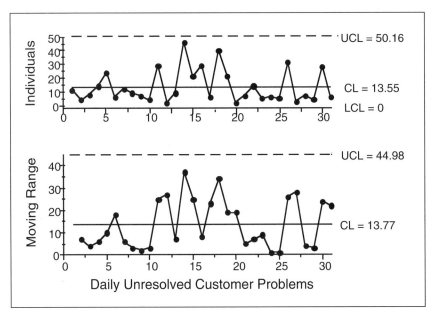

FIGURE 5.19   XmR Chart Showing Daily Unresolved Customer Problems

In light of the last quarter's process performance, Mr. James was surprised to find that the control chart did not reveal any assigned causes; to the contrary, the process appeared to be stable for the entire month. Nevertheless, Mr. James examined the chart more closely and observed that the moving range chart displayed very wide variation from one day to the next on days 10, 12, 13, 25, 27, and 29. He realized that if the process were in control, the median range ought to be close to the average range. Upon computing the median range, he found that it was about 50% lower than the average range. Also, when he examined the XmR chart again, he noticed that few of the actual daily ranges were close to the computed average range. He concluded that all these facts indicated that the average moving range had been inflated and expanded the individuals chart control limits. He constructed an XmR chart using the median range instead of the average range to see whether the chart would reveal any assigned causes. The results are shown in Figure 5.20.[7]

He noticed that the individuals and range chart limits using the median range were somewhat tighter than the limits in the initial XmR chart. Essentially, this was due to the reduction in the average range resulting from using the median moving range instead of the average moving range.

With the median range XmR chart in hand, Mr. James could see that the process had indeed exceeded the control limits, indicated by apparent assignable causes on the individuals and the range charts. He would need to undertake an

---

[7] The data used to construct the control chart limits and the related calculations are found in Appendix C.2.

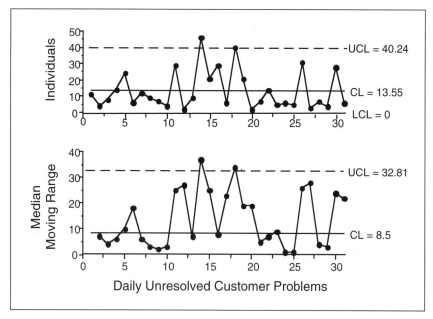

FIGURE 5.20   XmR Chart Using Median Moving Range Showing Daily Unresolved Customer Problems

investigation to determine the reasons for the assignable causes so that he could be confident that the process would return to its previous stable condition.

In this example, one can assume that the control chart received by Mr. James was not a continuation of the control chart covering the first quarter. If the previous quarter averaged approximately eight unresolved problems per day and the control chart continued into the month in question, the assigned causes would have been apparent on the continued control chart. Unless there has been a significant process change, there is no reason to restart a process control chart once reasonable control limits are established. We will discuss the topics of revising and updating control charts in Chapter 6.

5.1.8   MOVING AVERAGE AND MOVING RANGE CHARTS

Moving average and moving range charts are useful when the primary focus is on the trend of the process performance over time as opposed to the variance between individual measurements. For example, tracking the stability of software process performance that is expected to steadily rise (or fall) over time is an important project management activity to ensure adherence to schedule and quality targets. When the moving average and moving range control limits are used in conjunction with trend charts, they can be a useful tool in detecting shifts in process behavior without being overly sensitive to wide variations of individual measurements. (XmR control limits can be used to create trend charts as well; however, they are more sensitive to transitory variation in the process.) Because of the autocorrelation effects of the moving average, detection of assignable cause tests based on runs have no statistical basis. This means tests 2, 3, and 4 discussed in Chapter 4 and other similar tests based on runs should not be used to identify assignable causes when using moving average charts.

Selecting the group size n (the number of individual values) to use for the moving average depends on the amount of data available, the frequency of sampling, and the homogeneity of the data with the passage of time. As a general rule, with periodic data, the larger the subgroup, the less sensitive the control limits are to transitory variation, but the more susceptible the subgroups are to nonhomogeneity.

The procedure for calculating the moving average and moving range (MAMR) charts is essentially the same as that for average (X-bar) and range (R) charts, the first type of chart discussed in this chapter (Section 5.1.1). The difference in procedure is in deriving the moving average ($\overline{mX}$). To calculate a moving average of group size n, the individual measurements are displayed in n rows (or columns), each row (or column) offset by one. The rows (or columns) are summed and divided by n to determine $\overline{mX}_k$, the moving average for each subgroup. The grand average $\overline{\overline{mX}}$ is calculated by averaging all the $\overline{mX}_k$. The average moving range $\overline{mR}$ is determined by finding the range in each subgroup and calculating the average. The equations for finding the moving average are as follows:

1. For subgroups of size n, the moving average of the kth subgroup is

$$\overline{mX}_k = \frac{X_k + X_{k-1} + \ldots X_{k-n+1}}{n} \text{ for } k \geq n \geq 3 \text{ and } \frac{X_k + X_{k-1}}{2} \text{ for } k \geq n = 2$$

2. The grand average is

$$\overline{\overline{mX}} = \sum_{k=n}^{k=N} \frac{\overline{mX}_k}{N - n + 1}, \text{ where } N = \text{total number of individual observations}$$

The following example illustrates the calculation of the moving average and moving range control limits and their application to a trend chart.

Example 5.7: **Moving Average and Moving Range Charts**

A software development project manager is tracking the progress of detailed design of modules required for the product in development. The data in Figure 5.21

Design Completion Data									
Month	1	2	3	4	5	6	7	8	9
Monthly production	5	5	10	15	30	15	20	35	25
Cumulative production	5	10	20	35	65	80	100	135	160

FIGURE 5.21 History of Completed Design Units (Monthly and Cumulative)

shows the cumulative progress of unit (module) design completion since the start of the module design activity.

To calculate the moving average of the monthly production for $n = 2$, the data is displayed as shown in Figure 5.22. From the data,

Grand Average $\overline{\overline{mX}}$ = 18.125

Average Moving Range $\overline{mR}$ = 8.75

From the equations for average and range control limits,

$$\text{UCL}_{mX} = 18.125 + A_2(8.75) = 18.125 + 16.45 = 34.575$$

$$\text{LCL}_{mX} = 18.125 - A_2(8.75) = 18.125 - 16.45 = 1.675$$

$$\text{UCL}_R = D_4(8.75) = 28.55$$

The difference between the grand average and either the upper or lower control limits tells us the value of 3 sigma is 16.45 units.

The control chart for the data using moving average and moving range limits, shown in Figure 5.23, graphically displays the trend for the past nine months. The moving average chart reflects a growth in the rate of modules attaining the "completed design" status. However, the format of the control chart makes it difficult to project a trend indicating when the total or cumulative number of modules will be completed, whereas plotting the trend of the cumulative completions would do so. In addition, plotting control limits on the cumulative trend would be helpful in determining whether future monthly production is within limits and how future assignable causes may affect the time it takes to complete the work.

We first must calculate the moving average of the cumulative production to obtain a trend. We then can apply the limits to the trend for future guidance. The moving average for the cumulative production is seen in Figure 5.24.

The values labeled "Avg. cum. mX" are plotted on a values-versus-time grid as in Figure 5.25. The trend of the process can be calculated by using regression analysis of the plotted moving average values. In this case, a simple and reasonably accurate estimate of the trend line can be determined by using the last eight points, dividing them in half, and using the average of the two halves to establish the trend mean. The average of the first four values is 25. The average of the second half of the values is 106.9. By plotting these values halfway between the first and second average intervals, respectively, and connecting them with a straight line, the trend is readily apparent. The control limits of the trend are determined

k	1	2	3	4	5	6	7	8	9	
$n-1$	5	5	10	15	30	15	20	35	25	
n		5	5	10	15	30	15	20	35	25
Avg. mX		5	7.5	12.5	22.5	22.5	17.5	27.5	30	
mR		0	5	5	15	15	5	15	10	

FIGURE 5.22 Moving Average and Moving Range for Design Completion Data

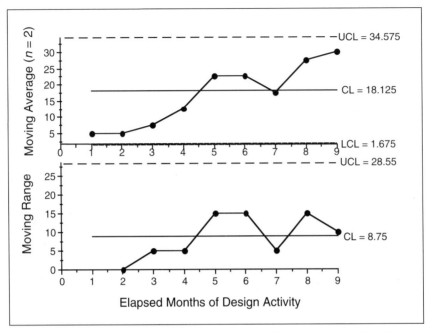

FIGURE 5.23   Moving Average and Moving Range Control Chart for Unit Design Monthly Progress

k		1	2	3	4	5	6	7	8	9	
n − 1		5	10	20	35	65	80	100	135	160	*
n			5	10	20	35	65	80	100	135	160
Avg. cum. mX			7.5	15	27.5	50	72.5	90	118	148	*

FIGURE 5.24   Chart of Moving Average and Moving Range Values

by adding the 3-sigma value of the monthly moving average to each side of the trend line. Figure 5.25 illustrates a trend-line graph of the example data.

Charts of this type not only are useful for monitoring the process stability but also provide status information to project management relative to development progress compared to plans. The control limits serve as an alert mechanism to project management should future values exceed the limits on either side of the mean. We know from the control chart in Figure 5.23 that the cumulative sum will increase an average of about 18 units per period (plus or minus 16.45 units) as long as the design process is reasonably stable. Exceeding the limits means that the process performance rate has changed significantly and could mean that quality will suffer or that schedules will not be met. The chart can also be used to forecast future process performance, assuming the process remains stable. In this example, the chart forecasts about 200 complete design units (plus or minus 16 or 17 units) by the end of the 12-month period.

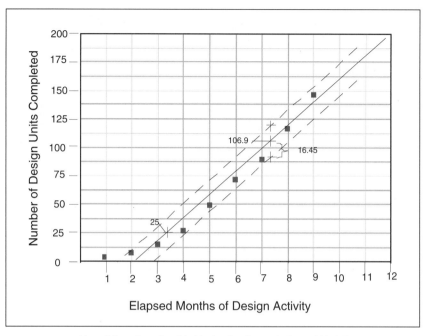

FIGURE 5.25   Trend-line Graph with Limits for Completion of Unit Design

5.2   Control Charts for Attributes Data

Thus far, our discussions on using control charts to analyze process stability have focused on variables data. These data usually consist of observations of continuous phenomena or of counts that describe size or status. Counts related to occurrences of events or sets of characteristics, on the other hand, are traditionally referred to as *attributes data*. Examples include the number of defects in a module or test, the percentage of people with specified characteristics, the number of priority-one customer complaints, and the percentage of nonconforming products in the output of an activity or a process.

When attributes data are used for direct comparisons, they must be based on consistent "areas of opportunity" if the comparisons are to be meaningful. For example, if the number of defects that are likely to be observed depends on the size of a module or component, all sizes must be nearly equal. The same holds true for elapsed times if the probabilities associated with defect discovery depend on the time spent inspecting or testing.

In general, when the areas of opportunity for observing a specific event are not equal or nearly so, the chances for observing the event will differ across the observations. When this happens, the number of occurrences must be normalized (converted to rates) by dividing each count by its area of opportunity before valid comparisons can be made.

Although constant areas of opportunity occur fairly often in manufacturing situations, where product sizes and complexities are often relatively consistent from item to item, conditions that make us willing to assume constant areas of opportunity seem to be less common in software environments. This means that normalization will almost always be needed when using attributes data to evaluate software products and processes.

When areas of opportunity can change from observation to observation, measuring and recording the size of each area is something that must be addressed when you define procedures for counting the occurrences of events that interest you. For example, if defects are being counted and the size of the item inspected influences the number of defects found, some measure of item size will also be needed to convert defect counts to relative rates that can be compared in meaningful ways. Similarly, if variations in the amount of time spent inspecting or testing can influence the number of defects found, these times should be clearly defined and measured as well. If both size and inspection time can influence the number of defects found, models more elaborate than simple division will be needed to normalize defect counts so that they can be plotted meaningfully on control charts.

Two cautionary notes: As Wheeler and Chambers point out, one of the keys to making effective use of attributes data lies in preserving the ordering of each count in space and time. Sequence information (the order in time or space in which the data are collected) is almost always needed to correctly interpret counts of attributes. When people think of attributes data as simple tallies, they often fail to impose a useful structure on their data. This failure is a major cause of disappointing results in the use of attributes data [Wheeler 1992].

Wheeler and Chambers also stress the importance of making counts specific. This is not a major problem with continuous data because the act of measuring usually makes the values specific enough. But, with attributes data and other counts, the act of counting easily allows vagueness to creep in. There must be an operational definition (a clear set of rules and procedures) for recognizing an attribute or entity if what gets counted is to be what the user of the data expects the data to be. Checklists like the ones illustrated earlier in Chapter 2 of this book are examples of structured approaches that can be used to address this need [Florac 1992; Goethert 1992; Park 1992].

5.2.1 DISTRIBUTIONAL MODELS AND THEIR RELATIONSHIPS TO CHART TYPES

To set the stage for the discussions that follow, it helps to have an understanding of the different kinds of control charts that are used with attributes data. Figure 5.26[8] lists the most frequently used chart types according to Wheeler and Chambers.

---

[8] Figure adapted from *Understanding Statistical Process Control,* 2nd ed., by Donald J. Wheeler and David S. Chambers, © 1992 SPC Press, Inc., Knoxville, Tenn.

Data Characterized by a Binomial Model		Data Characterized by a Poisson Model		Other Data Based on Counts	
Area of Opportunity		Area of Opportunity		Area of Opportunity	
n constant	*n* variable	constant	variable	constant	variable
np chart	p chart	c chart	u chart	XmR	XmR
or XmR	or XmR	or XmR	or XmR	charts for counts	charts for rates

FIGURE 5.26   Table of Control Charts for Attributes Data

Each type of chart is related to a set of assumptions (a distributional model) that must hold for that type of chart to be valid. There are six types of charts for attributes data: np, p, c, and u charts, as well as XmR charts for counts and XmR charts for rates.

XmR charts have an advantage over np, p, c, and u charts in that they require fewer and less stringent assumptions. They are also easier to plot and use. This gives XmR charts wide applicability, and many quality-control professionals recommend their use almost exclusively over np, p, c, and u charts. Nevertheless, when the assumptions of the underlying statistical model are met, the more specialized np, p, c, and u charts can give better bounds for control limits. Hence, in the right situations, they offer definite advantages.

The control charts listed in Figure 5.26 are categorized according to the underlying distribution model they rely on and the nature of the area of opportunity as follows:

1. An np chart is used when the count data are binomially distributed and all samples have equal areas of opportunity. These conditions can occur in manufacturing settings—for example, when there is 100% inspection of lots of size *n* (*n* constant) and the number of defective units in each lot is recorded.

2. A p chart is used in lieu of an np chart when the data are binomially distributed but the areas of opportunity vary from sample to sample. A p chart could be appropriate in the inspection example just given if the lot size *n* were to change from lot to lot. In software settings, for instance, it might be possible to use p charts to study coding practices, where the use of a practice is characterized by the percent of code in a module that contains a given construct—a comment, "uses" clause, or "with" clause, for instance. To do this, though, we should first ascertain that the conditions for a binomial model are satisfied—namely, that the event counted is matched to individual lines of code in a way such that each line can be treated as an independently drawn sample from a population with a constant probability of event occurrence from line to line (like tossing an unbalanced coin). Thus, the inclusion of headers in comment counts would likely invalidate the use of a binomial model, since headers tend to cluster at the start of modules. This illustrates the kind of care and caution that are needed when using the traditional charts for attributes data.

3. A c chart is used when the count data are samples from a Poisson distribution and the samples all have equal-sized areas of opportunity. Under the right situations, c charts can be appropriate charts to use when tracking the number of defects found in lengths, areas, or volumes of fixed (constant) size. As when using a binomial distribution, the justification for assuming a Poisson process should always be examined carefully, and the validity of the assumptions should be verified by empirical evidence wherever possible.

4. A u chart is used in place of a c chart when the count data are samples from a Poisson distribution and the areas of opportunity are not constant. Here, the counts are divided by the respective areas of opportunity to convert them to rates. Defects per thousand lines of code or defects per function point are possible examples.

5. An XmR chart can be used in any of the preceding situations. It can also be used when neither a Poisson nor a binomial model fits the underlying phenomena. Thus, XmR charts are especially useful when little is known about the underlying distribution or when the justification for assuming a binomial or Poisson process is questionable.

The first four charts (np, p, c, and u charts) are the traditional control charts used with attributes data. Each assumes that variation (as measured by sigma) is a function of the mean of the underlying distribution.[9] This suggests that caution is in order. Whenever a binomial or Poisson model is truly appropriate, the opportunities for process improvement will be somewhat constrained. The linking between sigma and the mean says that you cannot reduce variability without changing the centerline, nor can you move the centerline without affecting the variability. If these constraints on process improvement do not make sense, you should not use the traditional charts.

Because attributes data are individual values, XmR charts are almost always a reasonable choice. The exception occurs when the events are so rare that the counts are small and values of zero are common. Then, the discreteness of the counts can affect the reliability of the control limits in XmR charts. Still, whenever the average of the counts exceeds 1.00, XmR charts offer a feasible alternative to the traditional control charts just described. And, when the average count exceeds 2.00, the discreteness of the counts will have only negligible effects on the effectiveness of the control limits [Wheeler 1995].

5.2.2 C CHARTS AND U CHARTS

Of the control charts that rely on distributional models, the u chart seems to have the greatest prospects for use in software settings. A u chart is more flexible than

---

[9] In situations where the underlying distribution of the population is unknown, it would be useful to have a procedure for testing the hypothesis that a particular distribution will be satisfactory as a model of the process or population [Montgomery 1996]. This is referred to as *goodness-of-fit testing*. For a description of these analytical methods, refer to Montgomery's *Applied Statistics and Probability for Engineers* [Montgomery 1994].

a c chart because the normalizations (conversions to rates) that it employs enable it to be used when the areas of opportunity are not constant.

Both u charts and c charts assume that the events that are counted follow a Poisson process. One situation where a Poisson model might be appropriate occurs when counting the numbers of defects found in modules during inspection or testing. If the areas of opportunity for observing defects are the same across all modules or tested components, c charts may be appropriate charts to use. However, if the areas of opportunity are not constant (they rarely are), then the raw counts must be converted to rates by dividing each count by the size of its area of opportunity.

When areas of opportunity are appropriately measured and a Poisson model applies, u charts are the tool of choice. Defects per thousand lines of source code, defects per function point, and system failures per day in steady-state operation are all examples of attributes data that are candidates for u charts.[10] Defects per module and defects per test, on the other hand, are unlikely candidates for u charts, c charts, or any other charts for that matter. These ratios are not based on equal areas of opportunity, and there is no reason to expect them to be constant across all modules or tests when the process is in statistical control.

By virtue of their dependence on Poisson distributions, both u charts and c charts must satisfy the following conditions[11] [Wheeler 1992]:

- They must be based on counts of discrete events.
- The discrete events must occur within some well-defined, finite region of space, time, or product.
- The events must occur independently of one another.
- The events must be rare relative to the opportunity for their occurrence.

We suggest adding two more tests to Wheeler's list:

- The measure used to describe the size of the area of opportunity should be such that the expected (average) number of events observed will be proportional to the area of opportunity.
- No other factor that varies from one examined entity to another materially affects the number of events observed.

---

[10] Although u charts may be appropriate for studying software defect densities in an operational environment, we are not aware of any empirical studies that have generally validated the use of Poisson models for nonoperational environments (such as inspections). We can conceive of situations, such as variations in the complexity of internal logic or in the ratios of executable to nonexecutable statements, where simply dividing by module size provides inadequate normalization to account for unequal areas of opportunity. For example, if modules are deliberately made small when the tasks that they perform are inherently difficult to design and program, then simple defect densities are unlikely to follow the same Poisson process across all modules.

[11] Adapted from *Understanding Statistical Process Control,* 2nd ed., by Donald J. Wheeler and David S. Chambers, © 1992 SPC Press, Inc., Knoxville, Tenn.

One way to test whether or not a Poisson model might be appropriate is this: If you can count the nonconformities but find it impossible to count the conformities, you may have a Poisson situation. (The conditions that were just listed must apply as well.)

c Chart

When the area of opportunity is constant, the c chart may be used to track the process behavior. The equations for calculating c chart limits are given in Figure 5.27.

$$\bar{c} = \frac{\text{Total count of defects in sample events}}{\text{Sum of sample events}}$$

$$\text{Upper Control Limit} = \text{UCL}_c = \bar{c} + 3\sqrt{\bar{c}}$$

$$\text{Centerline} = \bar{c}$$

$$\text{Lower Control Limit} = \text{LCL}_c = \bar{c} - 3\sqrt{\bar{c}}$$

FIGURE 5.27 Equations for Calculating Control Limits for a c Chart

Example 5.8: c Chart

The number of unscheduled shutdowns of a computer system used to support a software development team is recorded each workday over a 12-hour period. The number of unscheduled shutdowns for one month (21 workdays) is shown in Figure 5.28.

From the equations in Figure 5.27,

$$\bar{c} = \frac{\text{Total count of defects in sample events}}{\text{Sum of sample events}} = \frac{13}{21} = 0.62$$

$$UCL_c = \bar{c} + 3\sqrt{\bar{c}} = 0.62 + 3\sqrt{.062} = 2.98$$

$$LCL_c = \bar{c} - 3\sqrt{\bar{c}} = 0.62 - 3\sqrt{.062} = 0$$

The resulting control chart, shown in Figure 5.29, indicates two assignable causes during the past 21 workdays. Steps must be taken to avoid the situation

Unscheduled Shutdown Data																				
Workday	1	2	3	4	5	6	7	8	9	10	11	12	13	14	15	16	17	18	19	20	21
Number of unscheduled shutdowns	0	0	0	4	0	0	0	1	0	0	0	0	3	1	1	0	2	0	1	0	0

FIGURE 5.28 Unscheduled Computer System Shutdowns Each Day

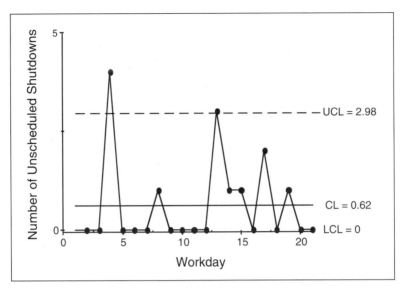

FIGURE 5.29   c Chart of Unscheduled Computer System Shutdowns

causing these two assigned causes to stabilize the number of unscheduled shutdowns. In this case, by excluding the two assignable causes, recalculating the control limits will reduce the control limits and centerline, resulting in a third assignable cause to show up. The third assignable cause will have to be removed before the process stabilizes for the 21-day period.

u Chart

When the opportunities for observing the event are not constant, as when differently sized portions of code are examined or tested for defects, the counts must be converted into rates—such as defects per thousand lines of code or defects per thousand source statements—before they can be compared. The rates are computed by dividing the value of the ith count (c_i) by its area of opportunity (a_i), and the rate that results is denoted by the symbol u_i:

$$u_i = \frac{c_i}{a_i}$$

Once values for u_i have been calculated, they can be plotted as a running record on a chart, as shown in Figure 5.30.

The centerline and control limits for u charts are obtained by finding $\bar{u}$, the average rate over all the areas of opportunity, and using the equations in Figure 5.31. The presence of the area of opportunity a_i in the equations for the control limits for u charts means that the limits will be different for each different area of opportunity. This can be disconcerting when the results are presented to people who are not familiar with these kinds of charts or the implications of a Poisson distribution.

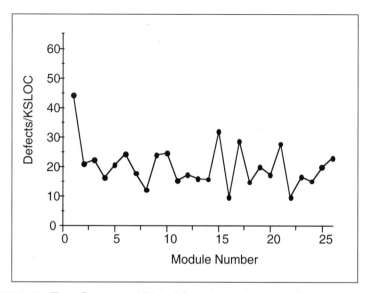

FIGURE 5.30 Time-Sequenced Plot of Code Inspection Results

$$\bar{u} = \frac{\sum c_i}{\sum a_i}$$

$$\text{Upper Control Limit} \;=\; \text{UCL}_u = \bar{u} + 3\sqrt{\frac{\bar{u}}{a_i}}$$

$$\text{Centerline} \;=\; \text{CL}_u = \bar{u}$$

$$\text{Lower control Limit} \;=\; \text{LCL}_u = \bar{u} - 3\sqrt{\frac{\bar{u}}{a_i}}$$

FIGURE 5.31 Equations for Calculating Control Limits for u Charts

The following example illustrates the use of u charts to investigate the stability of a code inspection process.

<hr>

Example 5.9: **u Chart**

Figure 5.32 shows a sequence of data obtained from inspecting 26 software modules. The data include the module identifier (its position in the sequence), the number of defects found that are attributable to coding errors, the size of the module (SLOC), and the density of defects per thousand lines of code (KSLOC). There are more than 100 other modules in various stages of development that are yet to be inspected, and the questions are, Are the inspection teams performing consistently? Are the results (the number of defects found by the inspection teams) within the historical ranges that we used when planning our resource and time allocations?

Module Number	Number of Defects	Module Size (SLOC)	Defects per KSLOC
1	19	430	44.2
2	8	380	21.1
3	3	134	22.4
4	6	369	16.3
5	9	436	20.6
6	4	165	24.2
7	2	112	17.9
8	4	329	12.2
9	12	500	24.0
10	8	324	24.7
11	6	391	15.3
12	6	346	17.3
13	2	125	16.0
14	8	503	15.9
15	8	250	32.0
16	3	312	9.6
17	12	419	28.6
18	6	403	14.9
19	3	150	20.0
20	6	344	17.4
21	11	396	27.8
22	2	204	9.8
23	8	478	16.7
24	2	132	15.2
25	5	249	20.1
26	10	435	23.0
Total	173	8316	—

FIGURE 5.32   Data from Code Inspections

To address these questions, which implicitly deal with relations of cause to effect and predicting future performance, we must include the defect insertion (code generation) subprocess within the envelope of the process we are examining. We do this because, based on the data alone, there is no basis for attributing the number of defects found solely to the performance of the inspection teams. The variations we see could easily be caused by differences in the quality of code produced for different modules. When defects are scarce, inspection teams may have a hard time finding them. If so, it would be incorrect to attribute low discovery rates solely to the performance of the inspection teams.

The question, then, is whether the overall system is performing consistently over time and across all modules with respect to the combined operation of the subprocesses that insert and discover defects. If it is not, early detection of process instability could point us toward assignable causes and let us make corrections to the coding and inspection processes that would make the remaining work predictable.

When we plot the data from the first 26 modules in the sequence in which the inspections were performed, we get the results shown previously in Figure 5.30. To determine whether or not the inspection process is stable, we must now compute appropriate values for the control limits. To do this, the value for the centerline $\bar{u}$ is first calculated by dividing the total number of defects found by the total amount of software inspected:

$$\bar{u} = \frac{173}{8,316} = 20.8 \text{ defects per KSLOC}$$

The upper and lower control limits are then calculated for each point individually, using the equations stated previously. The calculation of the upper control limit for the first point is as follows:

$$a_1 = 0.430 \text{ KSLOC}$$

$$UCL_{u_1} = \bar{u} + 3\sqrt{\frac{\bar{u}}{a_1}} = 20.8 + 3\sqrt{\frac{20.8}{0.430}} = 20.8 + 20.9 = 41.7$$

Corresponding computations would then be made for the lower control limit. The two computations would be repeated for each point, using the value of a_i appropriate to the point ($a_2 = 0.380$, $a_3 = 0.134$, and so forth).

The completed u chart is shown in Figure 5.33. The first point in Figure 5.33 falls above its upper control limit. This suggests that the process might not have

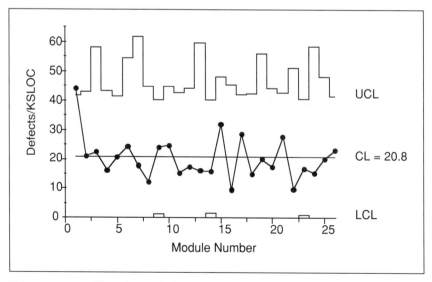

FIGURE 5.33   u Chart for a Module Inspection Process

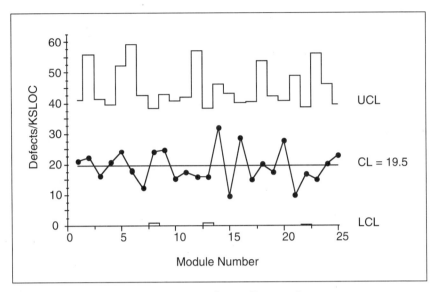

FIGURE 5.34   u Chart with Assignable Cause Removed

been in control when it started and that an assignable cause might be found. The reason for the out-of-control indication should be investigated. If an assignable cause can be found and if the process has changed (or been changed) so that the situation will not recur in the future, we can remove all values that were affected by the assignable cause and recalculate the centerline and control limits. This will give us a new centerline and control limits that will more accurately characterize the performance of the process as it currently exists.

The results of recalculating the control limits when the first point is removed are shown in Figure 5.34. All individual values are now within the limits, and the average defect rate has been reduced to 19.5 defects per KSLOC. The lowering of the centerline occurred as a result of omitting the point that was responsible for the initial instability. Omitting this point is a legitimate step if the situation that caused the out-of-limits point can never recur. From here on, improvements in the performance of the process will require changes to the process itself.

It may be, though, that the example we have just shown is not really a good illustration of the effective *use* of control charts. Since the point that we eliminated represents the discovery of a higher-than-usual number of defects, the inspection process used for module 1 may have been decidedly more effective than the process used for all modules that followed. If the investigation of assignable causes finds this to be the case, we should seriously consider reinstalling the initial process, throwing out the last 25 data points, and starting over again! This is one way that control charts can provoke process improvement.

On the other hand, if the reason for the high defect-discovery rate in the first module lies in the module itself or in the process that produced it, the example may be valid as given. It all depends on whether or not we can find the cause of the defect-rich module and prevent future recurrences. (No one ever said that investigating and correcting assignable causes would be automatic or easy!)

Figures 5.33 and 5.34 illustrate the variable control limits that are associated with using distribution models whose mean and standard deviation are determined by a single parameter. These variable control limits can make the chart seem difficult to analyze and interpret. This problem can be partially avoided when variations in the areas of opportunity are small—say less than 20%. Then, control limits can be approximated by constant limits that are based on the average area of opportunity. Exact control limits can always be calculated later, if any points fall near the approximate limits.

5.2.3 Z CHARTS

Another technique for avoiding variable control limits, and one that works for both large and small variations, is to convert the u chart into a Z chart. Here, the individual rates u_i and the average rate $\bar{u}$ are used to compute values that are scaled in terms of sigma units. To construct a Z chart, a sigma value is computed for each point from the equation

$$\text{sigma } u_i = \sqrt{\frac{\bar{u}}{a_i}}$$

The sigma-equivalent value for each rate is then

$$Z_i = \frac{u_i - \bar{u}}{\text{sigma } u_i}$$

These values can be plotted just as on any other control chart. The resultant Z chart for the data in Figure 5.32 is shown in Figure 5.35. This plot has the same general shape as that of Figure 5.33, except that the variation from the centerline is now expressed in sigma units. This makes it easier to see nonrandom patterns and test for conditions of instability, as illustrated in previous examples.

5.2.4 XMR CHARTS FOR ATTRIBUTES DATA

Perhaps the simplest technique for avoiding variable control limits when studying attributes data is to plot the data on individuals and moving range charts (XmR charts). When you do this, you will be abandoning the Poisson (or binomial) model and assuming instead that the standard deviation (sigma) of the phenomena you are studying is constant across all observations when the process is in statistical control. Be cautious, though. If you are plotting rates, and a Poisson or binomial model truly applies, this will *not* be the correct thing to do, unless the areas of opportunity are all nearly the same size. When the areas of opportunity vary by more than 20% or so, you must examine your assumptions carefully and test them

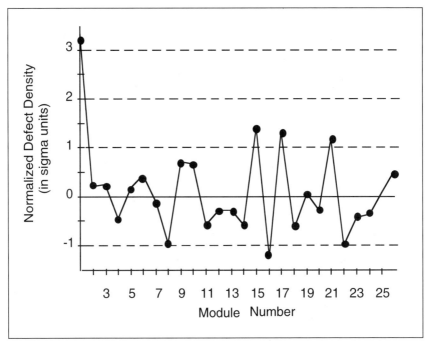

FIGURE 5.35   Example of a Z Chart

for validity. For example, XmR charts may not be the best tools to use for study-ing defect densities if your modules differ widely in size and you see or have rea-son to believe that the standard deviation of defect density decreases as the size of a module increases (as happens in Poisson processes).

Example 5.10:   **XmR Charts for Attributes Data**

Let us return to Example 5.9 (the u-chart example) and suppose for the moment that we have no theory or evidence that suggests that the standard deviation of defect density decreases as module size increases. Then, XmR charts may make more sense than u charts, and they are much easier to plot. The procedure for con-structing XmR charts for attributes data is exactly the same as that for variables data (see Section 5.1.4). If we use that procedure to analyze the defects per KSLOC data in Figure 5.32, we get the results shown in Figures 5.36 and 5.37.

Notice that, in this example, we arrive at the same conclusions that we reached when using u charts and Z charts alone. That is, with the first observation included, the charts signal an out-of-control condition at the initial point; with the first ob-servation removed, the data appear to describe a stable process.

So, which charts should you use? In practice, it is likely that none of the tra-ditional charts will be exactly right. The "rightness" of a control chart depends on the validity of the underlying probability model—and you cannot escape having

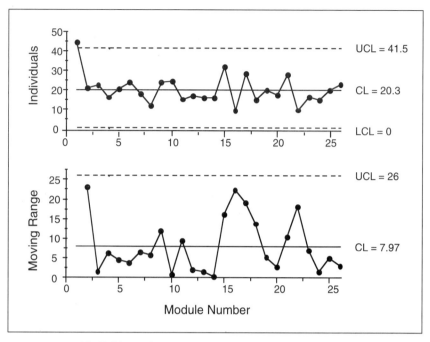

FIGURE 5.36   XmR Charts for a Module Inspection Process

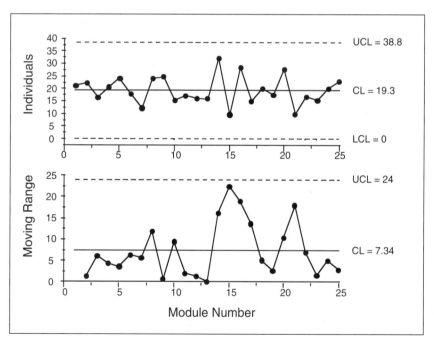

FIGURE 5.37   XmR Charts with Assignable Cause Removed

a model. A probability model is always there, even if you do not explicitly articulate it. Sometimes, the model has a specific distribution form, such as binomial or Poisson (there is seldom need to assume a normal distribution). At other times, the model simply assumes that sigma is independent of the mean or that the distribution is symmetric. In most (but not all) situations, the model requires that processes in statistical control produce observations that are independent and identically distributed random variables. Keep in mind, too, that all models are approximations. Real-world data seldom, if ever, follow any theoretical distribution.

If you are uncertain as to the model that applies, it can make sense to use more than one set of charts, as we have just done for the data in Figure 5.32. For instance, if you think that you may have a Poisson situation but are not sure that all conditions for a Poisson process are present, plotting both a u chart (or c chart) and the corresponding XmR charts should bracket the situation. If both charts point to the same conclusions, you are unlikely to be led astray. If the conclusions differ, then investigations of either the assumptions or the events are in order. If you choose to investigate the events, the worst that can happen is that you will expend resources examining an in-control process.

5.3 Summary

In this chapter, various control charts appropriate for software were discussed and illustrated with software process applications:

- Averages (X-bar) and range (R) charts
- Averages (X-bar) and standard deviation (S) charts
- Individuals and moving range (XmR) charts
- Individuals and median moving range charts
- Moving average and moving range charts
- c charts
- u charts
- Z charts

The X-bar and R charts apply to variables or discrete data, as do the X-bar and S charts. The c, u, and Z charts apply to attributes or count data, provided the underlying data distribution conforms to the Poisson distribution. The individuals and moving range charts may be used for either variables or attributes data and are particularly appropriate to use with periodic data (subgroups of $n = 1$).

When you have a stable process, the limits associated with a control chart or histogram for individual values describe what the process is able to do, as long as it continues to operate as it has in the past. These limits are called *natural process limits* because they represent the degree of variation inherent in the process once all assignable causes have been removed and prevented from recurring.

6

More About Process
Behavior Charts

*Discovering that a process is out of control is not a terrible event. It should not
be hidden from supervisors, managers, auditors, quality control experts, or, most
important, customers. In a sense, it is an event that should be celebrated because
it gives the process owner an opportunity to improve the process.*

Robert Hoyer & Wayne Ellis 1996

In Chapter 5, we discussed how to calculate control limits for several different
types of control charts. In this chapter, we discuss the sufficiency, organization,
and arrangement of process performance measures required for effective use of
control charts.

6.1   How Much Data Is Enough?

We have seen that, among the factors used to calculate control limits, the number
of subgroups k and the subgroup size n play an important role. The amount of data
you collect often determines both the number of subgroups that are possible and
the subgroup sizes, so you might ask, "How much data is enough?" That is, how
much data do you need to have before you can begin computing control limits?
For those who are comfortable with answers couched in terms of theory—for
example, coefficients of variation, degrees of freedom, and power curves showing the effects of the number and size of subgroups on the quality of the control
limits—we direct you to Wheeler's advanced text [Wheeler 1995]. Other interesting discussions can be found in papers by Proschan and Savage, Hillier, and
Quesenberry [Proschan 1960; Hillier 1969; Quesenberry 1993].[1] The following
paragraphs offer some advice based on the observations found in these references
and elsewhere.

---

[1] All of these analyses assume that the process is in statistical control.

6.1.1 CONSTRUCTING CONTROL CHARTS WITH LIMITED DATA

The answer to the question "How much data is enough?" has two parts. One answer addresses calculating control limits for the purpose of detecting assignable causes; the other answer deals with determining control limits of a stable process.

First, we will address the question in terms of determining the control limits for the purpose of detecting assignable causes. Out-of-control conditions may be detected with as few as three or four subgroups, even if the subgroup size (*n*) is 1. Limits calculated with limited data are often referred to as *trial limits*. Postponing the use of available data until you have collected 25 or more subgroups may cause you to miss opportunities for early discovery of out-of-control conditions. The advantage of calculating early trial limits is that even when you cannot yet demonstrate stability, you can get early indications that assignable causes of variation are present. At this stage of process analysis, the information gained from analyzing assignable causes is probably more important than that gained from a stable process.

When we address the question in terms of determining control limits for a stable process, the answer is quite different. The three main reasons for determining the control limits of a stable process are (1) to determine process capability, (2) to compare to standards or process requirements, and (3) to predict the process behavior. For these reasons, we want to be more confident of the limits.

In calculating control limits for a stable process, it is *desirable* to base the calculations on a minimum of 25 to 30 subgroups if you are using X-bar and R charts or 40 to 45 individual values if you are using XmR charts. The reason for this is that a large number of subgroups reduces the influence that a few extreme values can have on the calculated limits and increases the confidence in the control limit accuracy.

Note the emphasis on the word *desirable*. It is not mandatory to have the suggested minimum number of subgroups, especially when getting started. It usually pays to construct a run chart and begin plotting tentative, trial limits as soon as possible. You must be cautious in interpreting the initial results, though, because the limits you compute with small amounts of data may not be especially reliable. Concluding that a process is stable or nearly so, however, is risky with less than 20 to 30 subgroups. Often, even more observations are advisable.

In either of the two preceding cases, if you use only a few subgroups when you plot charts for averages and range, it is possible that an unusually large range within one subgroup can increase the distance between the centerline and the control limits on the chart for averages, thereby increasing the risk that you will miss an out-of-control signal. Keep in mind, though, that, even when control limits are inflated, values that fall outside the limits remain probable out-of-control signals.

Increasing the size (*n*) of the subgroup requires more observations to determine whether or not a process is in control and also affects the computation of control limits. Since

$$\text{sigma}_x = \frac{\overline{R}}{d_2 \sqrt{n}},$$

increasing the subgroup size (n) tightens the control limits and makes them more sensitive to small shifts in the process [Montgomery 1996]. While this may be desirable in some situations, increasing the subgroup size sometimes also increases the likelihood of including nonhomogeneous data. It is always more important to minimize the amount of variability within the subgroups. This is the principle of homogeneously subgrouped data that is so important to rational subgrouping. When we want to estimate process variability, we try to group the data so that assignable causes are more likely to occur between subgroups rather than within them. Control limits become wider and control charts less sensitive to assignable causes when large subgroup sizes contain nonhomogeneous data. Creating rational subgroups that minimize variation within groups always takes precedence over issues of subgroup size.[2]

Our advice, then, is the same as that given by Shewhart, Wheeler, Montgomery, and others. That is, when limited amounts of data are available, calculate and plot the limits, seek out the assignable causes that the data suggest, and then update the control limits as more data become available.

6.1.2 REVISING AND UPDATING CONTROL LIMITS

Revising and updating control charts both involve recalculating the control limits, but for different reasons and sometimes in different ways.

Revising

When you are *revising* control chart limits, you are generally working with an initial set of data for which you have calculated tentative or trial control limits, only to find that one or more data points fall outside the computed limits. If you believe that the out-of-limit values have assignable causes, you may want to set these points aside for investigation and compute new limits that are not contaminated by the out-of-limit values.[3] The new trial limits will be closer to the centerline, which may result in additional points being outside the limits. This process of removing points and recalculating can be repeated until all points without known assignable causes are within the recalculated limits. When revising control limits by omitting certain subgroups or values from the computation of the limits, we do not delete the out-of-limit subgroups or points from the chart but merely omit their values when calculating the limits.

Example 6.1: **Revising Control Limits**

Figures 6.1 and 6.2 illustrate the process just described. In this case, it was necessary to recalculate the limits twice. After the removal of the point at inspection

---

[2] We have already seen that it is possible to use a subgroup size as small as $n = 1$ (XmR charts).

[3] Subsequent discussion on rational sampling in this chapter illustrates the circumstances that make this action rational.

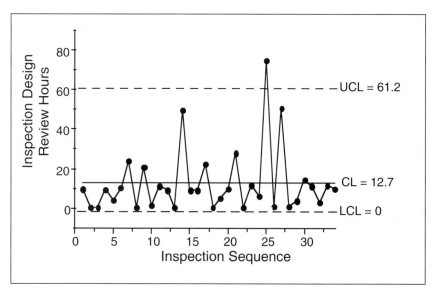

FIGURE 6.1   Individuals (X) Chart Control Limits Before Revision

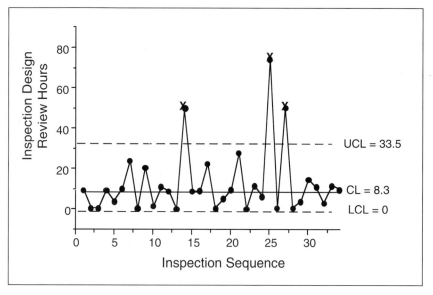

FIGURE 6.2   Individuals (X) Chart Control Limits After Revision

25, the recalculated limits dropped below the values at inspections 14 and 27. Upon removal of the values at 14 and 27, the revised limits resulted in the control chart in Figure 6.2.

When trial control limits are used, it is not unusual for many of the points to plot outside of the control limits. In these circumstances, it is better to look for a pattern of such points rather than try to determine the cause of each individual out-of-control point. Often, unnatural patterns can provide much information about the process behavior and lead to a more direct and rapid course of action to stabilize the process. Certain unnatural patterns will suggest rearranging and reorganizing the data, which will tend to eliminate many of the out-of-control points upon recalculation of the control limits. This will be discussed in more detail later in this chapter.

There is an argument that says rather than revise the limits, go to work on removing the assignable causes or unnatural patterns from the process since you will have to collect new data and compute new limits after the assignable causes are removed anyway. This is food for thought.

Updating

We talk about *updating* control chart limits when we use additional, more recently collected data to recompute the limits for an ongoing chart. The need to update can occur if you began the control chart with less data than you would have liked (see the previous section), if the process is observed to have shifted, or if a deliberate change has been made to the process. In these cases, you should recalculate the limits by using the newly collected data plus any measurements obtained previously that remain applicable. When the process has shifted, though, or when you have made a deliberate change to the process, previously collected data may no longer be applicable.

Example 6.2: | **Updating Control Limits**

Figures 6.3, 6.4, and 6.5 illustrate the updating of control chart limits when the process has shifted. The change request history is plotted for a twelve-month period

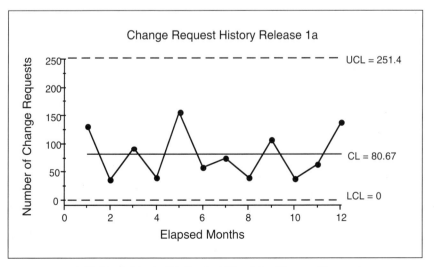

FIGURE 6.3   Initial Individuals (X) Control Chart for Change Requests

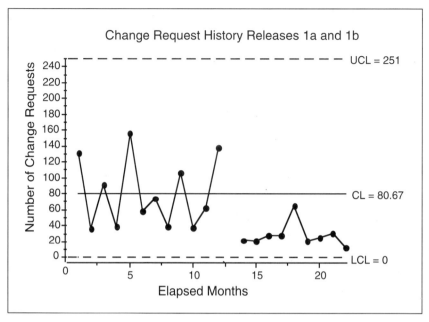

FIGURE 6.4 Initial Individuals (X) Control Chart Limits with Apparent Process Shift with Release 1b

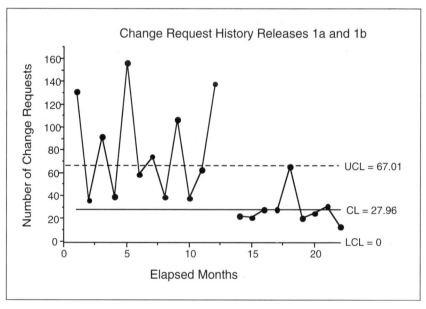

FIGURE 6.5 Updated Individuals (X) Control Chart Limits Based on Release 1b Observations

in Figure 6.3. The change request history for the next nine months is plotted in Figure 6.4 using the initial control chart limits. Note that the change requests at this point are for the next release of the software (release 1b). It appears that a significant process change has taken place due to the long run of sequential points on one side of the centerline (test 4). In Figure 6.5, the control limits have been recalculated to reflect the process shift using the initial nine values of change requests for release 1b.

Note that updating the control chart limits is based on evidence that a significant change in the process occurred. The new control limits will make it possible to measure future process performance with respect to the latest performance level. Updating the control limits without evidence of significant change will quickly lead to false alarms—or worse, to no distinction between signal and noise.

6.1.3   TESTING FOR AND SUSTAINING STATISTICAL CONTROL

Although it is possible (and practical) to establish control limits on a trial basis with relatively small amounts of data, you should be cautious about concluding that any process has demonstrated statistical control until sufficient data are plotted to provide an adequate historical record of stable process performance.

The data you have, when plotted on control charts, are infinitely better than no data at all. Nothing can change the fact that you will have to plan based on your predictions of the future performance of your processes. If your control charts signal out-of-control histories, you have little basis for extrapolating historical performance to the future. But, as you identify and permanently eliminate assignable causes of unusual variation, your willingness to rely on extrapolation increases. Reliable predictions of process performance and the setting of achievable goals then become reasonable possibilities.

One important corollary to your caution in concluding that a process is stable is that you should almost never stop control charting any process, especially one that has had a history of going out of control. How else can you be assured that, once stabilized and made predictable, the process has not fallen back into its old ways?

6.2   Anomalous Process Behavior Patterns

We have previously addressed detecting process instability and out-of-control situations by testing for assignable causes using the four Western Electric *Handbook* test rules cited in Chapter 4. Examination of the rules reminds us that a process can exhibit a lack of control without exceeding the control limits—test 4 is an example. There are many cases where recognition of an unnatural or anomalous pattern of points, whether exceeding the limits or not, points to process symptoms useful for the diagnoses that are required to make process improvement modifications or, at the very least, points to more effective ways of organizing the data for more effective analysis. The Western Electric *Handbook* [Western Electric 1958] provides descriptions of fifteen common control chart patterns as a guide to interpreting control charts. Six of these patterns, which seem to appear frequently in a software environment, are discussed briefly next.

6.2.1 CYCLES

Cycles are characterized by data that occur in relatively short, repeated patterns as in Figure 6.6. Values tend to repeat with a series of highs and lows, and nearly the same values at regular intervals are an indication of the presence of an assignable cause. Process variables that come and go on a periodic basis are generally the chief reasons for the cyclic performance. The intervals between peaks or valleys can sometimes point to the process variable causing the pattern. This pattern may be observed on average (X-bar), range (R), c, u, and individuals charts. Process variables such as effort, support systems, personnel rotation, schedule demands, and system-build cycles are likely sources of this type of assignable cause.

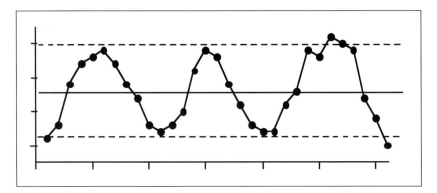

FIGURE 6.6 Cycles Pattern Example

6.2.2 TRENDS

Trends are typified by a gradual change in level, constantly in the same direction, either up or down, seemingly without settling at a new level. In a software development or support environment, trends such as that in Figure 6.7 generally are not considered anomalous unless the trend is not going in the direction or at the rate expected or desired. At times, the rate and direction of the plotted points are not readily determined by visual examination due to the arrangement of the points. When this occurs, use of regression analysis or a similar analytical method is necessary to determine the slope of the trend. Limits for the trend can be calculated using equations for either the averages or individuals charts. Establishing limits for the trend provides guidance on whether or not action is required to correct a

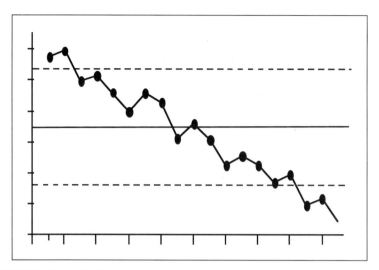

FIGURE 6.7   Trend Pattern Example

process performance problem. Trends seen on the average and individuals charts generally mean a gradual change in one of the principal process variables. A trend on the range charts signals a gradual change in the variation of a process variable. For example, we expect to see trends on average and individuals charts that are used to track progress of product completion or reduction of defects and changes. Trends on the range chart will mean that the variation in product completion or defect reduction is increasing or decreasing depending on the trend direction.

6.2.3   RAPID SHIFT IN LEVEL

A rapid shift in level occurs when there is a sudden and seemingly lasting change in values in one direction, most of which are assignable causes to the process. The values on the right side of the chart in Figure 6.8 are all assignable causes since they violate assignable cause detection tests 2, 3, and 4. This pattern, either a shift up or down, indicates a shift in the process mean on average and individuals charts.

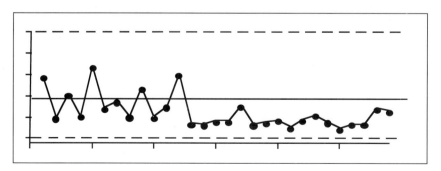

FIGURE 6.8   Shift in Process Level Example

On range charts, the pattern indicates a change in the process variation. If the shift is sustained, a new element or cause has been introduced into the process. A significant change to any one of the process variables may be responsible. New procedures, change of personnel, new or different product characteristics, and changes in the support system or programming tools are examples of process changes that may result in this pattern.

6.2.4   UNSTABLE MIXTURE

A mixture is evidence of the presence of several different distributions caused by the existence of two or more cause systems in the process performance data under consideration. We can think of mixtures existing due to the presence of one or more subprocesses within the measured process. The subprocesses may operate randomly, intermittently in clusters or groups, or consistently over time. The plots in Figures 6.9 through 6.11 depict mixtures in operation in each of these circumstances.

An example of mixtures occurring in a software environment might be the measurement of the effort or time taken to repair a defect. Suppose most of the defects are repaired in a short time or with little effort, but others take significantly more time or effort because of degree of difficulty or unavailable resources. If the occurrence of defects requiring significant time or effort is not high, the control chart will identify them as "freaks" (test-1 type of assignable causes). On the other hand, if the long-time, high-effort defects occur more frequently, the process performance data are likely to result in a control chart plot pattern as an unstable mixture or a bunched mixture.

When mixtures are apparent, the most effective way to analyze the process performance is to first separate data for each of the cause systems. One way to do this is to plot histograms or frequency charts of the data and look for collections of data within different distributions. Another way is to plot all the points above the centerline on one chart and all the points below the line on another. Either way essentially unscrambles the mixed data and organizes it so that the subprocesses involved in the overall process under measurement can be analyzed for assignable causes.

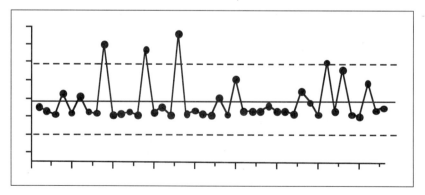

FIGURE 6.9   Unstable Mixture Example

6.2.5 BUNCHING OR GROUPING

The bunching or grouping pattern, as shown in Figure 6.10, is typified by the occurrence of all or most of the similar values in a cluster or quite close together. Values in a natural or random pattern are scattered uniformly throughout the data. The bunching or grouping of these values indicates a sudden introduction of new or different causes often occurring in doublet or triplet sequences. When bunching or grouping occurs, examination of the grouped signals are likely to identify the reason for the assignable causes.

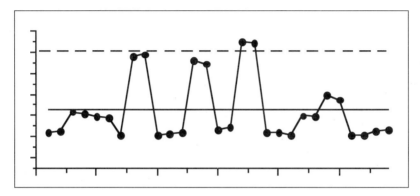

FIGURE 6.10 Bunching or Grouping Example

6.2.6 STRATIFICATION

A stratification pattern, like the one in Figure 6.11, typically has small variations between data points hugging the centerline and few to no values close to the limits. Stratification occurs on average charts when data from two different cause systems are mixed together in the same subgroup so as to artificially increase the subgroup range and thereby widen the average limits. (Incorrect calculation of control limits has been known to cause stratified patterns.) Range charts will display stratification

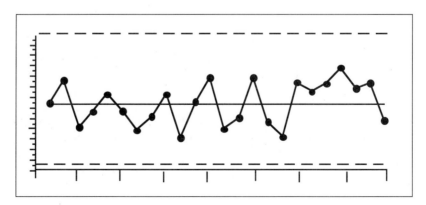

FIGURE 6.11 Stratification Example

when the subgroup range changes very little from one subgroup to the next. This means that the variation between the two cause systems is nearly constant. Stratification will not occur on an individuals chart, but the control limits may become inflated in any event if the process data represents two or more cause systems.

6.3   Rational Sampling and Homogeneity of Subgroups

The purpose of rational sampling is to obtain and use data that are representative of the performance of the process with respect to the issues being studied. Rational sampling is concerned with the what, where, when, how, and why of measurements that are plotted and used to compute control limits. The context in which the data are collected will always be the largest factor in determining the best ways to analyze the data.

Rational sampling is not limited to just collecting data. It also involves understanding the events associated with the data that are collected. This understanding will guide you in selecting the observations and subgroups that you will use for computing control limits.

For example, in measuring process performance drawn from a production stream, the performance should be measured in such a way as to preserve information relative to the process. If, for instance, outflows of parallel operations are combined without retaining such information, you will not be able to identify which of the operations gave rise to a result seen in a sampled item. When identifying the operation that caused the result is important, as it is when you are looking for assignable causes, this kind of sampling is not rational. This is a particularly important consideration when dealing with software processes because of the prevalence of parallel operations in many of the processes. If the process performance factor is based on parallel operations (such as a several-person team), and we do not have good reason to believe the parallel operation is homogeneous, the control charts may hide significant signals and may well give comfort when none is due. Before combining outflows of a parallel process, it is wise to confirm that all of the parallel outputs are, in themselves, consistent and homogeneous with one another. (An example in the ensuing section discussing rational subgrouping illustrates this point in terms of team production.)

Another example occurs when a subset of the data is known to be unrepresentative of the process. Rational sampling says that the unrepresentative subset should be removed from the computation of control limits. This point can be controversial. The key to resolving the controversy lies in the word *unrepresentative*. It is certainly wrong to omit a value or set of values just because you do not like what you see. There must be a stronger (rational) reason, perhaps of the sort, "Oh, yes—on that occasion, X (not a normal part of the process) happened. We know that is an assignable cause, and we want control limits that will detect any similar occurrences." As we pointed out in the discussion of analytic studies, this is the kind of decision that only a subject-matter expert can make. Neither analysts by themselves nor any statistical tool can ever tell whether or not a particular set of data should be excluded from a study.

A third example of rational sampling deals with sampling frequency and its relation to the rates with which performance can change. Observations that are too far apart in time or space can permit substantial shifts, drifts, or changes in variability to occur between observations. When this happens, the variability within subgroups that is used to compute control limits will be too large, regardless of how the data are grouped. The process may then appear to be in control even though it is not. A good deal of judgment and knowledge of the process are necessary to know when it is rational to group data. If you can consider that the observations (measurements) have been made under essentially the same conditions and that the differences between the measurements are due primarily to common cause variation, then you may rationally group the observations.

The nature of the process often dictates how the data may be rationally sampled and grouped. If the process operation is such that the frequency of sampling is not constrained and the subgroup size is independent of the sampling frequency, then we have the option of sampling at time periods matching potential process changes and collecting as much data as necessary to calculate sensitive control limits. This is the type of rational sampling associated with average and range charts, for example.

On the other hand, if the process does not allow complete freedom in sampling frequency and subgroup size is not independent of sampling frequency, a trade-off must be made between subgroup size and sampling frequency. Processes that provide data periodically—once a day, once a week, once a month—typify this situation. Each value is associated with a specific period of time. Accounting figures, shipments, efficiencies, absences, losses, inspection ratios, maintenance costs, accident reports, and records of tests exemplify the types of periodic process data. Increasing the subgroup size will, of necessity, increase the time covered by the subgroup. When this time exceeds that of potential process changes, we no longer have rational sampling since the principle of homogeneous subgrouping is not in effect. For processes providing periodic data, the individuals chart is the chart used to measure process behavior. As we have seen previously, the XmR chart allows us to plot a point every time a value becomes available, using a logical subgroup size of 1.

6.4   Rational Subgrouping

Rational subgrouping is concerned with organizing the data so that the control charts answer the right questions. The first requirement for rational subgroups is that, insofar as possible, subgroups should be selected so that the variations within any given subgroup all come from the same system of chance causes. This means that, in a practical sense, rational subgroups should consist of measured values from small regions of time or space. The purpose of small regions is to have sets of data that, within themselves, are relatively homogeneous with respect to potential causes of variation.

Selecting homogeneous subgroups is important because it is the variation *within* the subgroups that is used to compute the control limits for the process. Minimizing this variation makes detecting changes between subgroups easier and more reliable.

For example, if you look at how control limits are derived from range data, you will see that the ranges within subgroups are used to compute an average range across all subgroups. This average range is then used to compute the upper and lower control limits. When subgroups have been chosen so that variation within groups is small, the control limits will be as close to the centerline as you can make them. Changes in process performance, such as shifts and trends, will then be more easily detected.

In effect, the variation *within* subgroups puts limits on the amount of variation that can exist *between* subgroups for the process to be stable. The larger the variation within groups, the wider the limits and the less effective the control chart will be in detecting instabilities. Another way of thinking about this is to understand that control charts ask the following questions:

- Control charts for averages ask the question, Do the subgroup averages vary more than they should based on the observed variation within subgroups?
- Control charts for ranges ask the question, Is the variation within subgroups consistent from subgroup to subgroup?

In short, the ways in which data are collected and organized determine the behavior you see reflected on a control chart. Inappropriate groupings and the wide limits associated with them will affect your ability to detect patterns and out-of-limit conditions. Variation within subgroups is what determines the sensitivity of the control chart to variation between subgroups. One of your principal objectives when choosing subgroups is to make the opportunity for variation within groups as small as possible. This means paying attention to not only how observations are grouped but also how and when the data are collected.

Thus, it is important to consider the potential sources of variation and organize your data into subgroups that will help you address the questions you have relative to stability, capability, and process improvement. In some cases, there will be a single, natural way to group the data. In other cases, there may be several ways. When many ways are possible, you should select subgroups that will permit the questions of interest to be answered. The following example illustrates some of these issues.

Example 6.3: **Rational Subgrouping**[4]

The software organization of Alphabetronics, Inc., is developing a product consisting of four major components. There is a different design team for each major component. The leader of the design group has asked the four design teams to

---

[4] This example is based on a comparable example given by Wheeler [Wheeler 1992].

count the number of fan-outs (calls to other modules) as the designs for each of their modules are completed. The leader suspects that the number of fan-outs per module might be a useful factor for characterizing system complexity. In particular, she anticipates that there may be a relationship between high fan-out counts and defects [Card 1990]. As a result, she wants to keep the number of fan-outs low. Also, there are new members in each of the design teams, and the group leader wants to be sure that the designers, as a group, are producing consistent designs relative to the overall system structure.

The fan-out counts for the first 20 modules designed by each team are shown in Figure 6.12. The counts were recorded in the sequence in which each team completed its designs. Knowing that the sequence is a production sequence is important. If the sequences were recorded in the order inspected or reported instead of the order produced, the conclusions about stability and assignable causes that could be derived from the data could easily be different and perhaps less useful. This is part of what we mean when we say that traceability of values to the events that produced them is essential to valid analyses.

The data in Figure 6.12 have two identifiable sources of variation. There is variation between teams, and there is variation over time in the number of fan-outs produced by each team. The variation within each team over time is shown in the columns labeled A, B, C, and D. The design group leader must decide how to group the data so that the sources of variation can be isolated and characterized. For purposes of illustration, we will do this in three different ways.

Module Sequence Number	Fan-out Counts for Team				Average (X-bar)	Range (R)
	A	**B**	**C**	**D**		
1	1	4	6	4	3.75	5
2	3	7	5	5	5.00	4
3	4	5	5	7	5.25	3
4	2	6	4	5	4.25	4
5	1	6	7	3	4.25	6
6	3	8	6	4	5.25	5
7	5	7	6	6	6.00	2
8	3	5	4	6	4.50	3
9	2	5	9	4	5.00	7
10	5	5	6	7	5.75	2
11	4	5	6	5	5.00	2
12	5	7	8	6	6.50	3
13	3	3	7	3	4.00	4
14	2	3	6	9	5.00	7
15	3	7	4	3	4.25	4
16	4	6	6	5	5.25	2
17	0	5	5	5	3.75	5
18	3	4	6	6	4.75	3
19	0	4	4	6	3.50	6
20	2	6	5	4	4.25	4
Grand Averages					4.76	4.05

FIGURE 6.12   Module Fan-out Data

Since the design group leader wants to determine whether the overall frequency of fan-outs has been consistent as the design has been progressing, the counts will first be organized into subgroups of size $n = 4$ consisting of one value for each design team (subgroup 1 contains the first module produced by each of the teams, subgroup 2 the second, and so on). The averages and ranges for these subgroups are shown in the two rightmost columns of Figure 6.12.

The design group leader prepared the control charts from the data as follows:

grand average $\overline{\overline{X}} = 4.7625$

average range $\overline{R} = 4.05$

subgroup size $n = 4$

From the table in Appendix A (for $n = 4$),

$A_2 = 0.729, D_4 = 2.282, D_3 = $ undefined

From the equations for X-bar and R charts,

$$UCL_{\overline{X}} = \overline{\overline{X}} + A_2 \overline{R} = 4.763 + 0.729(4.05) = 7.715$$

$$CL_{\overline{X}} = \overline{\overline{X}} = 4.763$$

$$LCL_{\overline{X}} = \overline{\overline{X}} - A_2 \overline{R} = 4.763 - 0.729(4.05) = 1.811$$

$$UCL_R = D_4 \overline{R} = 2.282(4.05) = 9.24$$

$$CL_R = \overline{R} = 4.05$$

$$LCL_R = D_3 \overline{R} = \text{undefined (does not exist for } n = 4)$$

The results are shown in Figure 6.13. The averages and ranges of the subgroups plotted in Figure 6.13 all fall within the control limits, thus meeting the principal requirement for statistical control.

The design group leader found this interesting, but she was concerned that the average fan-out count was higher than desired. Also, the average range within subgroups was 4, suggesting that there was considerable variability across the four teams.

To examine the difference in performance between teams, the group leader knew that she would have to organize the data so that each team became a subgroup. This meant lumping together 20 observations for each team and raised substantial questions in her mind about homogeneity and the rationality for such groupings. If the system of chance causes was not constant within each team, there would be no rational basis for inferring that the results of this kind of analysis would have any predictive value.

To explore the question of homogeneity within teams, the design group leader organized the data so that she could plot XmR charts for each team. This organization reduced the size of the subgroups to $n = 1$. The table that resulted is shown in Figure 6.14.

The control charts that the group leader constructed are shown in Figure 6.15. The values for the teams are plotted on common coordinate systems to assist in

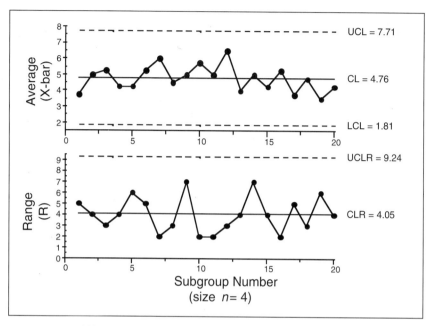

FIGURE 6.13 X-bar and R Charts for Module Fan-out Data (Fan-outs/Module)

Module	Team Fan-out Counts (X) and Moving Ranges (R)							
Sequence	A		B		C		D	
Number	X	R	X	R	X	R	X	R
1	1	—	4	—	6	—	4	—
2	3	2	7	3	5	1	5	1
3	4	1	5	2	5	0	7	2
4	2	2	6	1	4	1	5	2
5	1	1	6	0	7	3	3	2
6	3	2	8	2	6	1	4	1
7	5	2	7	1	6	0	6	2
8	3	2	5	2	4	2	6	0
9	2	2	5	0	9	5	4	2
10	5	3	5	0	6	3	7	3
11	4	1	5	0	6	0	5	2
12	5	1	7	2	8	2	6	1
13	3	2	3	4	7	1	3	3
14	2	1	3	0	6	1	9	6
15	3	1	7	4	4	2	3	6
16	4	1	6	1	6	2	5	2
17	0	4	5	1	5	1	5	0
18	3	3	4	1	6	1	6	1
19	0	3	4	1	4	2	6	0
20	2	2	6	2	5	1	4	2
Averages	2.75	1.8	5.4	1.35	5.75	1.45	5.15	1.9

FIGURE 6.14 Data Organization of Module Fan-out Counts for Constructing XmR Charts

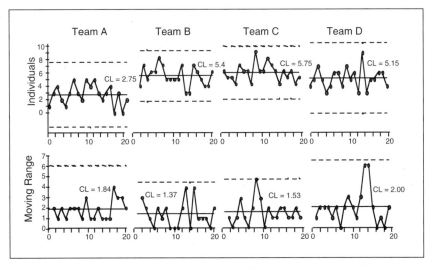

FIGURE 6.15 Individuals and Moving Range Charts for the Four Design Teams (Fan-outs/Modules)

comparing the results. The charts for individual values show no signs of out-of-control conditions for any of the teams. The range chart for team C, however, shows one point that borders on its control limit. This point corresponds to the highest point (and biggest jump) on team C's chart for individual values. Since this point is within its control limits and no other moving range appears unusual, the group leader saw no strong reason to say that team C's performance was out of control.

The group leader was interested to see that Figure 6.15 showed the average fan-out count for team A's modules to be about half that of the other teams. This reinforced her suspicion that there were differences among the processes that the teams were using to design software modules. She knew, however, that the evidence so far was inconclusive.

Since the processes that the teams were using showed no evidence of trends and appeared to be in statistical control, the group leader felt that it would be justifiable to treat the data within each team as having come from a constant system of chance causes. This meant that she could combine the observations into four groups and proceed to the next step—comparing the performance of the teams.

To explore the question of variation in performance across teams, the group leader organized the data into four subgroups, as shown in Figure 6.16. Each subgroup is now of size $n = 20$, and the performance within the groups is known to be reasonably homogeneous.

The resulting control charts are shown in Figure 6.17. The average fan-out count per module is the same as in Figure 6.15, but the limits are much closer to the centerlines. This is not surprising since we know that, in general, the standard deviation for the average of n values is proportional to $1/\sqrt{n}$.

Module Sequence Number	Fanout Counts for Team			
	A	B	C	D
1	1	4	6	4
2	3	7	5	5
3	4	5	5	7
4	2	6	4	5
5	1	6	7	3
6	3	8	6	4
7	5	7	6	6
8	3	5	4	6
9	2	5	9	4
10	5	5	6	7
11	4	5	6	5
12	5	7	8	6
13	3	3	7	3
14	2	3	6	9
15	3	7	4	3
16	4	6	6	5
17	0	5	5	5
18	3	4	6	6
19	0	4	4	6
20	2	6	5	4
X-bar	2.75	5.4	5.75	5.15
R	5	5	5	6

FIGURE 6.16 Data Organization for Measuring Fan-out Variation Between Design Teams

Figure 6.17 shows that the average fan-out counts for teams A and C fall outside the control limits. This suggests that real differences exist between the teams, despite the performance of each team being under statistical control. The group leader would not be justified in reaching this conclusion had she not verified that each of the teams had a stable process.

Strictly speaking, because the sample size is bigger than 10, the group leader should have used an S chart rather than an R chart as the basis for assessing variability and computing control limits. Just to be safe, we verified her conclusions by making those computations. The results, as shown in Figure 6.18, are essentially the same.

What is going on here? The range charts in Figures 6.13 and 6.15 provide a clue, but first let us review the questions the control charts are answering compared to the questions the design leader was asking.

The subgrouping of data shown in Figure 6.12 was aimed at examining the variation in fan-out counts as the design progressed over time. This subgrouping assumed that, at any point in the sequence, the variability across teams would be

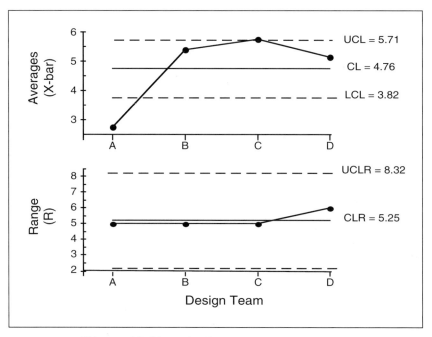

FIGURE 6.17   X-bar and R Charts for Fan-out Variation Between Design Teams

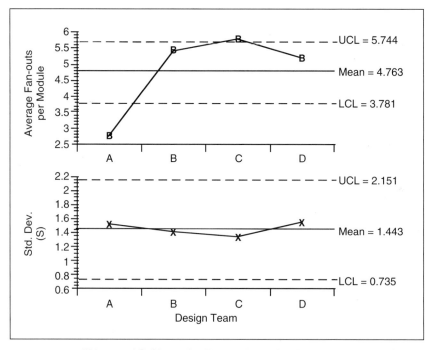

FIGURE 6.18   X-bar and S Charts for Fan-out Variation Between Design Teams

less than the variability over time. When this assumption is true, it is rational to use the variations observed among the four teams to compute control limits that describe the inherent variability in the average fan-out count for groups of four at any point in time. These control limits can then be used to examine the stability of the overall process. Thus, the charts resulting from the organization of data in Figure 6.12 examine these questions:

- X-bar chart: Have there been detectable differences in the average fan-out counts as the design has progressed?
- R chart: Has the team-to-team variability in fan-out counts been consistent across the 20 groups of modules?

This organization of the data did not ask the question, Are there detectable differences in the fan-out counts between the respective design teams? In fact, there were implicit assumptions that the variation would be less across teams than it would be over time and that the performance of each team's design process would be evolving at the same rate.

The second organization of the data (Figure 6.14) made fewer assumptions. It addressed the problem of subgroup homogeneity by using XmR charts individually for each of the four teams. This data organization asked questions similar to the first organization but aimed at the design teams individually. Because the subgroup size was $n = 1$, two-point moving ranges were used to estimate sigma and set the control limits. The questions that this organization of data asked were these:

- individuals chart: Have there been detectable differences within any team's fan-out counts as the design has progressed?
- mR chart: Has the variability in fan-out counts for each of the teams been consistent across their 20 modules?

The third organization of the data used the fan-out counts for each team's 20 modules as the subgroups ($n = 20$). The justification for doing this was that the XmR charts showed that each team's results appeared to come from a process with a constant system of chance causes. When the performance is consistent within teams (is in statistical control), the average of the variations in the teams (the subgroups) can be used to set limits for comparing the differences in performance among the teams. The questions being addressed with this data organization were these:

- X-bar chart: Were there detectable differences in the module fan-out counts among the teams?
- R chart: Was the variability in fan-out counts consistent from team to team?

The X-bar chart in Figure 6.17 shows the average performance of each of the four design teams, and the R chart shows the respective ranges of performance within each team. Although the ranges are remarkably consistent across the teams, the chart for averages (X-bar) shows significant differences among the teams' average performance. When significant differences exist, there may be assignable causes. Whether or not team A's process leads to an unusually small number of fanouts or team C's to an unusually large number are things to be investigated. If the design group leader wants to obtain lower fan-out counts from teams B, C, and D, she must now determine the process changes that will be needed for the three teams to achieve results comparable to those of team A.

Notice that sequence was not an issue in the third analysis. Thus, in a sense, this analysis does not illustrate a classical use of control charts. Instead, it effectively uses a technique called *analysis of variance*. The difference is that before the team leader performed her analysis, she verified that one of the necessary conditions—the existence of a single distribution within each team—appeared to hold. In ordinary analysis of variance, this is often just assumed. Now that you have seen how easy it is for data produced by processes to be corrupted by assignable causes, you can appreciate how easy it is for simple analyses of variance to lead you astray in dynamic environments like the ones that we often find in analytic studies.

The three approaches in this example show that there can be several ways to organize data into subgroups and that each way makes different assumptions and leads to answering different questions. Clearly, the choice of subgroups determines what you can learn from the data. In general, the sources of variation of least concern (those closest to the inherent variation in the process) should be represented by differences within subgroups. The sources of variation that you wish to detect, on the other hand, should be represented by differences between the subgroups. Rational subgrouping keeps the variation within subgroups small so that the tightest possible limits can be set. Narrow limits are what make control charts sensitive to the nonrandom variations you want to detect. Rational subgrouping enables you to set narrow limits without an uneconomical number of false alarms.

Thus, rational subgrouping is about common sense and efficiency in the use of data obtained from a process. The frequency of sampling should reflect both the nature of the process and the frequency with which actions or decisions are needed. If multiple measurements are collected at the same time and there are no structural reasons for the values to be different, they may be grouped together and used to estimate the inherent process variability. If only single values are collected, subgroups of size 1 and their associated moving ranges are likely to be most appropriate. When only limited amounts of data are available, you should look first to plotting a running record of the individual values. Automatically subgrouping limited amounts of data is not a good practice.

6.5   The Problem of Insufficient Granularity in Recorded Values

When measured values of continuous variables have insufficient granularity—that is, are coarse and imprecise—the discreteness that results can mask the underlying process variation. Computations for $\overline{X}$ and sigma can then be affected, and individual values that are rounded or truncated in the direction of the nearest control limit can easily give false out-of-control signals.

There are four main causes of coarse data: (1) inadequate measurement in-struments, (2) imprecise reading of the instruments, (3) rounding, and (4) taking measurements at intervals that are too short to permit detectable variation to oc-cur. When measurements are not obtained and recorded with sufficient precision to describe the underlying variability, digits that contain useful information will be lost. If the truncation or rounding reduces the precision in recorded results to only one or two digits that change, the running record of measured values will show only a few levels of possible outcomes. Fortunately, when this problem oc-curs, it is easy to identify.

Example 6.4:   Insufficient Granularity

Figure 6.19 shows two sets of values for X (the measured process performance) and mR (the moving range of X). The leftmost set of values lists 32 observations as they were recorded; the rightmost set lists the observations after rounding (or

	Measured		Rounded	
Observation	X	mR	X	mR
1	1.08	—	1.1	—
2	1.09	.01	1.1	0
3	1.15	.06	1.2	0.1
4	1.07	.08	1.0	0.2
5	1.03	.04	1.0	0
6	1.08	.05	1.1	0.1
7	1.1	.02	1.1	0
8	1.04	.06	1.0	0.1
9	1.07	.03	1.1	0.1
10	1.1	.03	1.1	0
11	1.12	.02	1.1	0
12	1.09	.03	1.1	0
13	1.03	.06	1.0	0.1
14	1.03	.0	1.0	0
15	1.09	.06	1.1	0.1
16	1.13	.04	1.1	0
17	1.02	.11	1.0	0.1
18	1.04	.02	1.0	0
19	1.03	.01	1.0	0
20	1.04	.01	1.0	0
21	1.14	.1	1.1	0.1
22	1.07	.07	1.1	0
23	1.08	.01	1.1	0
24	1.13	.05	1.2	0.1
25	1.08	.05	1.1	0.1
26	1.03	.05	1.0	0.1
27	1.02	.01	1.0	0
28	1.04	.02	1.0	0
29	1.03	.01	1.0	0
30	1.06	.03	1.1	0.1
31	1.02	.04	1.0	0.1

FIGURE 6.19   Measured Values as Originally Recorded and Subsequently Rounded

as they might have been recorded if the measurements were insufficiently precise). The XmR charts produced from the two sets of values are shown in Figures 6.20 and 6.21. Notice that the charts do not appear to describe the same process. The

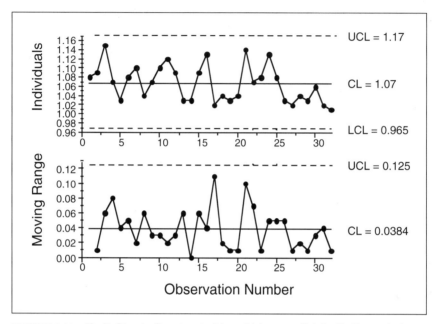

FIGURE 6.20 XmR Charts Constructed from Values as Originally Recorded

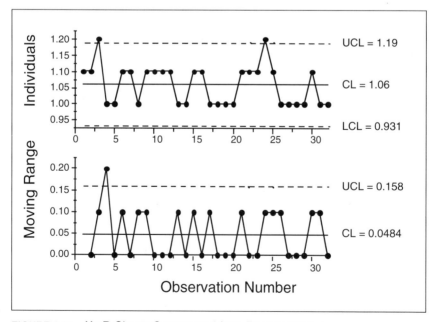

FIGURE 6.21 XmR Charts Constructed from Rounded Values

out-of-control points in Figure 6.21 appear solely because the data do not correctly reflect the underlying process variation.

The solution to the problem of insufficient granularity is to ensure that the data used for control charts have a resolution that is smaller than the process standard deviation. A good rule of thumb for achieving this is to ensure that the set of points that are plotted always takes on values that range over at least five possible levels of discreteness (the charts in Figure 6.21, for example, have stepped appearances because the values in them have only three possible levels). Increasing the number of levels can be accomplished by measuring more precisely, by decreasing the frequency of measurement to allow for variation to occur between measured values, or by increasing the size of subgroups to allow for more variation within a subgroup.

Never round data to the point where the values that result span less than five attainable levels. If this rule must be violated, the data can be plotted in a running record, but they should not be used to calculate control limits.

Additional examples and guidelines related to this subject can be found under the topic of "Inadequate Measurement Units" in Wheeler's books [Wheeler 1989, 1992, 1995].

6.6   Aggregation and Decomposition of Process Performance Data

When analyzing process performance data, you must be constantly concerned that you have identified all sources of variation in the process. If a conscious effort is not made to account for the potential sources of variation, you may inadvertently hide or obscure variation that will help you improve the process. Even worse, you may mislead yourself and others with a faulty analysis.

When data are aggregated, your process will be particularly susceptible to overlooked or hidden sources of variation. Overly aggregated data come about in many ways, but the most common causes are

- Inadequately formulated operational definitions of product and process measures.
- Inadequate description and recording of context information.
- Lack of traceability from data back to the context from whence it originated.
- Working with data whose elements are combinations (mixtures) of values from nonhomogeneous sources.

  Overly aggregated data easily lead to

- Difficulty in identifying instabilities in process performance.

- Difficulty in tracking instabilities to assignable causes.
- Using results from unstable processes to draw inferences or make predictions about capability or performance.

We addressed issues associated with the causes and avoidance of overly aggregated data in Chapters 3 and 4. The example that follows shows some of the advantages that accrue when full traceability is present so that data can be disaggregated and used to probe the underlying structure of a process. The example uses orthogonal attribute definitions to help identify sources of variation and provide insights to potential process improvement [Chillarege 1992, 1996].

Example 6.5: **Aggregation and Decomposition of Process Performance Data**

The top two rows in Figure 6.22 show the number of defects found during design inspections for each of 21 components of a new system. Each component is believed to possess the same area of opportunity in terms of the potential for defects to occur and be found.

The XmR charts of Figure 6.23, constructed for the total number of defects found in each component, show no signs of instability from component to component. Based on this cursory examination, it would appear that the combined process of design and inspection was stable and under control.

The next activity that the organization had planned was to classify the defects according to the types listed in Figure 6.22 and determine whether the number of defects found, by type, were within the target limits obtained from previous experience [Chillarege 1992; Bhandari 1993]. The bottom eight rows of Figure 6.22 show the number of defects of each type found in each component.

Before we embark on this activity, it is important to know whether or not the component design process is in control for the different types of defects found. Therefore, XmR charts were constructed by plotting the number of defects for each type in the sequence in which the components were completed. The control charts for these individual values are shown in Figure 6.24.

Here, we see that the disaggregated data for the number of defects found suggests unstable conditions in seven of the eight control charts. Several points are out of bounds, and one chart shows a run of eight points below the centerline. (There were no signs of instability in the respective moving range charts.) The

Component	1	2	3	4	5	6	7	8	9	10	11	12	13	14	15	16	17	18	19	20	21	Totals
Defects	12	16	18	32	22	16	23	35	15	27	16	25	20	26	20	23	23	36	22	27	17	471
Defect Type	Number of Defects per Type per Component																					
Function	3	5	4	4	4	3	3	20	4	11	2	3	3	5	3	7	4	5	5	15	2	115
Interface	2	2	4	4	3	4	2	3	3	4	2	3	5	3	3	3	2	16	6	2	4	80
Timing	1	1	0	1	0	2	1	0	0	2	0	1	1	1	1	1	0	1	0	0	15
Algorithm	0	0	1	14	2	0	0	0	0	0	0	1	5	2	7	6	5	1	2	0	1	47
Checking	1	1	5	1	7	1	1	2	0	1	6	3	1	12	1	0	2	4	3	5	2	59
Assignment	0	2	0	4	1	2	1	3	2	3	2	8	1	0	2	1	2	1	0	1	1	37
Build/Pkg.	3	1	1	2	1	0	0	4	3	6	1	0	2	1	1	1	3	2	2	2	1	37
Document.	2	4	3	2	3	6	14	2	3	2	1	7	2	2	2	4	4	7	3	2	6	81

FIGURE 6.22   A Summary of Defect Types Found During Component Inspections

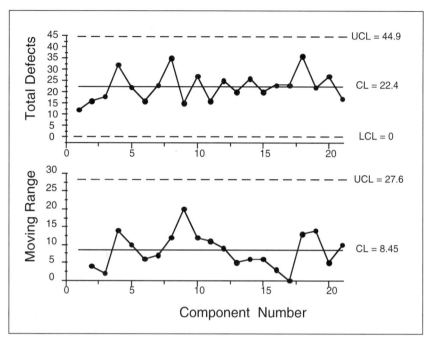

FIGURE 6.23   XmR Charts for Total Number of Defects Found in Component Inspections

charts for individuals show that as many as eight different components may have been associated with the instabilities. This suggests that reasons for the unusual variations be sought. If reasons are found, actions can be taken to fix the problems that caused the unusual variations.

Note that, when assignable causes are found and the corresponding points are removed from the charts, the control limits will become narrower, and the performance of the process will be more predictable for each defect type. The organization will then be in a position to make changes in a controlled fashion or to project future performance if it desires.

Example 6.5 shows that a single control chart of aggregated data, as in Figure 6.23, may be ineffective for identifying instabilities or for pointing to potential opportunities for improvement unless the aggregated data are demonstrably stable as well. As Wheeler and Chambers point out when discussing a similar example, the more sources of nonconformity that are combined on one chart, the greater the likelihood that the chart will appear to be in control [Wheeler 1992]. Thus, although charts such as the one in Figure 6.23 may provide a useful record of what is happening, they are not very useful for improving a process. Due to the smoothing produced by aggregating the effects of several sources of error, control charts for the total number of defects can easily fail to identify both the timing of instabilities and the potential sources of assignable causes.

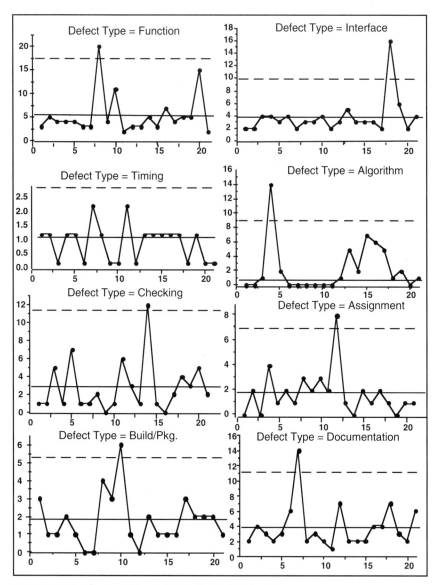

FIGURE 6.24 Control Charts for Individual Defect Types

6.7 Summary

A number of topics arise when one moves from reading about control charts to actually using control charts to measure process performance. How much data is enough? The guidelines offered in this chapter can best be summarized by taking the advice of Shewhart, Wheeler, Montgomery, and others. That is, when limited amounts of data are available, calculate and plot the limits, seek out the assignable causes that the data suggest, and then update the control limits as more data become available.

The section on anomalous process behavior patterns identified and illustrated a number of data patterns that frequently occur when measuring unstable software processes. Trends, stratification, unstable mixtures, bunching or grouping, cycles, and rapid shift in levels are typical of many software processes by virtue of inadvertent combination of data representing more than one cause system.

The sections on rational sampling and subgrouping provided a detailed explanation of rational sampling, rational subgrouping, and homogeneity of data and were followed by an extensive illustration of these principles using a software process example. These sections might best be summarized by noting that the ways in which data are collected and organized determine the behavior you see reflected on a control chart. Inappropriate groupings and the wide limits associated with them will affect your ability to detect patterns and out-of-limit conditions. Variation within subgroups is what determines the sensitivity of the control chart to variation between subgroups. One of your principal objectives when choosing subgroups is to make the opportunity for variation within groups as small as possible. This means paying attention to not only how observations are grouped but also how and when the data are collected.

Lastly, the chapter alerted the reader to two frequently encountered issues dealing with the data used to create control charts: aggregation of data and insufficient data granularity. The first issue gives you the possibility of a control chart that appears to indicate a stable process when there is none (a close relative of a stratification anomaly); the second, the appearance of assignable causes when there are none (due to coarse measurements).

7

Three Paths to Process Improvement

When process performance measurements are plotted on process behavior charts and analyzed as discussed and illustrated in Chapters 4, 5, and 6, the results point to one of three investigative directions:

1. **Remove assignable causes.** When the process is not stable (or nearly so), the proper action is to identify the assignable causes of instability and take steps to prevent the causes from recurring.

2. **Change the process.** If the process is stable but not capable (not meeting organizational or customer needs), the proper action is to identify, design, and implement necessary changes that will make the process capable. Keep in mind that changing a process transforms it into a new process and that the new process must be brought under control and made stable before its capability can be assessed.

3. **Continually improve.** If the process is both stable and capable, the proper action is to seek ways to continually improve the process so that variability is reduced and quality, cost, and cycle time are improved. Once more, any changes to a process will transform the process into a new process whose stability must be established before you can rely on predictions of future performance.

In the sections that follow, we explore the three investigative directions summarized in the shaded box of the flowchart in Figure 7.1. We focus on establishing process stability by examining anomalous process variables and relating them to characteristic assignable causes in a software environment. In addition, we discuss methods used to determine process capability and explore various avenues to improve process capability.

Perceptive readers will observe that the flowchart in Figure 7.1 exposes the recursive nature of process improvement. Discovering that a problem exists is only the start of a journey. The next questions are these: Why? What can we do about it? How much is it worth? Taking action to improve the process will, more often

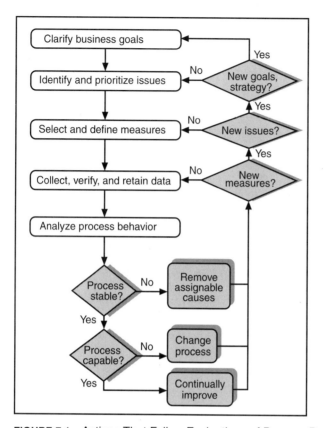

FIGURE 7.1   Actions That Follow Evaluations of Process Performance

than not, require process knowledge, information, and data beyond the process performance measurements used to arrive at the three investigative directions just listed.

Once you find that a process is either unstable or performing at an unacceptable level, you may find that you need additional information to help you find and remedy assignable causes. Additional information may be needed to visualize and implement actions to make the process capable or improve the process. Getting this information may mean measuring additional attributes of the product, process, or environment if it has not been gathered previously. There are three reasons for needing additional data:

1. To support or invalidate hypotheses about possible causes of instability. Data may be required to find, confirm, and eliminate root causes of instabilities and inadequate performance. (What is causing the problems we see?)

2. To identify, verify, or quantify cause-and-effect relationships. So that the right amounts of the right changes can be made to improve the process,

additional data may be needed to identify and quantify cause-and-effect relationships. (Which factors should we change when we wish to improve? How large a change should we make? What are the other characteristics of the product, process, system, environment, resources, and customer that we are addressing?) You will likely need data (and perhaps experiments) to test the hypotheses and to support or eliminate specific factors. This means that measurement, with all its subactivities—selecting, defining, collecting, retaining, analyzing, and acting—will once again be needed.

3. To estimate (or confirm) the business value of the actions that are proposed (or taken) to improve the process. Data is needed to estimate costs and benefits associated with present levels of performance and proposed improvements. (What are the costs and benefits now? What will they be after the changes? What will it cost to make the changes? How long will it take?) There is always the pragmatic reason that, whatever action you propose, you will have to convince others to assist you in implementing and funding the changes. Without factual evidence to support the rationale for proposed actions, people will have every right to challenge your proposals.

The method of analysis used to identify root causes and solutions or to estimate costs and benefits, though, may be different from the ones you used for measuring process stability and capability. In particular, enumerative studies may well come into play. (Chapter 3 illustrates several of the more commonly used analytic tools for such an analysis.)

7.1 Finding and Correcting Assignable Causes

When you find that a process is not stable, you should try to find the reasons for assignable causes and take actions to prevent their recurrence. It is important to recognize that correcting assignable causes is not the same as changing a process. Eliminating assignable causes essentially repairs the process and brings it to a repeatable state—but this is a very important state to achieve. When a process is not stable, it seldom makes sense to introduce changes to improve capability or performance. Without stability as a baseline to start from, you are likely to simply trade one unstable condition for another.

Finding and correcting assignable causes calls for detective work that is not unlike that of debugging a failing software component. You will not be far off track if you think of the hunt for an assignable cause as the equivalent of the hunt for the cause of a software failure. As with software, when process outputs vary erratically, one of the best things to do is to look for familiar patterns and try to isolate the problem (or problems).

One of the characteristics of process behavior charts (control charts) is that each type of chart is responsible for reporting the state of the process with respect to the mean and the amount of variability over time. So, when we see assignable causes occurring on an averages chart, a range chart, an individuals chart, or any one of the attributes charts, we can tell immediately whether the assigned cause is due to abnormalities in the product or process attributes, excess variation of the attributes, or both. By looking for anomalous patterns, like those described in Chapter 6, we can determine other characteristics of process behavior that will help "debug" the process.

7.1.1   AVERAGE OR X-BAR CHARTS

Average or X-bar charts show the average of the process performance attribute(s) being measured. The X-bar pattern will shift with the center of distribution of the attribute. Changes in the process common cause system will tend to affect the process performance all at once, all in the same way.

Examples of changes in cause systems occur when a computer support system or a database fails, when there is a large increase in requirements, or when there is a sudden absence or increase in personnel or decrease in product size or increase in product defects. Changes like these almost always affect the entire process and will be reflected on an X-bar chart. An X-bar chart also can be affected by assignable causes that appear on the R chart but primarily as a reflection of the R chart values. If there is a change in the mix proportion of cause systems (such as the ratio of duplicate problem reports to total problem reports), the average can be raised or lowered accordingly. This type of change would be seen on the R chart and reflected on the X-bar chart. Also, if the R chart contains assignable causes, this may cause the X-bar average to look like it is out of control. Always read the X-bar chart and the R chart together, and do not try to interpret the X-bar chart if the R chart has assignable causes.

7.1.2   R CHARTS

R charts measure the amount of variation or spread of the process performance. If the same process performance attribute is measured over two separate processes, the process with the lowest average range will produce more consistent results (less variation) than the other. If an R chart does not remain in control or if the average range changes, it is a sign of erratic process performance and often means that a separate system of causes has come into play. The R chart is the chart of choice to detect mixtures of all types, erratic conditions, and interactions with other cause systems.

The R chart is sensitive to changes that affect only a part of the product or process performance over time. Inconsistency in process performance of any kind will be seen on the R chart. Examples of such changes are larger code units leading to more defects per unit; inexperienced or poorly trained engineers resulting in inconsistent work products; intermittent disruption of support systems; and changes in software complexity from one unit to another leading to inconsistent design effort and inspection reviews, delays in receiving material, and missing or incomplete product parts.

7.1.3   ATTRIBUTES CHARTS

Attributes charts (p, np, c, and u charts) are all based on theoretical models to compute limits about the process mean and therefore are more limited in their capacity to provide information about processes showing a lack of control. Attributes charts showing assignable causes can be interpreted in much the same way as X-bar charts. That is, changes in the process elements or cause systems should be investigated. Examples would include changes in material, personnel, and support systems including tools or procedures.

7.1.4   INDIVIDUALS CHARTS

Many of the conditions that are detected on X-bar charts and R charts also show up on individuals charts for the same reasons. Individuals charts are not as sensitive as X-bar or R charts in detecting assignable causes, but certain patterns show up more plainly on individuals charts. Cycles, trends, and mixtures often will show up on an individuals chart sooner than on an X-bar or R chart. In addition, an individuals chart plainly shows the relationship between the voice of the process and the voice of the customer and is often the basis for computing process capability. (Note that we are addressing the X part of an XmR chart, not the mR part. These comments do not apply to the mR chart.)

A summary of the control charts discussed in the preceding subsections and the use of these charts for interpreting process behavior is given in Figure 7.2.

7.1.5   NONCOMPLIANCE AS AN ASSIGNABLE CAUSE

When a process component is not performing consistently, lack of compliance to process standards may be the cause of the instabilities you see in process results. Processes get designed, either implicitly or explicitly, around four kinds of knowledge: (1) the desired transformation of process input; (2) the known or estimated performance of process components; (3) the existence and effectiveness of support systems; and (4) the anticipated effects of organizational factors such as management support, organizational changes, and personnel policies and actions. Therefore, when you are investigating assignable causes, a potential source of process instability may be compliance (or the lack thereof) to the process. The following aspects of compliance should be examined:

- Adherence to the process.
- Fitness and use of people, tools, technology, and procedures.
- Fitness and use of support systems.
- Organizational factors, such as management support, organizational changes, personnel turnover, relocations, downsizing, and so forth.

Figure 7.3 lists some of the things to examine when searching for causes of noncompliance. Note that the concept of fitness to execute a process applies to

Control Chart	Function	Interpretation
Average or X-bar charts	Show the average of the process performance attributes being measured. X-bar pattern will shift with the center of the distribution of the attribute. Changes in the process common cause system will tend to affect the process performance all at once, all in the same way. Can also be affected by assignable causes that appear on R charts.	Examples of changes in cause systems: large increase in requirements; sudden absence or increase in personnel, decrease in product size, or increase in product defects.
R charts	Measure the amount of variation or spread of the process performance. Are sensitive to intermittent or systematic changes that affect only a part of the product or process performance over time.	Inconsistency in process performance of any kind will be seen. (Note: Always read the X-bar chart and R chart together.) Examples: larger code units leading to more defects per unit; inexperienced engineers resulting in inconsistent work products; changes in software complexity from one unit to another leading to inconsistent design effort and inspection reviews.
Attributes charts (p, np, c, and u charts)	Based on theoretical models to compute limits about the process mean and therefore are more limited in their capacity to provide information about processes showing a lack of control.	Similar to average charts. Reflect changes to cause systems. Examples: changes in material, personnel, and support systems including tools or procedures.
Individuals charts	Show the average and variation of single-point measures of process variables taken over time. Show the relationship between the voice of the process and voice of the customer and are often the basis for computing process capability.	Useful for periodic data or single-point samples taken over time. Not as sensitive as X-bar or R charts in detecting assignable causes, but detect certain patterns more promptly. Examples: general trends, large fluctuations, and mixtures of cause systems, including cycles, stratification, and grouping.

FIGURE 7.2 Summary of Control Charts and Their Use for Interpreting Process Behavior

Compliance Issues	Things to Examine When Seeking Reasons for Noncompliance
Adherence to the process	Awareness and understanding of the process
	Existence of explicit standards
	Adequate and effective training
	Appropriate and adequate tools
	Conflicting or excessively aggressive goals or schedules
Fitness and use of people, tools, technology, and procedures	Availability of qualified people, tools, and technology
	Experience
	Education
	Training
	Assimilation
Fitness and use of support systems	Availability
	Capacity
	Responsiveness
	Reliability
Organizational factors	Lack of management support
	Personnel turnover
	Organizational changes
	Relocation
	Downsizing
	Disruptive personnel
	Morale problems

FIGURE 7.3   Compliance Issues and Potential Sources of Noncompliance

people, resources, methods, technologies, and other support related to the process. Although an organization may have defined a process, there is no guarantee that its people can actually use it or properly execute it. There are many reasons why this may be so. Examples include lack of awareness, insufficient training, inadequate tools or facilities, difficulties in transferring technology, inadequate management support, and mismatches between the process and the software domain characteristics.

If we determine that the performance of the process is not stable (not in control), one reason may be that the process is not being executed as defined. If the intended tools are not being used, if there is a wide disparity of experience or skills within the set of people executing the process, or if procedures other than those contained in the process definition are sometimes substituted, the process is likely to be unstable.

All processes are subject to forces of entropy. That is, if left alone, processes tend to deteriorate from a controlled state to a chaotic state. Unless we make a conscious effort to sustain our processes by reinforcing their proper use and by repairing the effects of entropy, we tend to lose control. Organizational factors, like those listed in Figure 7.3, are often the reason for process instability.

7.1.6   MAPPING SIGNALS AND ANOMALOUS PATTERNS TO ASSIGNABLE CAUSES

In Chapters 4, 5, and 6, we drew your attention to the more frequently encountered patterns and signals that are symptomatic of assignable causes. Summarized in Figure 7.4, these symptoms can occur in any unstable process—they are not unique to software processes. We also have discussed various types of generic assignable causes, such as those listed in Figure 7.5. A reasonable question is, How

Symptoms or Signals
Freaks
Mixed processes/nonconstant system of causes
• Stratification
• Bunching/grouping
• Unstable mixtures
Process shifts of mean or variance
Cycles
Trends

FIGURE 7.4   Summary of Process Behavior Chart Symptoms or Signals

Assignable Causes
Erroneous data
• Data collection mishaps
• Poor or loose operational definitions of measures causing misinterpretation and misunderstanding leading to incorrect data recording
Data organization and analysis issues
• Lack of rational sampling
• Irrational subgrouping
• Nonhomogeneity in subgroups
• Parallel streams, use of averages from out-of-control processes, and so on
Process noncompliance
• People, skill mix, resources, support, management
• Careless or inconsistent process execution
• Work environment changes
Flawed or inadequate process design
Change in characteristics of one or more process elements or causes

FIGURE 7.5   Summary of Generic Assignable Causes

do these signals relate to the generic assignable causes, and how is this applied to a process behavior chart for a specific software process? Unfortunately, there is not a one-to-one relationship between the signals and assignable causes. There is not even a finite list of signals or of assignable causes. In short, there is no formula or transformation algorithm that one can apply to this question. In practice, intimate knowledge of the process, combined with understanding of control chart fundamentals and being a reasonably good investigator, turns out to be the key to relating process behavior chart signals to specific process assignable causes.

We can pass along the benefit of experience of those who have used control charts and been successful in determining reasons for assignable causes for various processes. We will do this by outlining a rather general approach to finding assignable cause reasons and illustrating the results using a number of examples based on data from actual software processes.

7.1.7 APPROACHES TO DETERMINING ASSIGNABLE CAUSE REASONS

As a first step, examine process performance data against the four data validation criteria described in Chapter 3. Knowing the extent to which the data satisfy these criteria will provide a basis for including or excluding data having an unusual relationship to the rest of the data. Plotting the data using XmR charts sometimes can help you identify outlandish and other freakish data that escapes the eye in a data listing. These data should not be ignored, but rather tracked down to understand how the data came to be in error so that erroneous data can be avoided in the future.

When you start to measure a process, your process behavior chart is very likely to consist of a reasonably complex pattern after you have plotted the first twenty or so values. If this occurs, take the time to reexamine your assumptions about the process, your selection of process performance data, and the resulting data organization you have selected for plotting on control charts. (Is the organization of the data such that it truly measures the process variation of interest? Did you inadvertently allow multiple cause systems to be merged?) Since it is very easy to make assumptions about what the process data represent based on the way the process is supposed to operate, you should verify your assumptions about the process before spending effort on chasing down other presumed assignable causes.

If the control chart pattern indicates a mixture, try simplifying the pattern by reorganizing the data into two sets—one set containing the values above the centerline, the other set the values from below. Plot separate control charts for each of the data sets. This often will reveal an underlying or a hidden process that is affecting the process common cause system.

You may want to assemble a group of people who work within the process to explore possible reasons for the unusual behavior. Ishikawa charts, Pareto diagrams, and most of the analysis tools discussed in Chapter 4 can help to focus the discussions and summarize the results. The process control charts will put the process behavior in context with time, thereby allowing the group to relate to events that may be relevant to the assignable causes. The group may point out process idiosyncrasies explaining process behavior or assignable causes.

You may also find that you want to measure key parameters of some of the inputs to the process and plot run charts (or control charts) to see whether anything unusual is happening. Out-of-control inputs, for example, can cause out-of-control outputs. When out-of-control inputs are found, this could push your search for root causes and corrective actions to points earlier in the overall process, or it may indicate that the process under study has two or more "invisible" processes (ways of dealing with the input that are not recognized by the process description).

Sometimes, assignable causes, once found, can point the way to improving process performance. For example, an unusual series of events or an inadvertent change to the process may cause the process not only to become unstable but also to improve—at least momentarily—certain aspects of quality. When this happens and the assignable causes can be replicated, it may be profitable to incorporate the causes of the beneficial results as permanent parts of the process. Finding and making process changes that will improve process performance is the topic of an ensuing section of this chapter. For the moment, when instabilities are present, the first order of business is to isolate and eliminate the elements that are making the process unstable.

The scenario and data in the following example is adapted from the results of a joint study conducted by the Software Engineering Institute (SEI) and the Onboard Space Shuttle Software Project to evaluate the use of statistical process control to assess and predict and ultimately improve their software processes.[1] The example follows a set of events analogous to that experienced in the joint study and uses Onboard Space Shuttle Software Project software inspection process performance data. The example is presented here to illustrate how combining knowledge of the process, recognition of process behavior patterns, and application of statistical control methods not only can find assignable causes but also can point the way to process improvements.

---

[1] In this example, we discuss a portion of the work conducted under a collaborative study between the Onboard Space Shuttle Project at Lockheed-Martin Corporation and the Software Engineering Measurement and Analysis team at the Software Engineering Institute, Carnegie Mellon University. This work was conducted from September 1997 to May 1998. The primary objective of the collaboration was to address the practical application of statistical process control techniques in an organizational software setting. Specifically, the focus of the study was to better understand and improve software processes and be able to better predict results and outcomes. We are indebted to Ted Keller and Tom Peterson, who sponsored this collaboration, encouraged and supported our work, and challenged us to think outside of the box. The authors are also grateful to have had the opportunity to work with Julie Barnard, Ricardo de la Fuente, and Calvin Armstrong. We appreciated their enthusiasm, willingness, and openness in working with their data and experimenting and learning with us. Other aspects of this work were reported at the 1998 SEI Software Engineering Symposium. The figures presented in this example are used with permission of the Onboard Space Shuttle Software Project (now a part of United Space Alliance).

| Example 7.1: | **Finding and Correcting Assignable Causes** |

The onboard space shuttle software consists of six major components that are used to control and support systems, maneuvers, and payloads of the space shuttle vehicle from liftoff to touchdown. Needless to say, software quality is of prime importance. The software is modified to match each space mission as required and is upgraded periodically with new or additional features to meet the expanding function of the space shuttle.

Each of the six major software components has its own development team, and each team is guided by a common system architecture group and a software engineering process group (SEPG). The components are integrated, tested, verified, and released by a separate system evaluation team. Since human life is dependent on reliable and accurate operation of the shuttle and its components to say nothing of the tremendous cost of failure—NASA reviews various quality records collected during development and testing to support the Onboard Space Shuttle Software Project's prediction of accuracy and reliability.

The purpose of this part of the joint study was to determine whether, by using SPC to analyze selected processes, predictions of the already highly reliable space shuttle software could be reinforced and enhanced earlier in the development cycle. The SEPG selected the software inspection process as the trial process because it is a well-documented, common process across all six software components, it has been practiced by all personnel since early in the project, and it has proven to be a cost-effective process in terms of producing an exceptionally high-quality product. Another reason for selecting the inspection process was the fact that a database existed that contained an extensive number of inspection process attributes covering several years of activity. The existing database allowed the examination of a very large number of inspection process attributes without having to invoke a data collection process and avoided having to wait for weeks or months for access to the data. Thus, the initial task of the joint study team was to review the database contents and select appropriate measures for analysis.

Selecting Measures

The SEPG considered consistency of inspection review effort as a key issue of the inspection process. Because the number of inspectors and the size of the inspection package varied with each inspection, it was important to establish whether or not the review effort was consistent from one inspection to the next. Demonstrating that the review effort was consistent (stable) was considered a prerequisite to examining the process performance in terms of escaped errors.

After conferring with each of the software development teams, the SEPG selected the software inspection process attributes listed in Figure 7.6 as the initial set of attributes that would usefully quantify the process behavior in terms of review effort.[2] The inspection package material consisted of a requirements description,

---

[2] This set of attributes was later amended to include the inspection review time for each inspector for each inspection so that the stability of each inspector's review effort could be ascertained from inspection to inspection and release to release.

Initial Set of Attributes
Release ID
Build ID
Component name
Date of inspection
Inspection type
Number of inspectors
Inspection preparation effort total
Modified and new SLOC in inspection package

FIGURE 7.6 Software Inspection Process Performance Data

a listing of modules changed or added, design statements and a source program listing, and the number of modified and new source lines of code (SLOC). The number of new and modified SLOC was chosen to be the key measurement factor to determine the review rate since it highly correlated to the inspection preparation effort.

The inspection rate for each inspection was expressed as SLOC reviewed per average preparation hour, where

SLOC reviewed = Modified and new SLOC in inspection package

$$\text{Average preparation hour per inspector} = \frac{\text{inspection preparation effort total}}{\text{number of inspectors}}$$

In effect, this expressed the rate that modified and new SLOC were reviewed by the average inspector.

Plotting Initial Control Charts

The process analyst first grouped the inspection data by release to preserve the homogeneity of the data. This allowed an analysis of process performance consistency of each inspection within a release and allowed comparisons among each of the releases demonstrating stability. The analyst initially used the data from one release to plot the first 30 inspections from all six components, calculating and plotting the SLOC review rate using the XmR control chart in Figure 7.7.

Two discrepancies are immediately apparent on the chart. The first is a missing value for inspection 5. The second (indicated in both charts) is the absurdly high value for inspection 8. Examination of the data revealed that both discrepancies are due to key entry errors by inexperienced personnel, and it was necessary to obtain the correct data from the moderator's original records. The long run of data points below the centerline is due to the influence of the erroneous data of inspection 8 on the average and does not represent an assignable cause.

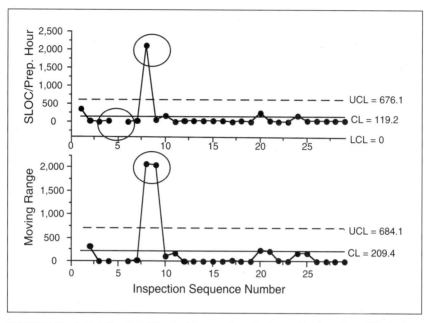

FIGURE 7.7 Initial Control Chart of Inspection Package Review Rate (SLOC/ Prep. Hour) for all Product Components

Identifying Mixtures and Separate Cause Systems

When reviewing the data, the process analyst remembered that the plot included data from all six major components. Since the development and inspection processes for each of the components represent separate cause systems (the set of personnel, skills, resources, products, and support systems was not the same across all six components), the process analyst separated the inspection data into six groups—one for each component. The review rate data for each of the components was plotted on a separate chart. The data for component A is plotted as shown in Figure 7.8.

The control chart in Figure 7.8 indicates that there are several assignable causes signaled by both the individuals chart and the moving range chart. Closer examination of the inspection data records revealed that the points exceeding the limits were calculated from inspections consisting solely of data lists, tables, and arrays. When questioned about the high review rate indicated by the points beyond the limits, the component A inspectors and developers informed the process analyst that the process for reviewing data lists, tables, and the like was not the same as that for inspecting design and program modules due to the use of several verification and validity-checking tools.

Since the inspection of data lists, tables, and the like apparently is truly a different process—even though the inspection process description did not recognize this difference—the process analyst removed all the plotted values based on

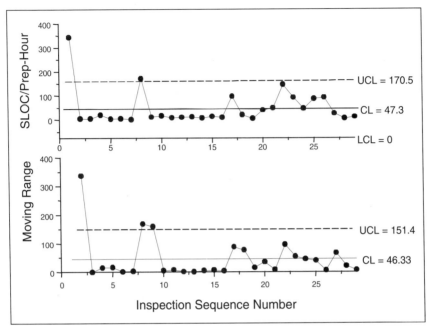

FIGURE 7.8   Control Chart of Inspection Package Review Rate for Component A

such inspections. The points removed are marked with an X in Figure 7.9. Note that more than just the points beyond the limits have been removed since they too are based on inspection of data lists and tables, even though they appear to be within the control limits. This is consistent with the notion of separation of different cause systems data to simplify and clarify process behavior.

The sequence of points from inspection 9 to inspection 16 also indicates a possible assignable cause (eight sequential points on the same side of the centerline). The process analyst decided to defer examining the reason for this sequence until she recalculated the control chart limits and replotted the control chart using the remaining data.

Finding Trial Limits

The revised control chart, shown in Figure 7.10, indicates that the inspection process for component A is not stable despite removing erroneous data and eliminating data values pertaining to other cause systems. The process analyst observed that the inspection review rate was less than 26 SLOC/preparation hour, for the first 15 inspections, then jumped to review rates in excess of 26 SLOC/preparation hour for the next 7 inspections, and then returned to a lower rate at the last recorded inspection.

Noting that this behavior was similar to a mixed pattern or a shift in process pattern, the analyst decided to separate the points into two categories—those with values of less than 26 SLOC/preparation hour and those with values equal to or greater than 26 SLOC/preparation hour. She then aligned the inspection package

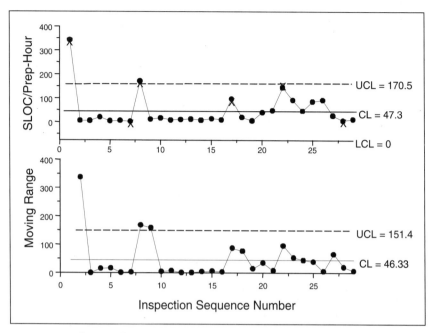

FIGURE 7.9 Control Chart of Figure 7.8 Showing Removal of Values from Separate Cause System

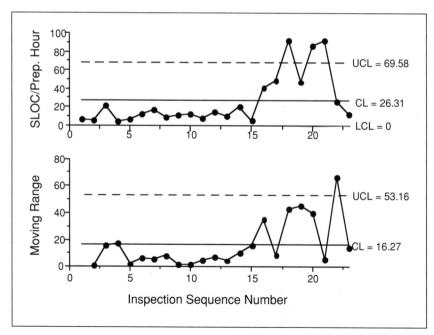

FIGURE 7.10 Revised Control Chart of Inspection Package Review Rate for Component A

size (modified and new SLOC) for comparison with the respective inspection review rates as shown in Figure 7.11.

The process analyst could see by examining the data that the inspection review rates appeared to significantly increase when the inspection package size was over 60 SLOC. The analyst reasoned that if the average preparation time was truly proportional to the size of the inspection package, there would not be changes of this magnitude in the review rate ratio. It appeared to the analyst that something was happening to change the inspection review rate when the inspection package size was larger than 60 SLOC. Discussions with the inspection moderators only verified that the inspection data was accurate and that there was nothing unusual about the inspections from their perspective.

Since there did not appear to be any obvious process noncompliance, the process analyst decided to prepare two control charts showing the inspection review rates—one for inspection packages of less than 60 SLOC and another for inspection packages equal to or greater than 60 SLOC. The results are given in Figures 7.12 and 7.13, respectively.

Neither control chart shows any assignable causes, but there appear to be two different review rates in operation. The inspection review rate averages about 10.7 SLOC/preparation hour when the amount of SLOC to be reviewed is 60 or less; otherwise, the review rate jumps to an average of nearly 62 SLOC/preparation hour

Review Rate SLOC/Prep. Hour	Inspection Package SLOC
6.00	6
5.33	4
20.83	15
4.00	4
6.00	3
11.93	24
17.07	14
8.95	17
10.71	15
12.17	20
7.22	7
14.23	51
9.90	17
20.31	22
5.09	14
11.60	58
40.47	86
48.86	86
92.11	75
46.96	90
86.77	188
92.50	185
26.00	130

FIGURE 7.11   Inspection Review Rates Compared to Inspection Package Size

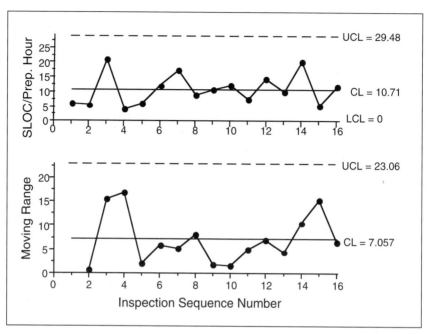

FIGURE 7.12   Process Performance for Inspection Packages of <60 SLOC for Component A

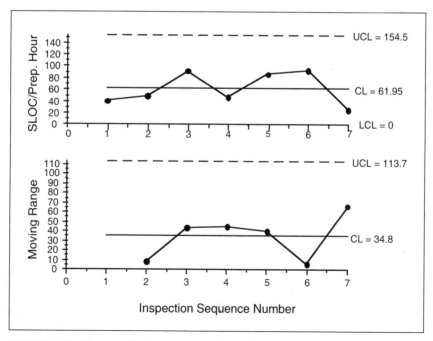

FIGURE 7.13   Process Performance for Inspection Packages of >60 SLOC for Component A

when the amount of SLOC in the inspection package is over 60 SLOC. If the next dozen or so inspection review rates followed this same pattern, the process analyst felt that the process behavior charts would be telling her that another "invisible" process was buried in the inspection process—in effect, that there were two separate cause systems resulting in a mixed pattern when all the inspection review rates were plotted on the same chart.

Since there were additional inspections to complete for this release, the process analyst decided to plot the future inspection rates on the charts she had just completed, keeping the centerline and the upper and lower control limits the same and essentially using them as trial control limits for the inspection process.

Testing the Limits

Inspection data collected over the next several weeks was added to the charts. The analyst plotted the inspection rates according to the size of the inspection package, just as she had done previously. An additional 26 inspection reports were added, including 16 with inspection packages of less than 60 SLOC and 10 with inspection packages of 60 or more SLOC. The control charts with the additional data plotted are shown in Figure 7.14a and b.

Both control charts contain apparent assignable causes. When the process analyst reviewed the inspection measurement data, she did not find any erroneous data, but she did notice that over half of the recent inspections were coded as "reinspections." When she spoke to the inspection moderators about the significance of this, she learned that the inspection packages sometimes require reinspection because portions of the design or code did not properly interpret the requirements or the requirements needed to be reconfirmed because of the design or code complexity. In such cases, the inspection packages were scheduled for reinspection when the requirements issues were resolved. As a result, the recorded package size (SLOC) did not necessarily represent the size of the material being reinspected since the original size was not changed to reflect the size of the material being reinspected.

Given the information about the reinspection measurement data, the process analyst decided to remove the reinspection control chart points since the measurements did not reflect the reinspection process. (She made a note to see that correct measurements of the reinspection process were instituted.) The points removed from each chart are marked with an X in Figure 7.15a and b.

Establishing Baseline Process Performance

After eliminating the reinspection data points, the process analyst plotted the remaining data points on the respective charts as shown in Figure 7.16a and b. All the remaining data points fall within the control chart limits, and no other anomalous patterns are apparent. The process analyst concluded that, while it was premature to consider the processes stable (especially the process for inspection packages over 60 SLOC), the processes did not display any instability either, and therefore she decided to continue using the respective average and limits as the baseline for

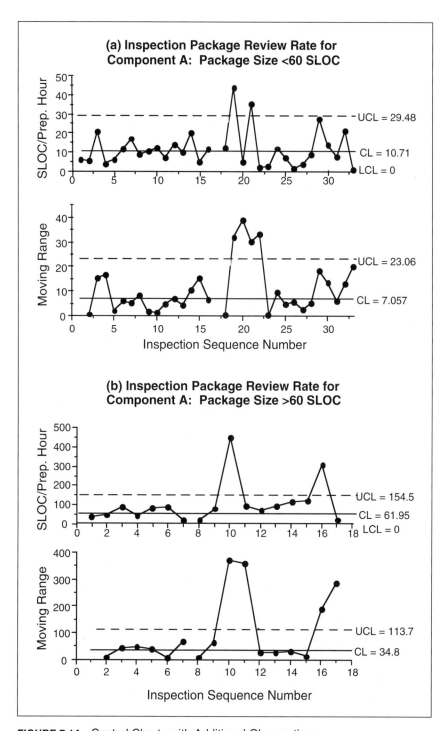

FIGURE 7.14   Control Charts with Additional Observations

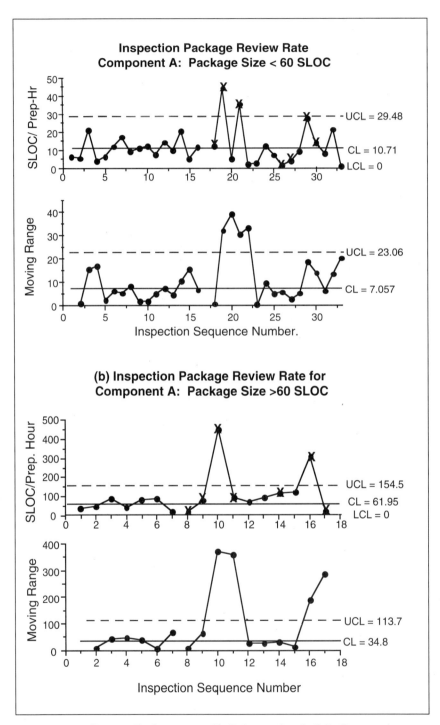

FIGURE 7.15 Process Performance with Reinspection Activity Removed

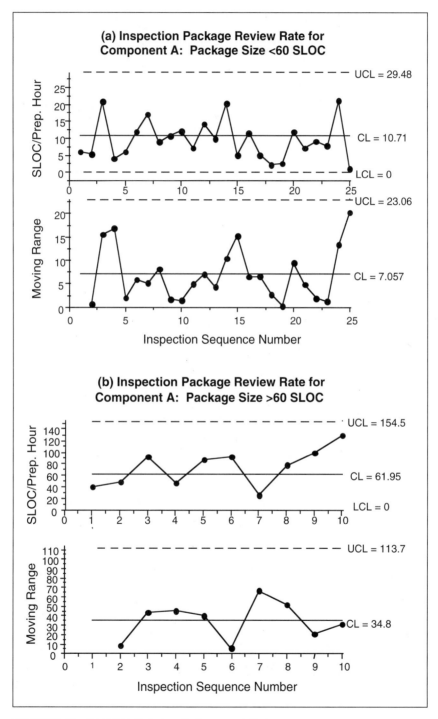

FIGURE 7.16   Baseline Process Performance Data

future analysis of the inspection processes' review rate. The process performance would continue to be tracked, the control charts updated with additional process inspection rates, and any assignable causes investigated to determine whether changes in the process had taken place.

At this point, the process analyst reviewed the results of her analysis with the inspection teams. As she did, she identified the factors that provided a new and more accurate understanding of the inspection process.

1. The existing inspection process contains several undocumented (invisible) subprocesses:

   - Inspection of data modules and tables
   - Reinspection inspections
   - Design/code inspections

2. The review rate of the design/code inspection process appears to be stable (consistent) when the inspection package is separated into two categories—less than 60 SLOC and equal to or greater than 60 SLOC.

3. Inspection packages of 60 SLOC or more were reviewed on average about 6 times faster than inspection packages with less than 60 SLOC.

The process analyst indicated that she would use the nearly stable inspection review rates as baseline data to investigate the several newly identified issues that could lead to improved process performance: Why are the larger packages reviewed so much faster? Is this good or bad? Is there a difference in effectiveness between the inspection package sizes—for example, does one find more errors or allow fewer escapes? How effective are the data inspections or the reinspections? Do the other components' inspection processes behave similarly? How do the components compare? How do the components compare from release to release? In addition, the following issues required action:

1. Documentation of the processes for reinspection and data/tables.

2. Training of key entry personnel, inspectors, and moderators regarding inspection data recording.

3. Establishment of data collection activity to capture the preparation time of each inspector for each inspection (which is necessary to validate the assumption that the inspection effort is consistent across all inspectors).

7.2   Process Capability

7.2.1   WHAT IS PROCESS CAPABILITY?

When we speak of process capability, we are referring to the predictable performance of a process under statistical control. When a process is in statistical control with respect to a given set of attributes, we have a valid basis for predicting, within limits, how the process will perform in the future. As long as the process continues to remain in the same state of statistical control, virtually all measurements of those attributes will fall within their natural process limits, which is defined as the *process capability*.

Attempting to assess the capability of a process that is not in statistical control is fruitless. Evaluations of capability invariably get interpreted as predictions of future performance, and it is unrealistic to expect records of past performance to be reliable predictors of the future unless you know that the underlying system of chance causes is stable. Therefore, before a process can be said to have a defined capability, it must display a reasonable degree of statistical control.

7.2.2 WHAT IS A CAPABLE PROCESS?

Whenever we propose to produce products to meet specifications or to meet deadlines at a specified cost with acceptable quality, we find ourselves using the concept of a *capable process*. For a process to be capable, it must meet two criteria:

1. The process must be brought into a state of statistical control for a period of time sufficient to detect any unusual behavior.
2. The capability of the process must meet or exceed the specifications that have to be satisfied to meet business or customer requirements.

The histogram in Figure 7.17 is a frequency plot of measurements obtained from a stable process. The histogram shows the empirical distribution of measurements of elapsed time between a problem's evaluation and its resolution in a problem-resolution process. Since the process is known to be stable, the results can be taken to reflect the process capability—that is, the ability of the process to perform in a

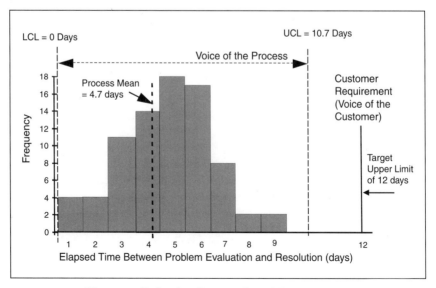

FIGURE 7.17 Histogram Reflecting Process Capability

timely fashion. As the variation is due solely to a constant system of chance causes (the definition of *stable*), the mean and control limits shown in the figure represent what the process is able to accomplish as it is currently defined and executed. In this sense, the histogram, the mean, and the limits together represent the "voice of the process" or the process capability.

If we superimpose the customer (or business) requirement on the histogram, we can compare what the process says it can do to what the business says it needs. For example, the dotted vertical line to the right of the histogram in Figure 7.17 depicts the customer requirement. Requirements (or specifications) like this are often referred to as the "voice of the customer."

When the variability shown by the voice of the process falls within the limits required by the customer, the process *conforms* to customer requirements. When a process is stable and conforming to requirements, it is termed *capable*.

If, on the other hand, the customer requirement was 8 days instead of 12, one of the natural process limits would fall outside the specification limits, and there would be frequent occasions where the process would not meet its requirements even though the process is stable. To change that situation, either the variability would have to be reduced or the process mean would have to be moved (or both). A third alternative may exist in some situations—relaxing the specifications to bring the requirements and the process limits into alignment. Figure 7.18 illustrates the three alternatives.

Analysis of process performance identifies areas where the capability of a process can be improved to better support business objectives. Even though a process

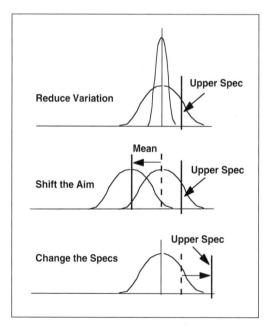

FIGURE 7.18 The Three Alternatives for Aligning Process Performance to Process Requirements

may be stable, its capability may need to be improved to satisfy competitive pressures or comply with customer needs.

Note that the concept of process capability is different from that of a product tolerance or planning target. Mistaking product tolerances and planning targets for process capability is a frequent cause of missed commitments.

Knowledge of process capability is essential for predicting the quality of products and the proportion of defective units that an organization produces. Projections of quality that are based on desires or wishful thinking, rather than statistically relevant historical data, are destined to cause problems down the road.

7.3   Process Capability Analysis

Capability analysis consists of two stages. First, the capability of the process under study must be determined. Second, the process capability must be compared to the specifications or requirements stipulated by the customer or business needs. The comparison is commonly addressed using one of the methods discussed in the remainder of this section.

7.3.1   CAPABILITY HISTOGRAMS

The simplest and easiest way to assess the performance of a stable process with respect to a given attribute is to plot a histogram of the individual values that have been observed during a period of stability. The *natural process limits* (the control limits for individual values) can then be used to characterize the performance. These limits can be computed from the grand average and average range of the measured values by using the following equation:

$$\text{Natural Process Limits} = \overline{\overline{X}} \pm 3\text{sigma}_X = \overline{\overline{X}} \pm 3\frac{\overline{R}}{d_2}$$

The ranges that are averaged can be either those of the subgroups used to construct an X-bar chart or the moving ranges used to plot an XmR chart. When two-point moving ranges associated with XmR charts are used, d_2 will equal 1.128, and the equation reduces to

$$\text{Natural Process Limits} = \overline{X} \pm 2.660\,\overline{R}$$

We can illustrate the use of histograms to determine process capability by returning to the Homogeonics example in Chapter 5. Figure 7.19 repeats the histogram of the 80 individual values recorded as shown in Figure 5.17. Since our analyses of these data in Figure 5.13 showed no signs of lack of control, we are justified in computing the natural process limits and plotting them on the histogram. These limits, which are the same as the upper and lower limits that would be used on a control chart for individual values, are designated in Figure 7.19 by

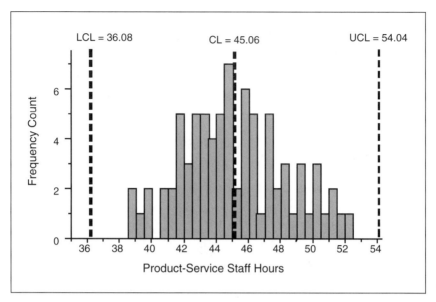

FIGURE 7.19   A Process Capability Histogram

UCL and LCL. For the Homogeonics data, all 80 of the measured values fall within the range given by the natural process limits.

The natural process limits in Figure 7.19 represent the voice of the process. They reflect what the process can be expected to do as long as it continues to operate as it has over the past 80 days. A stable process will continue to produce results that are almost always within its natural process limits until some event occurs that causes the process or its inputs to change.

The second stage of a capability analysis consists of comparing the natural process limits to the specifications imposed by business needs or customer requirements. When the natural limits fall entirely within the specification limits, almost every product that is produced will conform to specifications. Such a process is said to be *capable*. If a process is not capable, it will produce nonconforming results at rates that may be economically inefficient.

Thus, a simple way to assess whether or not a process is capable is to plot the specification limits on the histogram of measurements obtained from a stable process. The relationship of the natural process limits to the specification limits will portray the capability of the process.

Suppose, for instance, that the software manager at Homogeonics, Inc., requires product-service staff hours per day to fall between a value of 30 at the lower limit (to guarantee that customer requests are logged and acknowledged) and 50 at the upper limit (to ensure that critical skills are available for other activities). If the distribution is expected to be symmetric, the optimal value for the average daily product-service staff hours will be 40, the midpoint of the desired range, as used in his plans. The manager's requirements, which are effectively his specifications, are illustrated in Figure 7.20. LSL and USL are the lower and upper specification limits, respectively.

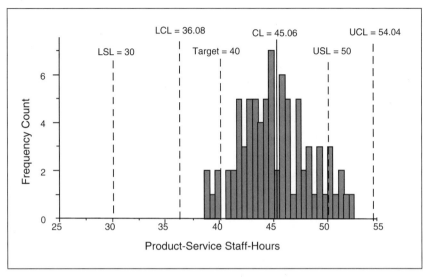

FIGURE 7.20 A Process Capability Histogram with Specification Limits

7.3.2 SPECIFICATION TOLERANCES

When one (or both) of the natural process limits falls outside the specification limits, as happens in Figure 7.20, the process is likely to produce nonconforming results more frequently than desired, even when it is in statistical control. For example, in Figure 7.20, the process is stable, but 6.25% of the results have fallen outside the specification limits.

Processes with a large number of nonconforming results can be *stable*, but they are not *capable*. To reduce the amount of nonconforming product or the frequency of nonconformance to other process standards, action must be taken to change the process. The changes must have one or more of the following objectives: to reduce process variation, to reset the process average, or to relax the specifications.

You can test whether or not specification limits are wide enough to allow for natural process variation by calculating the *specification tolerance* (the distance between the specification limits) as follows:[3]

Specification Tolerance =
Upper Specification Limit – Lower Specification Limit

Specification Tolerance (in sigma units) =
$$\frac{\text{Specification Tolerance}}{\text{sigma}_X}, \text{ where sigma}_X = \frac{\overline{R}}{d_2}$$

---

[3] Specification tolerances (sometimes called *engineering tolerances*) are related to statistical tolerance intervals only when the upper and lower specification limits have been chosen based on an analysis of statistical tolerance intervals.

When the tolerance exceeds 6 sigma units and the process is centered within the specification limits, the specification leaves sufficient room for process variation without producing large amounts of nonconforming product. When the specification tolerance is less than 6 sigma units, extreme values will frequently exceed the specification limits, regardless of the centering.

One reason that a process may not be capable is that it may not be sufficiently centered. That is, the average of its measured values may not fall at an appropriate point within the specification limits. For symmetric distributions, the way to remedy this problem is to change the process so that the process average is brought closer to a value midway between the limits. We can determine how much adjustment is needed to center the process average by calculating the distance to the nearest specification (DNS).

First, some background: The distance in sigma units between the process average and the upper and lower specification limits (USL and LSL) is given by

$$Z_U = \frac{\text{USL} - \text{process average}}{\text{sigma}_X}$$

$$Z_L = \frac{\text{process average} - \text{LSL}}{\text{sigma}_X}$$

If the process average is within the specification limits, the values of Z_U and Z_L will both be positive. If the process average is not within the specification limits, one of the Z values will be negative. To hold the number of nonconforming items to an economical value, it is desirable that both Z values be positive and greater than 3. When both values are positive, the smaller of the two is called the *distance to the nearest specification* (DNS).

Figure 7.20 shows a process limit that exceeds the specification limits, so we can use the example to illustrate the procedures just described. To satisfy the specifications, the tolerance must exceed 6 sigma units. To check this, we compute

$$\text{Specification Tolerance (in sigma units)} = \frac{\text{USL} - \text{LSL}}{\text{sigma}_X} = \frac{50 - 30}{mR/d_2}$$

$$= \frac{20}{(3.38/1.128)} = 6.67$$

Thus, the process is currently meeting this requirement. The distance to the nearest specification, however, is

$$\text{DNS} = \frac{\text{USL} - \overline{\overline{X}}}{\text{sigma}_X} = \frac{50 - 45.06}{2.996} = 1.65$$

This is well below the value of 3 needed to avoid an excessive number of nonconforming results.

To comply with the specifications, Mr. Smith, the manager at Homogeonics, Inc., will have to change the process so that the average number of product-service staff hours per day decreases. If the variability is symmetric about the average, the optimal value for the new average will be the point midway between the specification limits, coinciding with his original planning target of 40. If this change can be made, the DNS will become

$$DNS = \frac{USL - \bar{\bar{X}}}{sigma_X} = \frac{50 - 40}{2.996} = 3.34$$

The tactics that Mr. Smith might use to shift the mean include improving a number of attributes or subprocesses. Product quality, user documentation, customer training, the handling of service requests, and the process that assigns staff to service requests are possible examples. Of course, any changes that he introduces will create a new process. The performance of the new process should then be monitored and plotted on run charts, and new control limits should be constructed as soon as sufficient data are available. Once the process appears to be stable, its capability can be reevaluated.

The advantage of using the specification tolerance and the DNS to characterize the capability of a stable process is that the two measures focus attention on the areas that need improvement. Instead of using artificial index numbers or simple values for percent defective or percent nonconforming, the DNS relates directly to the data in ways that make it easy to understand just how the process is performing relative to the customer's specifications.

The flowchart in Figure 7.21[4] gives an orderly procedure for assessing process capability [Wheeler 1992].

7.3.3 FRACTION NONCONFORMING

Individual values that fall outside the specification limits are instances of nonconformance to specifications. The fraction of the total observed outcomes that are nonconforming in a stable process gives an unbiased estimate for the fraction of nonconforming outcomes associated with the process. The statistical term for this is *fraction nonconforming*. In the Homogeonics example, 5 out of the 80 days had nonconforming results (the data in Figure 7.19 show 5 values above 50 and none below 30). This suggests that about 6.25% of the days in the underlying population experience product-service staff hours that exceed specifications.

Use of this statistic is helpful when expressing the capability of a process in very quick, summary-report fashion. However, it does very little to help understand how the process mean and variation differ from the customer or business requirement.

7.3.4 CAPABILITY INDICES

In lieu of the graphical summary of capability that a histogram provides, many people compute numerical summaries. Values with names like C_p and C_{pk} are often

---

[4] Figure adapted from *Understanding Statistical Process Control,* 2nd ed., by Donald J. Wheeler and David S. Chambers, © 1992 SPC Press, Inc., Knoxville, Tenn.

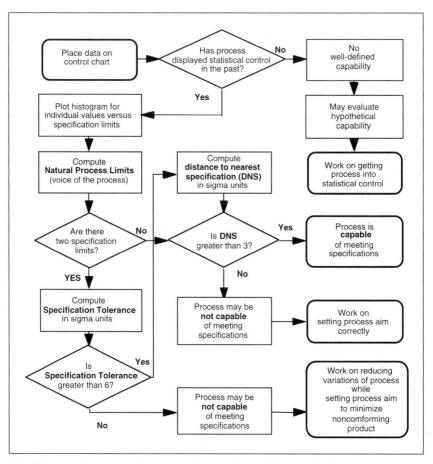

FIGURE 7.21   Procedure for Assessing the Capability of a Stable Process

used in an attempt to reduce measures of capability to a single index. Here are the equations for calculating these indices:

1. The capability ratio C_p is the ratio of the Specification Tolerance to 6 standard deviation units, or

$$C_p = \frac{Z_{USL} - Z_{LSL}}{6}$$

2. The centered capability ratio C_{pk} is the ratio of the distance to the nearest specification (DNS) to 3 standard deviation units, or

$$C_{pk} = \frac{\text{minimum of } \{Z_{USL} - Z_{LSL}\}}{3}$$

Although these indices are often used alone, they are more effective when combined with a histogram.

Our advice is to stick with graphical representations. They are not only more informative but also easier to explain than excessively condensed indices. If someone insists on having a value for C_p or C_{pk}, provide it, but provide the graphical summary as well. You will both be better served.

7.3.5   WORLD-CLASS QUALITY

In reading about the concept of process capability as we have introduced it, it would be easy to conclude, "Oh, that doesn't apply to me! I work on software, and we never have specification limits." While it may be true that few software processes have explicit specification limits, it is always true that excessive variability and off-target performance are inefficient and costly. The man most responsible for bringing this point to the world's attention is Genichi Taguchi. The situation he pictured for the classical concept of process capability is illustrated in Figure 7.22.[5] The figure shows the model implicitly used in industry when products are inspected and defective (nonconforming) items are discarded.

One of the characteristics that Taguchi observed in organizations that operate with this model is that processes that operate within specification limits get neglected. Taguchi recognized that this was inconsistent with the goal of continuous process improvement. He proposed an alternative model that recognized that all variation has economic consequences and that large variations are more detrimental than small variations. His model, in its simplest form, is shown in Figure 7.23.[6]

For both mathematical and practical reasons, Taguchi's model is often well approximated by a parabola, at least in the vicinity of the target value. This leads

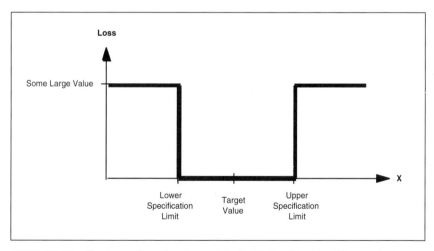

FIGURE 7.22   The Loss Function Associated with the Classical Concept of Process Capability

---

[5, 6] Figures adapted from *Understanding Statistical Process Control,* 2nd ed., by Donald J. Wheeler and David S. Chambers, © 1992 SPC Press, Inc., Knoxville, Tenn.

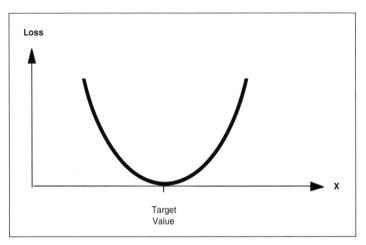

FIGURE 7.23   A Simple Loss Function Showing Taguchi's Concept of Capability

easily to analytic methods that, in conjunction with information about the distribution of outcomes, can be used to estimate the costs of being off target.

While the exact amounts of loss associated with being off target by given distances can be important, they need not concern us here. What is important, though, is to understand that any variability that exists causes deviations from the target, that each deviation has a cost, and that large deviations cost more than small deviations. All this is just as true in software settings as it is in manufacturing and service environments.

So, when you address issues of process performance that involve target values, do not conclude that the concept of capability does not apply just because no limits have been given to define an acceptable product or performance. Instead, we suggest that you picture Taguchi's model and adopt the view that

world-class quality = on target with minimum variability

When you adopt this view, the histograms you build with data from stable processes will give you much of the information that you need for assessing where you stand with respect to process quality and what the benefits would be from improving it. What is more, the attention of your organization will remain focused appropriately on opportunities for continuing to improve the process through additional reductions in variability.

7.4   Improving the Process

In the previous section, we discussed several methods for analyzing process capability. When the process is not capable, or even when we wish to improve an already capable process, it will be necessary to change the process to make improvements.

In our view, this is often more easily said than done, especially in a software setting. Aside from the potential issues of education, retraining, coordination with upstream and downstream processes, management approval, and funding, there are the fundamental issues of what to change, how much to change, and what magnitude of improvement can be expected.

In other disciplines—manufacturing, chemical processes, electronics, semiconductors, automotive, aerospace, medical devices, food-processing, and pharmaceuticals—techniques have been developed and used to determine the effects of process changes on the process performance. Process design and process capability analysis using designed experiment techniques are practiced in many of these industries. Various methods, such as analysis of variance, randomization and blocking, and factorial design have been developed to enhance process design and analysis. Those readers wishing to learn more about designed experiments may find Montgomery's discussion of process design and improvement with designed experiments of some interest [Montgomery 1996].

When it comes to process design and capability improvement, the use of designed experiments and associated analysis tools is considered an active statistical method, whereas sole reliance on SPC and control charts is viewed as a more passive method. This reason is that designed experiments actually make a series of carefully planned and purposeful changes to the process input or process elements, execute the process, and measure the corresponding changes in process performance. This is repeated until the changes produce the desired results with the optimum resources. With SPC and control charts, we measure an ongoing process, gathering and analyzing data to guide us in making appropriate changes to improve the process. In a software environment, we generally do not have the luxury or the capability of conducting designed experiments in the same way as they are traditionally used in other disciplines. Since the changes intended to improve the process will be made to an ongoing process, we must take exceptional care to select changes with a high probability of success or, alternatively, changes having a low likelihood of creating significant damage. To reduce risk and manage the scope of unexpected consequences, changes are frequently introduced as a pilot process within a single project for evaluation before implementing them across an entire organization.

While discussion of designed experiments and associated analytical methods is beyond the scope of this book, the guidelines and general approach used for process improvement by designed experiments are not entirely different when using the more passive approach with SPC tools and control charts. The following subsections discuss guidelines that assume the more passive SPC tools and control chart approach. This discussion is followed by suggested investigative directions with illustrative examples that rely on the use of SPC techniques, including control charts.

7.4.1   RECOGNITION OF THE PROCESS PERFORMANCE ISSUE

It is essential that all parties with a stake in the process understand and agree on the specific process performance attribute(s) that is at issue. Why do we wish to improve the process, and what is it about the process performance that we wish to improve? Generally, the issue will center around one or more of the process issues discussed in Chapter 2—product quality, process duration, product delivery, or process cost. A clearly written statement that addresses these questions such that it is acceptable to all those concerned with the process—those who may be affected by the change, those who must approve, and those who must implement the change—will aid in process understanding and lead to a successful solution.

7.4.2   SELECTION OF PROCESS PERFORMANCE VARIABLE

The process performance variable should provide useful and relevant information about the process. Sometimes, it may be necessary to select a process performance variable that is an indirect measure of process performance. Great care must be taken in such cases to relate the measured variable to the actual process performance with supporting data and analysis. Once a process performance variable is selected, a process performance target should be identified in terms of the desired mean and variability. This gives dimension to the magnitude of the change required. Is it a matter of reducing variability, or does the mean need to be shifted, or both?

7.4.3   CHANGES TO COMMON CAUSE ENTITIES AND ATTRIBUTES

There are two places to look when seeking ways to improve process performance:

1. The common cause system that comprises the process requiring improvement. (This consists of the people, tools, resources, procedures, and subprocesses required for process execution.)

2. Inputs to the process that are acted on or transformed by the process to yield process results.

The knowledge you have of your process (supported by evidence where available) and your analysis of the process behavior will guide you in directing your attentions to either of these two options.

Just like process instabilities, the characteristics of the people, tools, materials, resources, guidelines, and subprocesses that are used by the process can limit what your process can achieve. If you determine that the characteristics of one or more of these entities constrain the performance you seek to improve, you will have to go back to the origins of these entities and consider making changes to them to change your level of performance or reduce variation in process results. Figure 7.24 is an abbreviated list of some common process entities that should be considered. (See Chapter 2 for a more complete list.) These are things that you may want to examine when seeking ways to improve a process.

How do you determine which of the process entities to examine for change? Your choice of process performance variable will provide some guidance, assuming you have good reason to relate the effects of changing a process entity to the process variable of interest. Recall that, at the beginning of this chapter, we discussed

Common Cause Entities Whose Attributes Affect Process Performance	
Products and by-products from other processes	Guidelines and directions
	• Policies
Resources	• Procedures
• People	• Goals
• Facilities	• Constraints
• Tools	• Rules
• Raw Materials	• Laws
• Energy	• Regulations
• Money	• Training
• Time	• Instructions

FIGURE 7.24   Factors That Affect Process Performance

the situations where the need for additional data would become apparent. If you have additional data about the process performance, analysis may reveal cause-and-effect relationships that will single out the entities that must be changed to improve the process. You will find the tools described in Chapter 3 particularly useful in conducting such analyses.

If you do not already have data that supports a hypothesis about cause and effect, you will need to collect the data and conduct the analysis. The attributes associated with these entities can significantly affect the operation of your process; therefore, you may want to consider implementing measures that help quantify, control, and improve those attributes. This may easily lead you back to issues like the ones addressed in earlier chapters of this book, but with attention now directed to other parts of the software process.

Decomposing a stable but not capable process into its subprocesses and examining the subprocesses for stability is often a productive approach for pinpointing the roots of the variability. By breaking a process down into its component activities and subprocesses, you will often find points where intermediate products are produced. The output streams from these processes then become candidates for measurement and analysis, and control charts may once more be appropriate tools.

Finally, the products and by-products from other processes may be the limiting factor in improving the process performance. If the process under study is dependent on consistent input from another process, improving the process may not be possible until the processes producing the input product are stabilized. Sometimes, there are feedback loops where measured qualities of outputs from a process are used to control or specify attributes of its inputs. For example, high rates of defects found in testing can induce increased investment in inspection, thus changing the quality of outputs from earlier parts of the process.

As one example of the importance of looking upstream, consider a system-testing process. The best way to reduce the time, rework, and cost of system testing may lie not in the testing process itself, but in the quality of the incoming artifacts it tests. Improving the economics of testing may not be possible without improving key parts of the upstream processes—the activities where defects are inserted and the points where prevention, detection, and removal activities can be implemented or made more effective.

When examining the performance of upstream processes, you may find that they, in turn, are affected by elements that originate from outside. Dictated schedules (time) and tight budgets (money) are just two examples. Restrictions on time and money have been known to lead organizations to scrimp on the efforts they allocate to preventing and detecting defects during design and coding. The upstream processes may meet their time and budget goals, but the downstream impacts can easily outweigh the upstream benefits. In one sense, looking outside the testing process is an issue of balancing the performance of the overall software process (or the system). In another sense, if the organization knows that inspections work well, has data to suggest what the optimal levels of inspection might be, and would usually perform at that level, this may be just another instance of process noncompliance.

7.4.4 SELECTION OF A PILOT PROCESS

Ideally, the specific process selected as the pilot for evaluating process improvement changes should be the same process that was judged to need improvement. In large organizations where instantiations of the "same" process exist, the pilot process may not be the very same instantiation of the process that required improvement. In either case, the pilot process should exhibit essentially the same process performance as was measured when the process improvement activity was initiated. The process improvement changes should not be made to the candidate pilot process if it is not stable. If the process is stable but the performance mean and variability are significantly different from those observed when evaluating it for process improvement, then changes of some sort have been introduced in the meantime and need to be understood before implementation of the planned process improvements. Of course, before execution of the pilot process, all personnel involved in executing the process must be trained to properly use changes that involve new procedures, tools, different work flow, and support systems. It may be necessary to modify the related process measurement activities to include additional or revised data due to the process changes. All personnel connected to the process measurement activities should be aware of any measurement changes.

7.4.5 EXECUTION OF THE IMPROVED PROCESS

Once the process changes have been installed, you should measure and monitor all factors contributing to process performance to be sure that the process is being executed consistent with the process changes. This is especially important to track since there is a reasonable likelihood that the changes will not be completely or consistently understood by all involved. When the process is not consistently executed, you can expect your measurements of process performance to indicate that the process is not stable. Tracking the factors that contribute to the process will allow you to rapidly find the reason for assignable causes. Additionally, tracking the contributing factors to process performance will provide evidence supporting the effect the changes have on the process. There will be opportunities for assignable causes to occur for other reasons as well, so, in that sense, you will continue to be looking for assignable causes, removing them from the process, and striving for stability just as you would any other process.

7.4.6   DATA ANALYSIS

The data analysis portion of improving the process is not unlike the activities that we have discussed earlier in this chapter—specifically, validating assumptions, obtaining a stable process by elimination of assignable causes, and establishing the capability of the changed process (did the process improve and by how much?). Whatever the outcome, the analysis should stipulate the conditions that existed during the process execution. If the process changes are successful, this will enhance the adoption of the process changes by other instantiations of the process. If the process changes are less than successful, the information will be useful in reanalyzing the process for changes that will be more successful.

In addition to the analysis of the process performance in light of the changes made, the costs and benefits of fully implementing or retaining the changes as they affect the entire software organization must be assessed. The cost-benefit analysis should include assessments of impacts—positive or negative—on upstream and downstream processes as well. Changes that reduce variability while keeping the average about the same will usually be welcomed because they often improve the efficiency of downstream activities. Reductions in variability seldom have detrimental effects. Changes that shift the average, on the other hand, are more likely to affect downstream processes, and the consequences should be examined closely. When you propose actions that are intended to improve a process or adjust it to meet specifications, you should always examine the effects that the changes will have on other processes in the stream of work. (The law of unintended consequences is ubiquitous.)

7.4.7   CONCLUSIONS AND RECOMMENDATIONS

This portion of improving the process is largely a reporting of the facts, leading to a recommendation to implement or retain the process change to affect all of the instantiations of the process across the software organization. The mere reporting of facts relative to the changes is not always sufficient. Section 7.5 discusses the range of issues and how the relationship of departmental measures to organization strategies can be used to support conclusions about process improvements. First, however, let us consider the following two examples of process improvement.

Example 7.2: **Improvement Through Process Decomposition**

In the preceding discussion, we pointed out that one of the ways of improving a process is to decompose the process into subordinate processes and examine these processes for excessive variation, stability, and improvement. We can illustrate improvement through process decomposition by returning to an example found in Chapter 6—Example 6.5, Aggregation and Decomposition of Process Performance Data.

The control charts plotting the errors found in each component inspection are given again in Figure 7.25. As was pointed out in Example 6.5, the process appeared to be stable, but the average errors per inspection and variability inherent in the control limits were not satisfactory.

Fortunately, the inspection process used orthogonal defect definitions to provide traceability to the cause of defects. The control charts in Figure 7.26 show the average and control limits for each of eight different types of defects. Note that seven out of eight charts indicate assignable causes, and, hence, the process for finding these defect types is not stable. If we continue the analysis of the charts and revise the charts by eliminating the assignable causes and recalculating the limits (as we discussed in Chapter 6 with regard to revising control chart limits), we find that additional assignable causes become apparent in two of the control charts and that all the revised control charts have improved averages and limits.

Investigation of the instability indicated on these charts requires that the design process be studied for possible noncompliance of the process or design process improvements. In addition, the inspection process should be studied to find

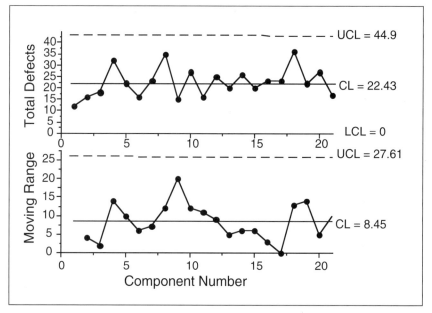

FIGURE 7.25 Original XmR Charts for Total Number of Defects Found in Component Inspections

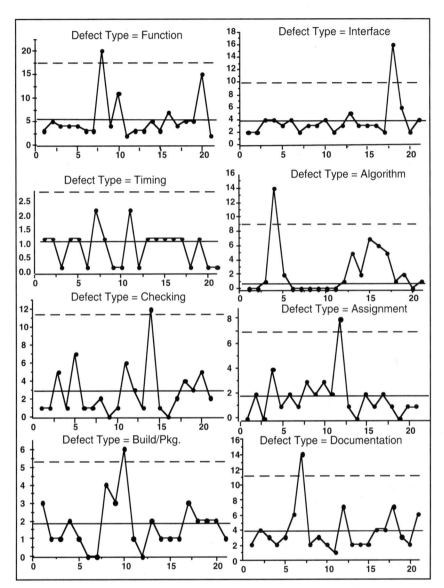

FIGURE 7.26 XmR Control Charts of Inspections for Each of the Defect Types

inspection errors resulting in assignable causes. Assuming that all the problems causing the instability are remedied, we can determine how much the total number of defects will be reduced and establish trial control chart limits for future defect measurements. Note that the focus of the control charting will now be on each of the defect types as opposed to the total number of defects. The control chart limits for each of the defect types are indicated in each chart in Figure 7.27. The revised control charts for the total number of defects are shown in Figure 7.28.

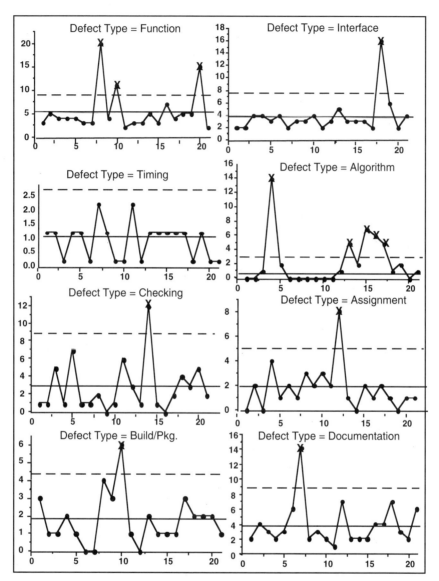

FIGURE 7.27 Revised XmR Control Charts of Inspections for Each of the Defect Types

Here, the average total defects per inspection is now reduced by nearly 5 defects per inspection, and the upper limits value is lower by about 20 defects per inspection. Since all the defect-type control charts are in control, further reduction in defects will have to come as a result of further improvements to the design process.

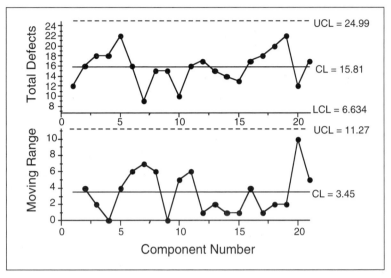

FIGURE 7.28   Revised XmR Charts for Total Number of Defects Found in Component Inspections

---

Example 7.3:   **Changing the Process for Improvement**

As we have illustrated with the previous example, often the best way to improve a stable process is by way of decomposition of the process variation. In the case of software development, one of the key elements in process variation is the activity of the software engineers engaged in executing the process. In this context, the Personal Software Process (PSP), developed by Watts S. Humphrey [Humphrey 1995] at the Software Engineering Institute, provides software engineers with a methodology for consistently and efficiently developing high-quality products. In addition, the PSP helps software engineers plan and track their work and enables them to make commitments they can meet. In the example of process improvement that follows, control charts are used to both visualize and quantify one aspect of improving the software process with PSP.

Figure 7.29 plots a history of the ratio of actual to estimated development (design and code) completion time of nine software components for a software application product.[7] The XmR chart indicates the process is apparently not in control at any point. The individuals chart indicates a sharp drop between point 3 and point 4. This is supported by an assignable cause at point 4 on the range chart. Together, this is indicative of a process shift. The process shift coincides with PSP training given to the component developers after completion of component 3 and before the start of component 4. The resulting improvement in the process is evident by comparing the two charts shown in Figures 7.30 and 7.31.

---

[7] The data for the three control charts in this example are based on the data found in "Results of Applying the Personal Software Process," *Computer* 30, no. 5 (1997):24–31.

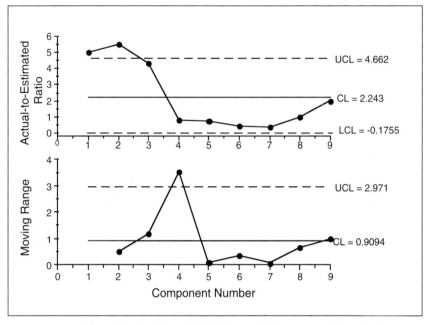

FIGURE 7.29 Plot of Ratio of Actual to Estimated Completion Time for Nine Components

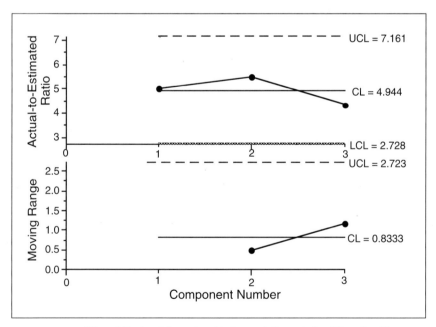

FIGURE 7.30 Plot of Ratio of Actual to Estimated Completion Time for First Three Components

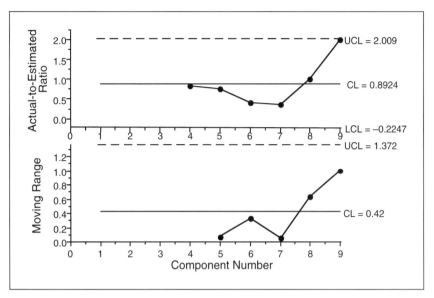

FIGURE 7.31   Plot of Ratio of Actual to Estimated Completion Time for Last Six Components

The chart in Figure 7.30, although containing only three points, indicates that the actual completion for each component is averaging nearly five times that of the estimate. Seeing that the actual time it would take to develop the remaining software would greatly exceed the time commitments made to the customer, the software development company renegotiated completion dates for the remaining components with the customer. The new estimates are based on the experience acquired in developing the first three components. While the process so far appeared to be in control, albeit not meeting targets (not capable), the company did not want to go back to the customer a second time to renegotiate schedules. Consequently, the software company sought to reduce the risk of having to renegotiate again by making improvements to the development process. The software company chose to give PSP training to the application development software engineers to improve their efficiency and effectiveness.

The chart in Figure 7.31 plots actual-to-estimated ratios of development time for the last six components. The chart shows an improvement in the development process by meeting or exceeding schedule commitments in all but one of the remaining components.

While there are not enough data points to establish stability, all of the existing points are within the control limits. More significantly, the actual development time is now about 10% less than the estimated time compared to nearly five times more than the estimate before the process improvements. If the next dozen or so actual-to-estimated ratios fall within the limits, the software company will have stabilized the process and implemented a process change that significantly increases their ability to accurately estimate the time to develop a software product.

7.5   Improvement and Investment

Business goals and strategies, together with factual data about attributes of product quality and process performance, are the key drivers that lead to actions that improve a software process. But just identifying the changes that are needed to improve a process is not sufficient. We must also look at the benefits that justify the costs associated with changing the process. This often means that measures that go beyond process performance may be required. Examples include training costs and costs for additional equipment, new programming tools, and so forth.

Economic payback may not be the only measure appropriate for quantifying the value of process changes. Recent studies have concluded that traditional financial indicators alone may be neither necessary nor sufficient to judge business performance or to justify investment in process changes [Kaplan 1992; Brodman 1995]. These studies cite operational measures of customer satisfaction, organizational innovation, competitive advantage, and improvement of core competence as important drivers of future business success.

For example, Richard L. Lynch and Kelvin F. Cross, in their book *Measure Up!*, suggest a number of measures that go beyond traditional financial measures like profitability, cash flow, and return on investment [Lynch 1995]. The measures that they propose relate to business operating systems, and they address the driving forces that guide the strategic objectives of the organization. Figure 7.32 illustrates their performance pyramid for business operating systems.[8]

Lynch and Cross suggest that customer satisfaction, flexibility, and productivity are the driving forces upon which company objectives are based. The status of these factors can be monitored by various indicators, as suggested in Figure 7.33.[9] These indicators can be derived, in turn, from lower-level (departmental) measures of waste, delivery, quality, and cycle time. The concept is illustrated in Figure 7.34. Figure 7.34 also points out that many measurements of process performance are obtained directly from measurements reported by the projects that make the organization's products.

The measures that you should use to rationalize and gain approval for software process improvement and investment are fundamentally the same as those suggested by Lynch and Cross. Departmental (and lower-level) measures can be related to software product and process measures with little difficulty. Rework, defect counts, schedules, development time, and service response time are just a few examples.

It is important, therefore, that people who propose improvements understand not only the business goals and strategies of the organization but also the priorities, risks, and issues associated with the goals and strategies. Identifying process

---

[8,9] Figures adapted from *Measure Up!*, by Richard L. Lynch and Kelvin F. Cross, © 1995 Blackwell Publishers, Basil Blackwell, Inc., Cambridge, Mass.

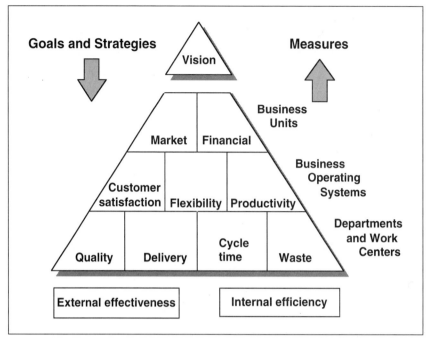

FIGURE 7.32 Lynch and Cross's Performance Pyramid for Business Operating Systems

measures that correspond to the business indicators in Figures 7.33 and 7.34 is challenging but doable. The key is to relate the costs and benefits of process improvement actions to the business indicators used in your own organization.

Experience has shown that measurements and analyses that can withstand the scrutiny of people not directly involved with the management and improvement of software processes are essential. One of the most important issues is that of demonstrating in a practical and statistical sense that the changes proposed can reasonably be expected to have the effects predicted. When we are able to show that process performance is stable and that changes are therefore needed if process capability is to be improved, and when we can predict the benefits of proposed process improvements based on sound evidence, then the credibility and confidence in proposals that require investment are enhanced significantly. These proposals then have a much better chance of being accepted and adequately funded. Proposals and plans that can be shown to measurably aid achievement of organizational goals are more readily approved and adapted than those that cannot.

> **Potential Indicators of Customer Satisfaction, Flexibility, and Productivity**
>
> Customer satisfaction
> - License renewal rate
> - Number of new licenses
> - Revenue per customer
> - Number of new customers
> - Number of complaints
> - Customer ratings of products or services (from surveys)
>
> Flexibility
> - Quoted lead times
> - On-time delivery
> - Time to market
> - Time to accommodate design changes
> - Number of change requests honored
> - Number of common processes
> - Number of new products
>
> Productivity
> - Reductions in product development or service cost
> - Rework as a percent of total work
> - Cost-to-revenue ratios
> - Ratios of development time to product life

FIGURE 7.33 Examples of Indicators for Business Operating Systems

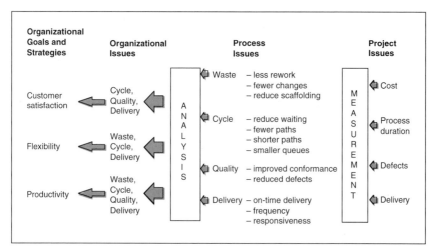

FIGURE 7.34 Sources of Early Indicators for Customer Satisfaction, Flexibility, and Productivity

7.6 Summary

After process performance measurements are analyzed and plotted on process behavior charts, our thoughts turn to evaluating the process. There are three paths to process improvement:

1. Removing assignable causes (taking the proper action to identify the assignable causes of instability and take steps to prevent the causes from recurring).

2. Changing the process (taking the proper action to identify, design, and implement necessary changes that will make the process capable).

3. Continually improving (taking the proper action to seek ways to continually improve the process so that variability is reduced and quality, cost, and cycle time are improved, after the process is both stable and capable).

We discussed that, when a process is not stable, you should try to find the reasons for assignable causes and take actions to prevent their recurrence. Eliminating assignable causes essentially repairs the process and brings it to a repeatable state. It does not make sense to introduce changes to improve capability or performance when a process is not stable. Without stability as a baseline to start from, you are likely to simply trade one unstable condition for another.

When process outputs vary erratically, one of the best things to do is to look for patterns and try to isolate the problem (or problems). Process behavior charts or control charts can be an effective tool to use in looking for trends and isolating the problem. Average or X-bar charts, R charts, attributes charts (p, np, c, and u charts), and individuals charts can be useful to understand the voice of the process.

We also discussed a number of ways to determine assignable cause reasons:

1. As a first step, examine process performance data against the four data validation criteria described in Chapter 3.

2. Plot the data using XmR charts. This may help you identify outlandish data that escapes the eye in a data listing. These data should not be ignored, but rather tracked down to understand how the data came to be in error so that erroneous data can be avoided in the future.

3. Examine process behavior charts for trends. If there is a complex pattern after you have plotted the first twenty or so values, reexamine your assumptions about the process, your selection of process performance data, and the resulting data organization you have selected for plotting on control charts.

4. Verify your assumptions before spending effort on chasing down other presumed assignable causes.

5. If the control chart pattern indicates a mixture, try simplifying the pattern by reorganizing the data into two sets—one set containing the values above the centerline, the other set the values from below. Plot separate

control charts for each of the data sets. This may reveal an underlying or a hidden process that is affecting the process common cause system.

6. Assemble a group of people who work within the process to explore possible reasons for the unusual behavior. The group may point out process idiosyncrasies explaining process behavior or assignable causes.

7. Measure key parameters of some of the inputs to the process and plot run charts (or control charts) to see whether anything unusual is happening. Out-of-control inputs, for example, can cause out-of-control outputs. When out-of-control inputs are found, this could push your search for root causes and corrective actions to points earlier in the overall process, or it may indicate that the process under study has two or more "invisible" processes (ways of dealing with the input that are not recognized by the process description).

8. Improve process performance. For example, an unusual series of events or an inadvertent change to the process may cause the process not only to become unstable but also to improve—at least momentarily—certain aspects of quality. When this happens and the assignable causes can be replicated, it may be profitable to incorporate the causes of the beneficial results as permanent parts of the process.

When a process is stable, it makes sense to introduce changes to improve the capability or performance. When we speak of process capability, we are referring to the predictable performance of a process under statistical control. When a process is in statistical control with respect to a given set of attributes, we have a valid basis for predicting, within limits, how the process will perform in the future.

Whenever we propose to produce products to meet specifications or to meet deadlines at a specified cost with acceptable quality, we find ourselves using the concept of a *capable process*. For a process to be capable, it must meet two criteria:

1. The process must be brought into a state of statistical control for a period of time sufficient to detect any unusual behavior.

2. The capability of the process must meet or exceed the specifications that have to be satisfied to meet business or customer requirements.

Capability analysis consist of two stages. First, the capability of the process under study must be determined. Second, the process capability must be compared to the specifications or requirements stipulated by the customer or business needs.

To succeed in finding ways to improve process performance, just as in searching for assignable causes, knowledge of the process—its activities, intermediate products, people, tools, and work flows—is paramount. It is this knowledge that points you to likely areas to investigate. This is one reason why responsibilities for process control and process improvement cannot be delegated to statisticians and staff scientists. Specialists can help, but responsibilities for improvement and for knowing the subject matter lie with those who own and operate the processes.

Remember that when you introduce improvements, the improvements will change the process. Changes mean instability, and instabilities lead—at least temporarily—to lack of predictability. You will not get the most from further improvement actions until you achieve stability at the new level of performance. Does this mean that you should be reluctant to introduce changes? Not at all! At least not when you have stable baselines against which to measure the results of your actions. Without stable baselines, though, you may have difficulty determining whether or not your actions have the effects intended. This means that the wisest first step is often to bring the existing process under control. Then, at least, you will know where you are starting from, and you can measure how well the improvements work. Without baselines, you will just be guessing.

8

Getting Started

Things may come to those who wait, but only the things left by those who hustle.
Abraham Lincoln

Now it is your turn to apply the techniques that we have discussed and to share your experiences with us. In this chapter, we have summarized our discussions into ten steps for applying SPC. We have also put together a section that you may find yourself referring to from time to time—the frequently asked questions section. We have compiled this list of questions from customers that we have worked with, from attendees of conference presentations, and from our colleagues trying to understand, interpret, and apply SPC techniques in software engineering organizations. These questions have helped us in addressing, organizing, and formulating examples so that people can make the translation from applications of SPC in manufacturing to issues in software engineering. And remember: The end goal, regardless of the application domain, is continuous improvement.

8.1 Ten Steps for Getting Started

So, how can you get started in applying SPC?

1. **Familiarize yourself with statistical process control techniques.** This book will help you to orient yourself with the key issues, concepts, and techniques for applying SPC to your software management and improvement activities. There is also a fairly extensive list of references at the end of the book that contains pointers to related books and technical papers that can serve as resources as well.

2. **Obtain a tool that can perform SPC calculations and generate the control charts.** While it is important to understand the concepts, formulas, and calculations, it will be useful to find a tool that can help to perform the analysis, especially on large amounts of data. Calculating control limits, centerlines, averages, and standard deviations by hand can be a tedious and

time-consuming activity. Whether you use a tool to help with the synthesis of the data or you generate the control charts by hand, be sure to understand the principles behind the calculations to avoid erroneous analyses.

3. **Identify critical process issues.** It is not practical or reasonable (or advisable) to apply SPC to analyze every software issue. However, it is important to identify the critical factors that determine whether or not your processes succeed in meeting the goals you (or your organization) set. Start by clarifying your business goals and objectives. Identify the critical processes. For example, processes that have experienced problems in the past, or are executed across organizational boundaries, or use a technology for the first time may all serve as prime candidates of critical processes. Next, list the objectives for each critical process in terms of the attributes of the products or processes that you want to control or improve. Then, list the potential problem areas associated with the processes. Finally, group the list of potential problems into common areas to help identify issues that can be described and quantified by closely related measurements.

4. **Identify process performance attributes.** The issues discussed in step 3 tie very closely to the process performance attributes that an organization will want to select for control or improvement. The attributes associated with product quality, process duration, product delivery, and process cost are important to most organizations and common to all software processes.

5. **Select and define measures.** Select measures to characterize a process or product that will provide information relevant to the issues you identified in step 3. Then, create operational definitions to ensure that different people will implement the measures correctly and consistently and also to ensure that data will be interpreted correctly. It is also helpful to frame your measurement selections in the context of a model that describes the process of interest.

6. **Collect data.** Once you have selected and defined your measures and planned your implementation actions, you are ready to begin collecting data. The complexity of your data collection processes will increase as additional projects or organizations are added or as additional processes to investigate are involved. For SPC analyses of process performance that are aimed at assessing process stability and capability, special attention needs to be paid to the time sequencing of the data, the contextual data, and rounding of data values.

7. **Organize the data and ensure that principles underlying SPC hold.** Here, we need to be concerned with issues of rational sampling, rational subgrouping, and homogeneity. The notion of rational sampling is to obtain and use data that is representative of the performance of the process with respect to the issues being studied. Rational subgrouping is organizing the data so that the control charts answer the right questions. That is, subgroups should be selected so that the variations within any given subgroup all come from the same system of chance causes.

8. **Plot/graph data.** Understand whether you are working with variables or attributes data (because control limits for attributes data are often computed in ways quite different from control limits for variables data). Select the appropriate control chart based on your process and data. Use appropriate calculations (based on the measurement data) to determine the centerline, control limits, and other statistics for the performance characteristics. Plot the data on the process behavior chart.

9. **Examine each plot/graph for process stability, process shifts, and assignable causes.** If the process is not stable, then we cannot determine the capability of the process. There is also no basis to predict outcomes. The resulting action is to understand why the process is not stable and determine what steps can be taken to achieve stability. If the process is stable, then the capability of the process can be determined and used to predict future process performance and/or examine other process constituents.

10. **Run additional analyses as the situation requires.** Of course, once the process is stable and capable, the objective is to continually improve. You will find that one question or issue leads to asking more "what if" questions and more analyses.

8.2   Frequently Asked Questions Regarding SPC

With so many types of control charts, which ones are relevant and applicable to software issues?

While all of the charts discussed in Chapter 5 may be used to measure software processes, we have found XmR charts and the average (X-bar) and range (R) charts to be the most useful—especially for those starting out. XmR charts offer wide applicability, and many quality-control professionals [Wheeler 1998] recommend their use almost exclusively with count data. Since much of the measurement data for software is count data (the number of defects in a module or test, the number of priority-one complaints from the customer, or the percentage of nonconforming products in the output of an activity or a phase), XmR charts are almost always a reasonable choice. Another reason that XmR charts are particularly useful is that they are the obvious choice to use for periodic data, allowing us to avoid the issue of sustaining subgroup homogeneity of measurements taken over wide intervals of time. The attributes charts (c and u charts) are often used to plot control limits for defects, but their use requires that the process behavior have an underlying Poisson distribution. XmR charts have no distribution requirement and can provide equally reliable insight into the process behavior.

Sometimes, however, there are advantages to grouping the data into subgroups versus plotting individual values. When the data is organized in subgroups, you can characterize the location of the process using the subgroup averages (the $\overline{X}$ values) and you can also understand the dispersion of the process with the subgroup ranges (the R values). The X-bar and R charts will have narrower control limits offering more sensitivity to assignable causes than the individuals data would offer.

Can I construct control charts with limited software data? How much data is enough?

Many have struggled with this issue because control charts conjure up images of needing large amounts of data. In fact, out-of-control conditions may be detected with as few as three or four subgroups, even if the subgroup size (n) is 1. It usually pays to construct a run chart and begin plotting tentative trial limits as soon as possible. You must be cautious in interpreting the initial results, though, because the limits you compute with small amounts of data may not be especially reliable.

The advantage of early trial limits is that even when you cannot yet demonstrate stability, you can get early indications that assignable causes of variation are present. Concluding that a process is stable or nearly so, though, is risky with less than 20 to 30 subgroups. Often, even more observations are advisable.

Our advice, then, is the same as that given by Shewhart, Wheeler, Montgomery, and others. When limited amounts of data are available, calculate and plot the limits, and seek out the assignable causes that the data suggest. Then, update the control limits as more data become available. (See Chapter 6 for more information regarding the construction of control charts with limited data and the techniques for updating and revising control limits.)

Why is 3 sigma sufficient?

Shewhart identified the need to establish efficient (statistical) methods for detecting the presence of variability that is not due simply to chance [Shewhart 1931, 1939]. He also pointed out that the choice of limits must be taken from empirical evidence—that is, must be based on what works well in practice. In his experience, 3-sigma tolerance limits, when used for control, provide an effective criterion for discriminating between common cause variability and assignable cause variability, regardless of the underlying distribution

Studies by Shewhart and others showed that using 3-sigma values for control limits reliability detects uncontrolled variation for the six distributions that were examined (uniform, right triangular, normal, Burr, chi-square, and exponential). Wheeler generalizes these results and combines them with other experience in the three-part empirical rule shown in Figure 8.1. Note that this rule assumes a homogeneous set of data.[1]

Part 3 of Wheeler's empirical rule shows why 3-sigma limits result in very few false alarms, regardless of the distribution. It also explains why points that fall outside the limits are highly likely to have assignable causes. Thus, any value for a measured attribute that falls outside 3-sigma limits sends a strong signal that

---

[1] *Homogeneous* means that the system of chance causes is constant. For data generated by a process, this means that the process must be in statistical control. Data from processes that are not in statistical control cannot be characterized by any probability distribution.

> **The Empirical Rule**
>
> Given a homogeneous set of data:
>
> Part 1: Roughly 60% to 70% of the data will be located within a distance of 1 sigma unit on either side of the average.
>
> Part 2: Roughly 90% to 98% of the data will be located within a distance of 2 sigma units on either side of the average.
>
> Part 3: Roughly 99% to 100% of the data will be located within a distance of 3 sigma units on either side of the average.

FIGURE 8.1 An Empirical Rule for the Dispersion of Data Produced by a Constant System of Chance Causes

investigation is warranted. Regardless of the underlying distribution, the event is sufficiently unusual to suggest that it has an assignable cause and that the process is not stable. This means that 3-sigma limits provide a robust criterion that works effectively for any underlying distribution.[2] You do not need to make assumptions of normality to use control charts to your advantage. (See Appendix B for a more detailed discussion of this question.)

Do I need to be a high-maturity organization to apply SPC techniques?

The issue is not one of high or low maturity as much as it is your ability to focus on improving your processes in a manageable way. If you are experienced in defining, collecting, and using measurements to plan and manage projects, then you are ready to use measurement data to control, improve, and predict process performance. It is advisable to have basic measurement practices defined initially and then use SPC to manage and improve your process performance.

Can I achieve homogeneity with software data?

For some, this can become a philosophical argument. Because of the nonrepetitive nature of software products and processes, some believe it is difficult to achieve homogeneity with software data. The idea is to understand the theoretical issues and, at the same time, work within some practical guidelines. We need to understand what conditions are necessary to consider the data homogeneous. When more than two data values are placed in a subgroup, we are making a judgment that these values are measurements taken under essentially the same conditions and that any difference between them is due to natural or common variation. The primary purpose of homogeneity is to limit the amount of variability within the subgroup data. One way to satisfy the homogeneity principle is to measure the subgroup variables within a reasonably short time period. Since we are not talking about producing widgets but software products, the issue of homogeneity of subgroup data is a judgment call that must be made by one with extensive knowledge of the process being measured.

---

[2] If you reduce your limits to 2-sigma values to make control charts more sensitive, as some people do, you lose much of this protection.

The principle of homogeneously subgrouped data is important when we consider the idea of rational subgrouping. That is, when we want to estimate process variability, we try to group the data so that assignable causes are more likely to occur between subgroups than within them. Control limits become wider and control charts less sensitive to assignable causes when they contain nonhomogeneous data. Creating rational subgroups that minimize variation within subgroups always takes precedence over issues of subgroup size.[3]

Where in the software process can I apply SPC?

Repeatability and predictability of processes are key to managing, forecasting, and planning [Keller 1998]. Keller points out that critical business decisions are made based on assumptions of process performance (such as cost, schedule, and quality). Therefore, utilizing SPC techniques can also help to establish bounds on management expectations—that is, to establish the voice of the process and to be able to discern variations that are signals requiring action from noise in the process. Understanding the patterns and causes of variation is critical for process management and improvement. Differentiating between people issues and process issues is important because fixing the wrong problem can be catastrophic. For example, SPC can be useful in the software environment to understand the reliability of human processes [Keller 1998]. Since there is a likelihood that humans will err, SPC can help us to understand how often they will err, or which root causes could be eliminated or minimized, or how we can desensitize our processes to human error.

Others view the application of SPC as shifting the emphasis from a defect detection system based on final inspection to a defect prevention system [Grabov 1998]. Grabov offers a comparative analysis of the defect detection view versus the defect prevention view seen in Figure 8.2.[4]

Defect Detection View	Defect Prevention View
Represents a kind of postmortem since it is applied after the production phase is over	Relies on monitoring process parameters to prevent defective items from being produced
Even 100% inspection never gives 100% detection of defects	Is based on sampling and provides a reliable basis for process management
Is expensive and time-consuming	Is relatively inexpensive and is performed in real time
Takes into account only specification limits and pays no attention to a target value	Recognizes that there is an economic loss for any deviation from a target and therefore tries to direct the product characteristics toward this target

FIGURE 8.2 Defect Detection Compared to Defect Prevention

---

[3] We have already seen that it is possible to use a subgroup size as small as $n = 1$ (XmR charts).

[4] Table adapted from *SPC's Effectiveness Prediction and Analysis* by Pavel Grabov, American Society for Quality 52nd Annual Quality Congress, May 1998.

From this perspective, SPC can serve as a tool to manage and improve the inspection and test processes. If, for example, an SPC analysis were used in determining the effectiveness of the inspection and test processes, the analyst could quantitatively assess the following:

- What is a signal versus what is not a signal (detection of anomalous behavior, reduction of false alarms).
- If a process change is better or worse than prior to the change.
- If a system is better or worse than a prior system.
- Performance of one system versus performance of another system.
- If inspection data is a predictor of field defects.

Gibson also voices the opinion that SPC is both practical and beneficial to software applications, especially for defining process stability for design, code, and inspection processes [Gibson 1998]. Gibson relates the idea of "intended process function" to measuring and assessing software processes. That is, what is it that you want the process and subprocesses to accomplish? The intended process function is used to establish appropriate measurements. The measurements are analyzed, using SPC and Shewhart's control charts, to assess whether processes are being conducted as intended. The idea of "intended function" can also be aligned to the concept of consistency. That is,

- Are the processes conducted in a consistent manner?
- Is the execution of the processes yielding consistent results?

Here, the control charts are useful to characterize the process and the associated range of performance.

In summary, Gibson uses SPC to address some useful questions:

- Is the observed amount of variation reasonable in process X? Does it matter?
- If the error quality were more consistent, would that make the process more stable and more predictable?

Gibson concludes that using SPC not only is practical, beneficial, and applicable to software development but also improves understanding and execution of software processes.

Is there a risk of using control charts for evaluation of personnel?

Austin discusses situations in which dysfunctional behavior may accompany measurement-based activities [Austin 1996]. The measurement experts interviewed by Austin strongly agreed that the primary reason to measure in software organizational settings was for informational purposes rather than motivational. The interviewees also shared the viewpoint that there was a potential for a host of problems when there was any thought that measurement would be used for personnel evaluations of any kind.

These points also apply regarding the use of control charts. Control charts can be used to serve many different purposes. Control charts can be helpful for monitoring processes from release to release to compare overall performance. They can be used for making process adjustments to ensure that stability is maintained for a process on a daily or weekly basis. Most importantly, control charts may be used for continuous improvement of a process that is stable and capable. It is important to keep in mind, however, that the control charts provide the most value to the people or team where the process knowledge resides.

Management can also help set the example of how not to use the control charts. While the control charts can be used to improve personal performance, management should not misuse this tool or the data. Management has to remember that the old saw "we will continue the beatings until morale improves" comes into play whenever measurements are used as part of the "beating." Clearly, dysfunctional behavior is likely to occur if employees perceive that measurements are being used in this way.

What is the difference between an enumerative study and an analytic study? Why is this distinction important?

When using measurements to manage and improve software processes, you will almost always be trying to predict or affect future performance. When you have these goals in mind, you will invariably find yourself in the realm of analytic studies. Understanding the implications of this will help you distinguish between valid and invalid use of measurements. It will also help you understand where responsibilities lie for making predictions come true.

An *enumerative* study is one in which action will be taken on the materials within the frame studied. The frame defines the population that is sampled. Software engineering examples of enumerative studies include

- Inspections of code modules to detect and count existing defects.

- Functional or system testing of a software product to ascertain the extent to which a product has certain qualities.

- Measurement of software size to determine project status or the amount of software under configuration control.

- Measurement of staff hours expended so that the results can be used to bill customers or track expenditures against budgets.

In each case, the aim of an enumerative study is descriptive—to determine "how many" as opposed to "why so many." An enumerative study answers questions like these:

- How many defects were found by inspecting the product code?

- How many problem reports have been received from customers?

- How many user manuals do we have on hand?

- How many employees are there in our organization?

- What percent have been trained in object-oriented design methods?
- How large were the last five products we delivered?
- What was the average size of our code inspection teams last year?
- How many staff hours were spent on software rework last month?

An *analytic* study differs from an enumerative study in that action will be taken on the process (or cause system) that produced the data, not on the materials within the frame from which the data came. Whereas enumerative studies are *not* designed to guide process change or predict results that might be obtained from different sampling frames either now or in the future, the aim of an analytic study *is* to predict or improve the behavior of the process in the future.

When we conduct an analytic study, we use data from an existing process to predict characteristics of future output or performance from either the same process or similar, perhaps modified, processes. Thus, an analytic study is always concerned with a process, not with a population.

Most analyses of measurements to support process management are analytic studies. This is not to say that enumerative studies are never used. They are often used to provide status reports that point to the need for management action. They can also be used to establish relationships among existing processes or products. Examples of analytic studies, on the other hand, include

- Evaluating software tools, technologies, or methods for the purpose of selecting among them for future use.
- Tracking defect discovery rates to predict product release dates.
- Evaluating defect discovery profiles to identify focal areas for process improvement.
- Predicting schedules, costs, or operational reliability.
- Using control charts to stabilize and improve software processes or to assess process capability.

In analytic studies, investigators are concerned with making inferences or predictions that go *beyond* the sampled data. This is inherently more complex than drawing conclusions from enumerative studies. The reason is that analytic studies require the added, often unverifiable assumption that the process about which one wishes to make inferences is statistically identical to the one from which the sample was selected [Hahn 1993].

In software settings, most studies will be aimed at predicting or guiding events that will take place in the future. Hence, they will be analytic, not enumerative. Before embarking on any data collection or analysis endeavor, you should have a clear understanding of the differences between the two types of studies so that you can design collection activities properly and not ask more of data than the data can deliver. Understanding the differences between enumerative and analytic studies will also help you explain why some questions that software managers ask are impossible to answer with statistical methods alone and why the managers themselves must assume much of the responsibility for ensuring the effectiveness of the results. (An expanded discussion of this topic is found in Appendix B.)

8.3   Final Remarks

We have used quotations at various places in this book to highlight important points and to give a sense of the importance that knowledgeable people attach to the concepts on which process measurement and improvement are founded. It seems fitting, then, to close with a particularly meaningful excerpt, like the following. Nothing that we could write could better summarize the message of interplay between context knowledge and statistical methods that this book has been trying to convey.

> *Every process and every product is maintained and improved by those who combine some underlying theory with some practical experience. More than that, they call upon an amazing backlog of ingenuity and know-how to amplify and support that theory. New-product ramrods are real "pioneers"; they also recognize the importance of their initiative and intuition and enjoy the dependence resting on their know-how. However, as scientific theory and background knowledge increase, dependence on native skill and initiative often decreases.[and] problems become more complicated. Although familiarity with scientific advances will sometimes be all that is needed to solve even complicated problems—whether for maintenance or for improvement—many important changes and problems cannot be recognized by simple observation and initiative no matter how competent the scientist. It should be understood that no process is so simple that data from it will not give added insight into its behavior. The typical . . . process has unrecognized complex behaviors which can be thoroughly understood only by studying data from the product it produces. The "pioneer" who accepts and learns methods of scientific investigation to support technical advances in knowledge can be an exceptionally able citizen in an area of expertise. Methods in this book can be a boon to such pioneers in their old age.*
>
> Ellis R. Ott and Edward G. Schilling 1990

Appendix **A**

Control Chart Tables and Formulas

Appendix A contains the following tables:

- Table A, which gives bias correction factors for values of subgroup size n.
- Table A.1, which presents formulas for determining control limits for average $\overline{\overline{X}}$ and average range $\overline{R}$ and includes constant factors used to find control limits.
- Table A.2, which provides formulas for determining control limits for average $\overline{\overline{X}}$ and median range $\tilde{R}$ and includes constant factors used to find control limits.
- Table A.3, which gives formulas for determining control limits for average $\overline{\overline{X}}$ and average standard deviation $\overline{S}$ and includes constant factors used to find control limits.

TABLE A Bias Correction Factors[1]

n	d_2	c_2	c_4	d_3	d_4	n	d_2	c_2	c_4	d_3	d_4
2	1.128	.5642	.7979	.8525	0.954	21	3.778	.9638	.9876	.7272	3.730
3	1.693	.7236	.8862	.8884	1.588	22	3.819	.9655	.9882	.7199	3.771
4	2.059	.7979	.9213	.8798	1.978	23	3.858	.9670	.9887	.7159	3.811
5	2.326	.8407	.9400	.8641	2.257	24	3.895	.9684	.9892	.7121	3.847
6	2.534	.8686	.9515	.8480	2.472	25	3.931	.9695	.9896	.7084	3.883
7	2.704	.8882	.9595	.8332	2.645	30	4.086	.9748	.9915	.6927	4.037
8	2.847	.9027	.9650	.8198	2.791	35	4.213	.9784	.9927	.6799	4.166
9	2.970	.9139	.9693	.8078	2.915	40	4.322	.9811	.9936	.6692	4.274
10	3.078	.9227	.9727	.7971	3.024	45	4.415	.9832	.9943	.6601	4.372
11	3.173	.9300	.9754	.7873	3.121	50	4.498	.9849	.9949	.6521	4.450
12	3.258	.9359	.9776	.7785	3.207	60	4.639	.9874	.9957	.6389	4.591
13	3.336	.9410	.9794	.7704	3.285	70	4.755	.9892	.9963	.6283	4.707
14	3.407	.9453	.9810	.7630	3.356	80	4.854	.9906	.9968	.6194	4.806
15	3.472	.9490	.9823	.7562	3.422	90	4.939	.9916	.9972	.6118	4.892
16	3.532	.9523	.9835	.7499	3.482	100	5.015	.9925	.9975	.6052	4.968
17	3.588	.9551	.9845	.7441	3.538						
18	3.640	.9576	.9854	.7386	3.591						
19	3.689	.9599	.9862	.7335	3.640						
20	3.735	.9619	.9869	.7287	3.686						

Given k subgroups of size n, the adjusted average dispersion statistics

$$\frac{\overline{S}}{c_4} \text{ or } \frac{\overline{R}}{d_2} \text{ or } \frac{\tilde{R}}{d_4}$$ will be denoted by the generic symbol sigma_X.

Likewise, the ratios

$$\frac{\overline{S}}{c_4\sqrt{n}} \text{ or } \frac{\overline{R}}{d_2\sqrt{n}} \text{ or } \frac{\tilde{R}}{d_4\sqrt{n}}$$ will be denoted by the generic symbol $\text{sigma}_{\overline{X}}$.

Let sigma_R denote

$$\frac{d_3\overline{R}}{d_2} \text{ or } \frac{d_3\tilde{R}}{d_4}$$

---

[1] Values for d_2, d_3, and d_4 are from H. L. Harter, "Tables of Range and Studentized Range," *Annals of Mathematical Statistics* 31 (1960):1122–1147. Values for c_2 and c_4 were computed from the following formulas:

$$c_2 = \sqrt{\frac{2}{n}} \frac{\Gamma\left(\frac{n}{2}\right)}{\Gamma\left(\frac{n-1}{2}\right)} \text{ and } c_4 = c_2\sqrt{\frac{n}{n-1}}$$

TABLE A.1 Computing Control Limits Using the Average Range[2]

Formulas for Determining Control Limits for Average $\overline{X}$ and Average Range $\overline{R}$

$\mathrm{UCL}_{\overline{X}} = \overline{\overline{X}} + A_2\overline{R}$ = grand average $+ A_2$ times average range

$\mathrm{CL}_{\overline{X}} = \overline{\overline{X}}$ = grand average

$\mathrm{LCL}_{\overline{X}} = \overline{\overline{X}} - A_2\overline{R}$ = grand average $- A_2$ times average range

$\mathrm{UCL}_{\overline{R}} = D_4\overline{R} = D_4$ times average range

$\mathrm{CL}_{\overline{R}} = \overline{R}$ = average range

$\mathrm{LCL}_{\overline{R}} = D_3\overline{R} = D_3$ times average range

Average Range Constants ($\overline{R}$) for Subgroups of Size n

n	A_2	D_3	D_4
2	1.880	—	3.268
3	1.023	—	2.574
4	0.729	—	2.282
5	0.577	—	2.114
6	0.483	—	2.004
7	0.419	0.076	1.924
8	0.373	0.136	1.864
9	0.337	0.184	1.816
10	0.308	0.223	1.777
11	0.285	0.256	1.744
12	0.266	0.283	1.717
13	0.249	0.307	1.693
14	0.235	0.328	1.672
15	0.223	0.347	1.653

For $n > 15$, use Table A to compute the following:

$$A_2 = \frac{3}{d_2\sqrt{n}}, \quad D_3 = 1 - \frac{3d_3}{d_2}, \quad D_4 = 1 + \frac{3d_3}{d_2}$$

---

[2] Formula and table values are from *Understanding Statistical Process Control*, 2nd ed., by Donald J. Wheeler and David S. Chambers, © 1992 SPC Press, Inc., Knoxville, Tenn.

TABLE A.2 Computing Control Limits Using the Median Range[3]

Formulas for Determining Control Limits for Average $\overline{X}$ and Median Range $\tilde{R}$

$$\text{UCL}_{\overline{X}} = \overline{\overline{X}} + A_4\tilde{R} = \text{grand average} + A_4 \text{ times median range}$$

$$\text{CL}_{\overline{X}} = \overline{\overline{X}} = \text{grand average}$$

$$\text{LCL}_{\overline{X}} = \overline{\overline{X}} - A_4\tilde{R} = \text{grand average} - A_4 \text{ times median range}$$

$$\text{UCL}_{\tilde{R}} = D_6\tilde{R} = D_6 \text{ times median range}$$

$$\text{CL}_{\tilde{R}} = \tilde{R} = \text{median range}$$

$$\text{LCL}_{\tilde{R}} = D_5\tilde{R} = D_5 \text{ times median range}$$

Median Range Constants ($\tilde{R}$) for Subgroups of Size n

n	A_4	D_5	D_6
2	2.224	—	3.865
3	1.091	—	2.745
4	0.758	—	2.375
5	0.594	—	2.179
6	0.495	—	2.055
7	0.429	0.078	1.967
8	0.380	0.139	1.901
9	0.343	0.187	1.850
10	0.314	0.227	1.809
11	0.290	0.260	1.773
12	0.270	.0288	1.744
13	0.253	0.312	1.719
14	0.239	0.333	1.697
15	0.226	0.352	1.678

For $n > 15$, use Table A to compute the following:

$$A_4 = \frac{3}{d_4\sqrt{n}}, \quad D_5 = \frac{d_2 - 3d_3}{d_4}, \quad D_6 = \frac{d_2 + 3d_3}{d_4}$$

---

[3] Formula and table values are from *Understanding Statistical Process Control*, 2nd ed., by Donald J. Wheeler and David S. Chambers, © 1992 SPC Press, Inc., Knoxville, Tenn.

TABLE A.3 Computing Control Limits Using the Average Standard Deviation[4]

Formulas for Determining Control Limits for Average $\overline{\overline{X}}$ and Average Standard Deviation $\overline{S}$

$$\text{UCL}_{\overline{X}} = \overline{\overline{X}} + A_3\overline{S} = \text{grand average} + A_3 \text{ times average standard deviation}$$

$$\text{CL}_{\overline{X}} = \overline{\overline{X}} = \text{grand average}$$

$$\text{LCL}_{\overline{X}} = \overline{\overline{X}} - A_3\overline{S} = \text{grand average} \pm A_3 \text{ times average standard deviation}$$

$$\text{UCL}_{\overline{S}} = B_4\overline{S} = B_4 \text{ times average standard deviation}$$

$$\text{CL}_{\overline{S}} = \overline{S} = \text{average standard deviation}$$

$$\text{LCL}_{\overline{S}} = B_3\overline{S} = B_3 \text{ times average standard deviation}$$

Average Standard Deviation Constants ($\overline{S}$) for Subgroups of Size _n_

_n_	A_3	B_3	B_4
2	2.659	—	3.267
3	1.954	—	2.568
4	1.628	—	2.266
5	1.427	—	2.089
6	1.287	0.030	1.970
7	1.182	0.118	1.882
8	1.099	0.185	1.815
9	1.032	0.239	1.761
10	0.975	0.284	1.716
11	0.927	0.322	1.678
12	0.886	0.354	1.646
13	0.850	0.382	1.619
14	0.817	0.407	1.593
15	0.789	0.428	1.572

For $n > 15$, use Table A to compute the following:

$$A_3 = \frac{3}{c_4\sqrt{n}}, \quad B_3 = 1 - \frac{3}{c_4}\sqrt{1-(c_4)^2}, \quad B_4 = 1 + \frac{3}{c_4}\sqrt{1-(c_4)^2}$$

---

[4] Formula and table values are from *Understanding Statistical Process Control*, 2nd ed., by Donald J. Wheeler and David S. Chambers, © 1992 SPC Press, Inc., Knoxville, Tenn.

Appendix **B**

More About Analyzing Process Behavior

Appendix B contains expanded and more detailed discussions of three major topics that were only briefly discussed in the main text of this book:

- Section B.1 defines enumerative and analytic studies and discusses the differences between them in terms of predictive capability and their applicability to process measurement.
- Section B.2 discusses the rationale and role of 3-sigma control limits as developed and explained by Walter A. Shewhart [Shewhart 1931].
- Section B.3 discusses the relationship of control limits to the central limit theorem and the normal distribution.

B.1 Enumerative Versus Analytic Studies

When using measurements to manage and improve software processes, you will almost always be trying to predict or affect future performance. When you have these goals in mind, you will invariably find yourself in the realm of analytic studies. Understanding the implications of this will help you distinguish between valid and invalid use of measurements. It will also help you understand what data you need, how to obtain the data you need, and the contextual information about the data.

The next two subsections describe the principal differences between enumerative and analytic studies and explain what the differences mean in practice. Textbooks in statistics have been slow to give the distinctions between these studies the attention they deserve [Hahn 1993]. Perhaps because of this, the advice you find here may seem unfamiliar and excessively conservative. If you are uncomfortable with the recommendations that follow, we strongly encourage you to supplement these discussions by reading what Deming, Hahn, Meeker, and Wheeler have to say on the topic [Deming 1975; Hahn 1993; Wheeler 1995].

B.1.1   ENUMERATIVE STUDIES

An *enumerative* study is one in which action will be taken on the materials within the frame studied. The frame defines the population that is sampled. Software engineering examples of enumerative studies include

- Inspections of code modules to detect and count existing defects.
- Functional or system testing of a software product to ascertain the extent to which a product has certain qualities.
- Measurement of software size to determine project status or the amount of software under configuration control.
- Measurement of staff hours expended so that the results can be used to bill customers or track expenditures against budgets.

In each case, the aim of an enumerative study is descriptive—to determine "how many" as opposed to "why so many." An enumerative study answers questions like these:

- How many defects were found by inspecting the product code?
- How many problem reports have been received from customers?
- How many user manuals do we have on hand?
- How many employees are there in our organization?
- What percent have been trained in object-oriented design methods?
- How large were the last five products we delivered?
- What was the average size of our code inspection teams last year?
- How many staff hours were spent on software rework last month?

Enumerative studies are not designed to guide process change or predict results that might be obtained from different sampling frames, either now or in the future. In an enumerative study, it is possible (although perhaps not practical) to reduce errors of sampling to arbitrarily low levels. In the limit, in theory, you could measure every element in the frame and thus have no sampling error whatsoever.[1] In an analytic study, on the other hand, it is impossible to compute the risk of making a wrong decision, no matter how many data points are obtained [Deming 1975].

The steps for collecting and analyzing measurement data for an enumerative study are as follows [Deming 1975; Hahn 1993; Park 1996]:

1. Define the goal of the study.
2. Define the characteristics or properties of interest.
3. Explicitly and precisely define the target population about which inferences are desired.

---

[1] Errors of measurement, however, can still be present, even when every element in the sampling frame is included in the sample. Rounding errors, approximations, biases, and errors in reading instruments or recording values are just a few examples.

4. Define the frame from which the sample will be taken by

- Obtaining or developing a specific listing or other enumeration of the population from which samples will be selected. (This population is often not identical to the target population.)
- Describing the environment in which the attributes will be measured.

5. Evaluate the differences between the sampling frame and the target population, and identify the possible effects that the differences could have on the conclusions of the study.

6. Define, clearly and precisely, the attribute(s) that will be measured, the measures and scales that will be used, and the manner in which measurements will be made.

7. Design and execute a sampling procedure that supplies entities to be measured that are appropriately randomized and as representative of the target population as possible.

8. Review and assess the collected data.

9. Identify the other assumptions that will be used in drawing inferences, including any assumption of a specific underlying distribution (such as the normal, binomial, Poisson, or exponential distribution) and all assumptions related to the representativeness of the sampled values.

10. Ensure that the tools and methods used for analysis are consistent with the nature of the data.

11. Ensure that the users of any inferences drawn from the study are made fully aware of the limitations implicit in the assumptions that underlie the inferences.

We refer you to the standard texts on statistics for guidance on using methods such as design of experiments, regression analysis, confidence intervals, correlation, multivariate analysis, and sampling when collecting and analyzing data for an enumerative study and presenting the results.

B.1.2 ANALYTIC STUDIES

An *analytic* study differs from an enumerative study in that action will be taken on the process (or cause system) that produced the data, not on the materials within the frame from which the data came. The aim of an analytic study is to predict or improve the behavior of the process in the future.

When we conduct an analytic study, we use data from an existing process to predict characteristics of future output or performance from either the same process or similar, perhaps modified, processes. Thus, an analytic study is always concerned with a process, not with a population. As Deming points out,

> There is a simple criterion by which to distinguish between enumerative and analytic studies. A 100 percent sample of the frame provides the complete answer to the question posed for an enumerative problem, subject of course to

the limitation of the method of investigation. In contrast, a 100 percent sample of a group of patients, or a section of land, or of last week's product, industrial or agricultural, is still inconclusive in an analytic problem.

W. Edwards Deming 1975

Most analyses of measurements to support process management are analytic studies. This is not to say that enumerative studies are never used. They are often used to provide status reports that point to the need for management action. They can also be used to establish relationships among existing processes or products. Examples of analytic studies, on the other hand, include

- Evaluating software tools, technologies, or methods for the purpose of selecting among them for future use.

- Tracking defect discovery rates to predict product release dates.

- Evaluating defect discovery profiles to identify focal areas for process improvement.

- Predicting schedules, costs, or operational reliability.

- Using control charts to stabilize and improve software processes or to assess process capability.

In analytic studies, investigators are concerned with making inferences or predictions that go *beyond* the sampled data. This is inherently more complex than drawing conclusions from enumerative studies. The reason is that analytic studies require the added, often unverifiable assumption that the process about which one wishes to make inferences is statistically identical to the one from which the sample was selected [Hahn 1993]. Whenever this assumption does not hold—and it almost never does—it will be impossible to make unconditional, quantitative statements about the probabilities or risks associated with future outcomes. The best that we can do is to make weak, conditional statements, subject to the assurances of subject-matter experts that *all* significant conditions in the future will be *exactly* as they were when the samples were obtained. Even these statements are at risk because all too often the samples that they are based on are convenience samples (and hence give biased views of the sampling frame) rather than representative samples of randomly occurring outcomes. Wheeler puts it this way:

In an Analytic Study there is no way to define a random sample of the future. All data, and all analyses of data, are historical. However, in an Analytic Study the inference of interest involves prediction, an extrapolation into the future. Probability theory offers no help here. All samples become "judgment samples," and there is no way to attach a probability to a specific future outcome.

Donald J. Wheeler 1995

Extrapolations to the future *always* go beyond what statistical methods alone can deliver. In addition to statistical methods, extrapolations require a model of the effects that changes will have on processes that are studied, together with assurances of the continued existence of all conditions not covered by the model (earthquakes, fires, strikes, unforeseen problems, changes in suppliers, raw materials, personnel, environments, etc.). Only subject-matter experts or people who manage and operate these processes can provide the models and make these assurances.

So, whenever you see a confidence, statistical tolerance, or prediction interval that is reported in the setting of an analytic study, you should understand that it is, at best, a lower (optimistic) bound on the true uncertainty [Hahn 1993]. The interval that expresses the total uncertainty is almost assuredly wider, and perhaps much wider, than the statistical intervals alone might lead you to believe. Analysts owe it to the users of their studies to make this point clear. Unfortunately, in the software world as in other business endeavors, this is seldom done.

The most critical issues in any statistical study are the models used to relate the target population to the sampled population and the assumptions associated with the representativeness of the data. These models and assumptions are often implicit, and hence hidden, from both analysts and users of the inferences. Departures from the (implicit) models and assumptions are common in practice. This can easily invalidate a formal statistical analysis. Failure to state and validate the models and assumptions can produce a false sense of security. This, in many instances, is the weakest link in the inference chain [Hahn 1993].

Consequently, when performing analytic studies, we are motivated to use statistical methods that require as few assumptions as possible. This is one reason for the well-deserved popularity of Shewhart's control charts and 3-sigma limits. Another is that control charts also address the problem of consistency of conditions over time. When you can demonstrate that a process has operated consistently in the past, you are on much sounder ground when you predict that the observed performance will continue into the future. The converse is also true. When a process you are examining is not in (or near) statistical control with respect to all characteristics of relevance, the applicability of statistical intervals or any other method for characterizing the process can be undermined easily by unpredicted trends, shifts, cycles, or other variations. Shewhart made this point very clear:

> *Sampling theory applies to samples arising under controlled conditions. Too much emphasis cannot be laid upon this fact. To be able to make accurate predictions from samples, we must secure control first just as to make accurate physical measurements, we must eliminate constant errors.*
>
> Walter A. Shewhart 1931

The steps for collecting and analyzing measurement data for an analytic study are essentially the same as those for enumerative studies. There are, however, some additional aspects that should be addressed. For instance, because we wish to draw conclusions about a process that may not even exist at the time of the study, the process that we sample is likely to differ in several ways from the process whose performance we seek to predict or describe. Moreover, instead of dealing with a set of identifiable units as in an enumerative study, we must deal with observations taken in some "representative" manner from an existing process.

What this means is that, in an analytic study, we have both greater opportunity and greater responsibility for defining the specific process to be sampled and the way the sampling will proceed [Hahn 1993]. In conducting analytic studies, you should always aim to consider as broad an environment as possible. This means addressing, insofar as possible, the full range over which inputs, resources, personnel, and operating conditions might be encountered in the future. This is contrary to the traditional advice applied to most scientific investigations, where one tries to hold all variables constant except those key to the study itself.

The reason for making an analytic study broad is to narrow the gap between the sampled process and the process of interest. This is especially important if there are possible interactions between the factors under investigation and any background or contextual conditions.

Another difference between enumerative and analytic studies is that, in an enumerative study, the probability model that you use to draw inferences is attached to the *selection* of the items in the sample. With such a probability model, you can work out formulas for induction and for estimating the uncertainties introduced by using a sample in place of a full census. In contrast, in an analytic study, the probability model must apply to the *behavior* of the phenomenon itself [Wheeler 1995]. Since you have less control of the behavioral process in analytic studies than you do of the sampling process in enumerative studies, the assumptions on which your inferences will be based are apt to be less justifiable, and there will be more (unknown) uncertainties in the inferences you draw.

Analytic studies can also differ from enumerative studies in that the sampling may take place over time. When this is the case, it is usually advisable to sample over relatively long periods. Observations taken over short periods are less likely to be representative of either average performance or long-run variability, unless the process is in strict statistical control.

The concept of statistical control is frequently important to analytic studies. When a process is in statistical control *and remains so,* the current data can be used to draw inferences about the future performance of the process. Data from a process in strict statistical control correspond to the commonly used (and at times misused) assumption of independent and identically distributed random variables.

Many analytic studies are dynamic in nature. Here, observed values are collected over a period of time, and the results are used to guide changes to an ongoing process. The changes may be for the purpose of stabilizing the process (statistical process control), hitting a desired target (industrial process control), or improving the process (reducing variability or resetting the process to a more profitable target). In these cases, an analytic study may also include steps like the following:

1. Analyze process performance data for stability:

- Find out what the process is doing now.
- Is the process stable?
- If the process is not stable, find all assignable causes and fix the assignable causes so that they cannot occur again.
- If the process is stable, either leave it alone and (if desired) proceed to capability evaluation or introduce adjustments (or improvements) and track the results.

2. Once stability is established, determine process capability by comparing the performance of the process to the requirements it is supposed to meet.

3. Use the results of stability and capability analyses to guide and evaluate investigations and decisions:

- Identify improvement opportunities.
- Assess probabilities of future outcomes.
- Determine the effectiveness of improvement actions.

In analytic studies, you should be mindful that statistical inferences are inherently limited to the conceptual population of entities that could, at least in theory, have been produced and measured at the same time and in the same manner as those in the study. However, as Hahn and Meeker point out,

> ... in the overwhelming majority of cases, the investigator's prime concern is not with the sampled process but with a different one. Any extrapolation of the inferences from the sampled process to some other process is generally beyond [the analyst's] area of competence. The validity of such an extrapolation needs to be assessed by the subject-matter expert. Under these circumstances, determining whether or not to use statistical inference methods requires a judgment call. If such methods are to be used, it is, moreover, the analyst's responsibility to clearly point out their limitations.
>
> Gerald J. Hahn and William Q. Meeker 1993

In software settings, most studies will be aimed at predicting or guiding events that will take place in the future. Hence, they will be analytic, not enumerative. Before embarking on any data collection or analysis endeavor, you should have a clear understanding of the differences between the two types of studies so that you can design collection activities properly and not ask more of data than the data can deliver. Understanding the differences between enumerative and analytic studies will also help you explain why some questions that software managers ask are impossible to answer with statistical methods alone and why the managers themselves must assume much of the responsibility for ensuring the effectiveness of the results.

B.2 Three-Sigma Control Limits

In his classic texts *Economic Control of Quality of Manufactured Product* and *Statistical Method from the Viewpoint of Quality Control,* Shewhart identifies the need to establish efficient methods for detecting the presence of variability that is not due simply to chance [Shewhart 1931, 1939]. He also points out that the choice of limits must be taken from empirical evidence. That is, it must be based on what works well in practice.

Shewhart uses the expression $\overline{X} \pm t\boldsymbol{\sigma}_X$ to characterize tolerance limits for variability due to chance causes.[2] He argues that, in practice, the method for establishing tolerance limits for observed data depends on statistical theory to furnish estimates for the mean $\overline{X}$ and standard deviation $\boldsymbol{\sigma}_X$ of the underlying distribution but requires empirical experience to justify the choice of t. Shewhart states that experience indicates that $t = 3$ provides acceptable economic value. By *economic*, he means that the costs resulting from missing assigned causes are balanced against the costs of looking for assigned causes when none exist (false alarms). In his experience, 3-sigma tolerance limits, when used for control, provide an effective criterion for discriminating between common cause variability and assignable cause variability, regardless of the underlying distribution.

Shewhart was guided to his view in part by Tchebycheff's inequality. This inequality says that when a process is stable with respect to a measured attribute X, the probability $P_{t\sigma_X}$ that any particular future observation will lie within the limits $\overline{X} \pm t\boldsymbol{\sigma}_X$ is greater than

$$1 - \frac{1}{t^2}$$

For $t = 3$, this says that at least 88.9% of all observations will fall, in the long run, within 3 standard deviations of the mean of the underlying distribution. The probability of false alarms will then be less than 0.111. Of course, this still leaves open the problem of obtaining good estimates for the mean and the standard deviation—topics that Shewhart and others have explored extensively.

Tchebycheff's inequality is important because it applies for any distribution. With it, there is no need to make additional assumptions—such as assuming normally distributed variables—that are so difficult to validate in practice.

When we do know something about the underlying distribution, we can be more precise in our statements about the probabilities associated with 3-sigma limits. For example, when a distribution has only one mode, when the mode is the same as the arithmetic mean (the expected value), and when the frequencies decline continuously on both sides of the mode, then the Camp-Meidell inequality applies. The Camp-Meidell inequality is similar to Tchebycheff's but is more exact. It says that the probability that a randomly selected future value will lie within the limits $\overline{X} \pm t\boldsymbol{\sigma}_X$ is greater than

$$1 - \frac{1}{2.25 t^2}$$

This means that when the Camp-Meidell conditions hold, and as long as the underlying distribution remains unchanged, the probability of false alarms with 3-sigma limits will be less than 0.049.

If you are willing to assume that your measured values follow a normal distribution, you can be even more precise. With normality, the probability $P_{3\sigma_X}$ that

---

[2] In Shewhart's notation, boldface type designates parameters of underlying distributions. In this section, these include the symbols $\boldsymbol{\sigma}_X$, $\overline{X}$, and $P_{t\sigma_X}$. Symbols for statistics calculated from measurements are printed in standard typefaces.

a given value will fall within $\overline{X} \pm 3\sigma_X$ is 0.9973.[3] Therefore, when an attribute that is measured has an observed value of X that is outside the 3-sigma limits, the probability is only 0.0027 that—for this single instance alone—this is *not* the result of an assignable cause.[4]

Note, however, that in real-world settings, we can never prove that a distribution is normal. Hence, the exact probabilities associated with any limits will always be at least somewhat in doubt. This, coupled with the robustness of Tchebycheff's inequality and with empirically related economic considerations, is the reason Shewhart and many others came to eschew probability-based limits and to prefer 3-sigma limits instead.

To test the consequences of this preference, Shewhart, Wheeler, and others have investigated the effectiveness of 3-sigma limits when the underlying distribution is not normal [Shewhart 1931; Wheeler 1992; Burr 1967]. Wheeler, for example, graphically illustrates the results of simulation studies in which 1,000 observations were drawn from each of six different distributions: uniform, right triangular, normal, Burr, chi-square, and exponential. His objective was to determine the extent to which 1-, 2-, and 3-sigma limits spanned the sets of data drawn from the six distributions. The sampling plan for each distribution was based on a random number generator, so the processes that produced the data were (a priori) in statistical control.

The studies showed that using 3-sigma values for control limits has little practical effect on the reliability with which the limits serve to identify uncontrolled variation for the distributions that were examined. Wheeler generalizes these results and combines them with other experience in the three-part empirical rule shown in Figure B.1[5] [Wheeler 1992]. Note that this rule assumes a homogenous set of data.[6]

Part 3 of Wheeler's empirical rule shows why 3-sigma limits result in very few false alarms, regardless of the distribution. It also explains why points that fall outside the limits are highly likely to have assignable causes. When we couple these empirical observations with the information provided by Tchebycheff's inequality and the Camp-Meidell inequality, it is safe to say that 3-sigma limits will never cause an excessive rate of false alarms, even when the underlying distribution is distinctly nonnormal.

---

[3] Be careful of your interpretations here. Just as with the Tchebycheff and Camp-Meidell inequalities, the probabilistic statement applies to randomly selected, single observations only. The probability that one or more points in a sequence of observations will fall outside the limits is considerably higher. For instance, even in a normally distributed process, the chances are greater than 50–50 that at least one point in the next 260 will fall outside the 3-sigma limits.

[4] These computations all assume that you know exactly what $\overline{X}$ and σ_X are. If you must estimate $\overline{X}$ and σ_X from the data, the probabilities will be different.

[5] Figure adapted from *Understanding Statistical Process Control*, 2nd ed., by Donald J. Wheeler and David S. Chambers, © 1992 SPC Press, Inc., Knoxville, Tenn.

[6] *Homogeneous* means that the system of chance causes is constant. For data generated by a process, this means that the process must be in statistical control. Data from processes that are not in statistical control cannot be characterized by any probability distribution.

The Empirical Rule

Given a homogeneous set of data:

Part 1: Roughly 60% to 70% of the data will be located within a distance of 1 sigma unit on either side of the average.

Part 2: Roughly 90% to 98% of the data will be located within a distance of 2 sigma units on either side of the average.

Part 3: Roughly 99% to 100% of the data will be located within a distance of 3 sigma units on either side of the average.

FIGURE B.1 An Empirical Rule for the Dispersion of Data Produced by a Constant System of Chance Causes

Thus, any value for a measured attribute that falls outside 3-sigma limits sends a strong signal that investigation is warranted. Regardless of the underlying distribution, the event is sufficiently unusual to suggest that it has an assignable cause and that the process is not stable. This means that 3-sigma limits provide a robust criterion that works effectively for any underlying distribution. You do not need to make assumptions of normality to use control charts to your advantage.[7]

B.3 Central Limit Theorem and Role of the Normal Distribution

It is true that some books on the statistical control of quality and many training manuals for teaching control charts show a graph of the normal curve and proportions of areas thereunder. Such tables and charts are misleading and derail effective study and use of control charts.

W. Edwards Deming 1986

We raise the issue of normal distributions and the central limit theorem because of an apparent misunderstanding by many people that data must be normally distributed to use control charts. This is not the case.

Assumptions of normality come into play when the factors used to adjust statistics for bias and compute control chart limits are calculated. For example, the constants A_2, D_3, and D_4 that are used to compute control limits for X-bar and R charts are based on the assumption that the chance causes come from a normal probability distribution.[8] Irving W. Burr, though, has examined 26 distributions and shown that this use of the normal probability model does not lead to values that

---

[7] If you reduce your limits to 2-sigma values to make control charts more sensitive, as some people do, you lose much of this protection.

[8] The tables in Appendix A of this book and in the appendixes of Wheeler's books show how these factors have been computed [Wheeler 1992, 1995].

are appreciably different from the constants that should be used for other distributions [Burr 1967]. Hence, using the usual, tabulated constants with nonnormal distributions has little affect on the location of the limits or their effectiveness for detecting unusual events.

Some people mistakenly believe that control charts work only when the central limit theorem applies, and many writers have propagated this misunderstanding. The central limit theorem says that, under very general conditions, when variation results from the sum of independent random elements and no small set of elements predominates, the distribution of the sum will approach a normal distribution as the number of terms in the sum increases. The convergence is often quite rapid. Thus, averages (such as $\overline{X}$) tend to be normally distributed, regardless of the underlying distribution. Ranges, however, always have distinctly nonnormal (skewed) distributions.

It is true that the theorem is relevant to many situations where data are grouped and averaged. In these cases, it is often valid to treat averages of observed values as at least approximately normally distributed, regardless of the underlying distribution. However, it is not necessary to make this assumption. As we illustrated previously, the normal distribution has no real bearing on the effectiveness of 3-sigma limits because nearly all values will fall within these limits for any process that is in statistical control, whatever the distribution. The conservative nature of 3-sigma limits makes the central limit theorem irrelevant. It is especially important to understand this when dealing with data obtained "one at a time" (subgroups of size 1). Sometimes, there are mistaken tendencies to forcibly average these data somehow, just to appeal to the central limit theorem. Better and more straightforward procedures, such as XmR charts, are almost always available.

Appendix C

Example Data and Calculations

Appendix C contains data and charts used by several of the examples in Chapter 5:

- Appendix C.1 illustrates the calculations used to determine the standard deviation for release 1 of the example illustrating the use of X-bar and S charts in Chapter 5.
- Appendix C.2 contains data and calculations for constructing the individuals and median range charts example in Chapter 5.

Appendix C.1

Calculations for determining the standard deviation (S) for release 1 data are given here using the formula

$$S = \sqrt{\frac{\sum_{i=1}^{i=n}\left(X_i - \overline{X}\right)^2}{n-1}}$$

The table in Figure C.1 lists the values (X_i) of SLOC/review hour for each inspection in release 1, the average SLOC/review hour ($\overline{X}$), and the values

$$X_i - \overline{X} \text{ and } \left(X_i - \overline{X}\right)^2.$$

First, calculating the numerator under the radical sign yields

$$\sum_{i=1}^{i=n}\left(X_i - \overline{X}\right)^2 = 26625.431$$

X_i	$\overline{X}$	$X_i - \overline{X}$	$(X_i - \overline{X})^2$
171.6	80.02526	91.6	8392.594
40.5	80.02526	−39.6	1564.572
98.0	80.02526	18.0	323.5678
48.9	80.02526	−31.2	971.0465
145.7	80.02526	65.6	4306.891
92.1	80.02526	12.1	145.9264
47.0	80.02526	−33.1	1093.542
86.8	80.02526	6.7	45.48114
92.5	80.02526	12.5	155.6192
26.0	80.02526	−54.0	2918.729
77.6	80.02526	−2.4	5.729701
129.2	80.02526	49.2	2418.934
73.8	80.02526	−6.3	39.37888
24.0	80.02526	−56.1	3144.121
46.9	80.02526	−33.2	1099.3

FIGURE C.1 Listing of Release 1 Calculations for Determining *S* for Release 1

Then, calculating *S* for release 1 gives

$$S = \sqrt{\frac{\sum_{i=1}^{i=n} (X_i - \overline{X})^2}{n-1}} = \sqrt{\frac{26625.431}{14}} = 43.61$$

And, $\overline{X}$ is 80.025 by averaging all the values of X_i in Figure C.1.

The calculations must be repeated to find *S* for releases 2, 3, and 4 using the appropriate values of X_i.

The XmR control charts in Figure C.2 indicate that the inspection review rate (SLOC/review hour) for each of the releases was under control and homogeneous, thus justifying the use of each of the release's data as a subgroup to calculate *S*.

Appendix C.2

The tables in Figures C.3 and C.4 contain data for one month reporting the number of unresolved problems per day, moving range (*mR*) from one day to the next, and ranked moving range to determine median range.

From Figure C.3, we see that

- The individuals average is 13.55.
- The average moving range (*mR*) is 13.77.

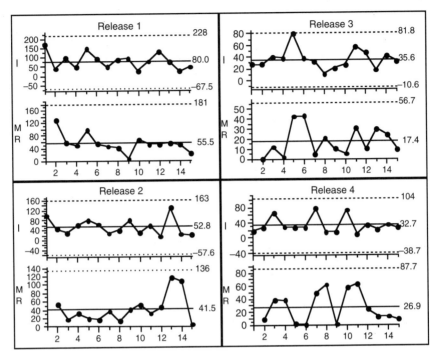

FIGURE C.2   Inspection Review Rates for Product Releases 1, 2, 3, and 4

From the ranking table in Figure C.4,

> rank $k = 30$
>
> $k/2 = 15$th number $= 8$
>
> $k/2+1 = 16$th number $= 9$
>
> median $m\tilde{R}$ = average $k/2$th and $k/2+1$st $= 8.5$

For moving range of $n = 2$,

$$\text{UNPL}_X = \overline{X} + \frac{3m\tilde{R}}{d_4} = \overline{X} + 3.145m\tilde{R} = 13.55 + 3.145(8.5) = 40.24$$

$$\text{CL}_X = \overline{X} = 13.55$$

$$\text{LNPL}_X = \overline{X} - \frac{3m\tilde{R}}{d_4} = \overline{X} - 3.145m\tilde{R} = 13.55 - 3.145(8.5) = -13.14$$

$$\text{UCL}_{\tilde{R}} = D_6\tilde{R} = 3.865m\tilde{R} = 3.865(8.5) = 32.81$$

$$\text{CL}_{\tilde{R}} = m\tilde{R} = 8.5$$

Day	URP=X	mR
1	11	
2	4	7
3	8	4
4	14	6
5	24	10
6	6	18
7	12	6
8	9	3
9	7	2
10	4	3
11	29	25
12	2	27
13	9	7
14	46	37
15	21	25
16	29	8
17	6	23
18	40	34
19	21	19
20	2	19
21	7	5
22	14	7
23	5	9
24	6	1
25	5	1
26	31	26
27	3	28
28	7	4
29	4	3
30	28	24
31	6	22
Averages	13.55	13.77

FIGURE C.3 Example Data of Unresolved Problems

Rank	mR
1	1
2	1
3	2
4	3
5	3
6	3
7	4
8	4
9	5
10	6
11	6
12	7
13	7
14	7
15	8
16	9
17	10
18	18
19	19
20	19
21	22
22	23
23	24
24	25
25	25
26	26
27	27
28	28
29	34
30	37

FIGURE C.4 Ranking of Ranges to Select Median Range

References

Austin, Robert D. *Measuring and Managing Performance in Organizations*. New York: Dorset House Publishing Company, 1996.

Basili, Victor R., and Green, Scott. "Software Process Evolution at the SEL." IEEE Software 11, 4 (July 1994):58–66.

Bhandari, I., et al. "A Case Study of Software Process Improvement During Development." *IEEE Transactions on Software Engineering* 19, no. 12 (1993):1157–1170.

Brassard, Michael, ed. *The Memory Jogger: A Pocket Guide of Tools for Continuous Improvement*, 2d ed. Methuen, Mass.: GOAL/QPC, 1988.

Brassard, Michael. *The Memory Jogger Plus+™: Featuring the Seven Management and Planning Tools*. Methuen, Mass.: GOAL/QPC, 1989.

Britz, Galen, et al. "How to Teach Others to Apply Statistical Thinking." *Quality Progress* (June 1997):67–78.

Brodman, Judith G., and Johnson, Donna L. "Return on Investment (ROI) from Software Process Improvement as Measured by U.S. Industry." *Software Process: Improvement and Practice* 1, pilot issue (August 1995):35–47.

Burr, Irving W. "The Effect of Non-Normality on Constants for X-bar and R Charts." *Industrial Quality Control* (1967):563–568.

Card, David N., and Glass, Robert L. *Measuring Software Design Quality*. Englewood Cliffs, N.J.: Prentice-Hall, 1990.

Card, David N. "The RAD Fad: Is Timing Really Everything?" IEEE Software 12, no. 5 (1995):19–22.

Champ, Charles W., and Woodall, William H. "Exact Results for Shewhart Control Charts with Supplementary Runs Rules." *Technometrics* 29, no. 4 (1987):393–399.

Chillarege, R., et al. "Orthogonal Defect Classification—A Concept for In-Process Measurements." *IEEE Transactions on Software Engineering* 18, no. 11 (1992):943–956.

Chillarege, R. Ch. 9, "Orthogonal Defect Classification," 359–400. In Michael R. Lyu, ed., *Handbook of Software Reliability Engineering*. Los Alamitos, Calif.: IEEE Computer Society Press, 1996. (Also available from McGraw-Hill, New York.)

Deming, W. Edwards. "On Probability as a Basis for Action." *The American Statistician* 29, no. 4 (1975):146–152.

Deming, W. Edwards. *Out of the Crisis.* Cambridge, Mass.: Massachusetts Institute of Technology, Center for Advanced Engineering, 1986.

Deming, W. Edwards. *The New Economics for Industry, Government, Education.* Cambridge, Mass.: Massachusetts Institute of Technology, Center for Advanced Engineering, 1993.

Duncan, Acheson J. *Quality Control and Industrial Statistics.* Homewood, Ill.: Richard D. Irwin, Inc., 1974.

Florac, William A., et al. *Software Quality Measurement: A Framework for Counting Problems and Defects* (CMU/SEI-92-TR-22, ADA258556). Pittsburgh, Pa.: Software Engineering Institute, Carnegie Mellon University, September 1992.

Florac, William A., Park, Robert E., and Carleton, Anita D. *Practical Software Measurement: Measuring for Process Management and Improvement* (CMU/SEI-997-HB-003). Pittsburgh, Pa.: Software Engineering Institute, Carnegie Mellon University, April 1997.

Gibson, John E. "Is the Software Industry Ready for Statistical Process Control?," a white paper. Gaithersburg, Md.: Lockheed Martin Mission Systems, April 1998.

Goethert, Wolfhart B., Bailey, Elizabeth K., and Busby, Mary B. *Software Effort and Schedule Measurement: A Framework for Counting Staff-Hours and Reporting Schedule Information* (CMU/SEI-92-TR-21, ADA258279). Pittsburgh, Pa.: Software Engineering Institute, Carnegie Mellon University, September 1992.

Grabov, Pavel. "SPC's Effectiveness Prediction and Analysis." American Society for Quality, 52nd Annual Quality Congress, May 1998.

Grady, Robert B., and Caswell, Deborah L. *Software Metrics: Establishing a Company-Wide Program.* Englewood Cliffs, N.J.: Prentice-Hall, 1987.

Grady, Robert B. *Practical Software Metrics for Project Management and Process Improvement.* Englewood Cliffs, N.J.: Prentice-Hall, 1992.

Grant, Eugene L., and Leavenworth, Richard S. *Statistical Quality Control,* 7th ed. New York: McGraw-Hill, 1996.

Hahn, Gerald J., and Meeker, William Q. "Assumptions for Statistical Inference." *The American Statistician* 47, no. 1 (1993):1–11.

Harter, H. L. "Tables of Range and Studentized Range." *Annals of Mathematical Statistics* 31 (1960):1122–1147.

Hayes, Will, and Over, James W. *The Personal Software Process™ (PSP™): An Empirical Study of the Impact of PSP on Individual Engineers.* (CMU/SEI-97-TR-001) Pittsburgh, Pa.: Software Engineering Institute, Carnegie Mellon University, December 1997.

Henry, Joel, and Blasewitz, Bob. "Process Definition: Theory and Reality." *IEEE Software* 9, no. 6 (1992):103–105.

Hillier, Frederick S. "$\overline{X}$ and R-Chart Control Limits Based on a Small Number of Subgroups." *Journal of Quality Technology* 1, no. 1 (1969):17–26.

Hoyer, Robert A., and Ellis, Wayne C. "A Graphical Exploration of SPC." *Quality Progress* 29, nos. 5 and 6 (1996):65–73, 57–64, respectively.

Humphrey, Watts S. *Managing the Software Process*. Reading, Mass.: Addison-Wesley, 1989.

Humphrey, Watts S. *A Discipline for Software Engineering*. Reading, Mass.: Addison-Wesley, 1995.

Ishikawa, Kaoru. *Guide to Quality Control,* 2d rev. ed. White Plains, N.Y.: UNIPUB—Kraus International Publications, 1986.

Juran, J. M., and Gryna, Frank M., eds. *Juran's Quality Control Handbook,* 4th ed. New York: McGraw-Hill, 1988.

Kaplan, R. S., and Norton, D. P. "The Balance Scorecard—Measures That Drive Performance." *Harvard Business Review* (January–February 1992):71–79.

Keller, Ted. *Applying SPC Techniques to Software Development—A Management Perspective*. Proceedings from the 1998 SEI Software Engineering Symposium. Pittsburgh, Pa.: Software Engineering Institute, Carnegie Mellon University, September 1998.

Kenett, Ron S. "Two Methods for Comparing Pareto Charts." *Journal of Quality Technology* 23, no. 1 (1991):27–31.

Lynch, Richard L., and Cross, Kelvin F. *Measure Up!* Cambridge, Mass.: Blackwell Publishers, Basil Blackwell, Inc., 1995.

McGarry, John, et al. *Practical Software Measurement: A Foundation for Objective Project Management, Version 3.1a*. Landing , N.J.: Picatinney Arsenal, April 1998.

Montgomery, Douglas C., and Runger, G. C. *Applied Statistics and Probability for Engineers*. New York: John Wiley & Sons, 1994.

Montgomery, Douglas C. *Introduction to Statistical Quality Control*, 3d ed. New York: John Wiley & Sons, 1996.

Mood, Alexander M., Graybill, Franklin A., and Boes, Duane C. *Introduction to the Theory of Statistics,* 3d ed. New York: McGraw-Hill, 1974.

Ott, Ellis R., and Schilling, Edward G. *Process Quality Control,* 2d ed. New York: McGraw-Hill, 1990.

Pall, Gabriel A. *Quality Process Management*. Englewood Cliffs, N.J.: Prentice-Hall, 1987.

Park, Robert E., et al. *Software Size Measurement: A Framework for Counting Source Statements* (CMU/SEI-92-TR-20, ADA258304). Pittsburgh, Pa.: Software Engineering Institute, Carnegie Mellon University, September 1992.

Park, Robert E., Goethert, Wolfhart B., and Florac, William A. *Goal-Driven Software Measurement—A Guidebook* (CMU/SEI-96-HB-002, ADA313946). Pittsburgh, Pa.: Software Engineering Institute, Carnegie Mellon University, July 1996.

Paulk, Mark C., et al. *Capability Maturity Model for Software, Version 1.1* (CMU/SEI-93-TR-24, ADA263403). Pittsburgh, Pa.: Software Engineering Institute, Carnegie Mellon University, February 1993.

Paulk, Mark C., et al. *Key Practices of the Capability Maturity Model, Version 1.1* (CMU/SEI-93-TR-25, ADA263432). Pittsburgh, Pa.: Software Engineering Institute, Carnegie Mellon University, February 1993.

Paulk, Mark C., et al. *The Capability Maturity Model: Guidelines for Improving the Software Process.* Reading, Mass.: Addison-Wesley, 1995.

Paulk, Mark C. "Practices of High Maturity Organizations." Proceedings of the 1999 Software Engineering Process Group Conference, Atlanta, Georgia, 28–31 March 1999.

Perry, Dewayne E., and Votta, Lawrence G. "People, Organizations, and Process Improvement." *IEEE Software* 11, no. 4 (1994):36–45.

Proschan, Frank, and Savage, I. R. "Starting a Control Chart: The Effect of Number and Size of Samples on the Level of Significance at the Start of a Control Chart for Sample Means." *Industrial Quality Control* (September 1960):12–13.

Pyzdek, Thomas. *Pyzdek's Guide to SPC: Volume One, Fundamentals.* Tucson, Ariz.: Quality Publishing, Inc., 1990.

Pyzdek, Thomas. *Pyzdek's Guide to SPC: Volume Two, Applications and Special Topics.* Tucson, Ariz.: Quality Publishing, Inc., 1992.

Quesenberry, Charles P. "The Effect of Sample Size on Estimated Limits for $\overline{X}$ and X Control Charts." *Journal of Quality Technology* 25, no. 4 (1993):237–247.

Rigdon, Steven E., Cruthis, Emma N., and Champ, Charles W. "Design Strategies for Individuals and Moving Range Control Charts." *Journal of Quality Technology* 26, no. 4 (1994):274–287.

Roes, Kit C. B., Does, Ronald J. M. M., and Schurink, Yvonne. "Shewhart-Type Control Charts for Individual Observations." *Journal of Quality Technology* 25, no. 3 (1993):188–198.

Scheuer, E. M. *Let's Teach More About Prediction,* 133–137. Proceedings of the Statistical Education Section, American Statistical Association. Washington, D.C.: American Statistical Association, 1990.

Senge, Peter M. *The Fifth Discipline Fieldbook.* New York: Doubleday, 1994.

Shewhart, Walter A. *Economic Control of Quality of Manufactured Product.* New York: Van Nostrand, 1931. (Reprinted in Milwaukee, Wisc.: American Society of Quality Control, 1980.)

Shewhart, Walter A. *Statistical Method from the Viewpoint of Quality Control.* Washington, D.C.: Graduate School of the Department of Agriculture, 1939. (Reprinted in Mineola, N.Y.: Dover Publications, Inc., 1986.)

Wadsworth, Harrison M., Stephens, Kenneth S., and Godfrey, A. Blanton. *Modern Methods for Quality Control and Improvement.* New York: John Wiley & Sons, 1986.

Western Electric Co., Inc. *Statistical Quality Control Handbook.* Indianapolis: AT&T Technologies, 1958.

Wheeler, Donald J., and Lyday, Richard W. *Evaluating the Measurement Process.* Knoxville, Tenn.: SPC Press, 1989.

Wheeler, Donald J., and Chambers, David S. *Understanding Statistical Process Control,* 2d ed. Knoxville, Tenn.: SPC Press, 1992.

Wheeler, Donald J. *Understanding Variation: The Key to Managing Chaos.* Knoxville, Tenn.: SPC Press, 1993.

Wheeler, Donald J. *Advanced Topics in Statistical Process Control.* Knoxville, Tenn.: SPC Press, 1995.

Wheeler, Donald J., and Poling, Sheila R. *Building Continual Improvement.* Knoxville, Tenn.: SPC Press, 1998.

Index

Action(s)
    "plans, preparing," 38–40
    to integrate measures, 35, 37–38
Aggregation and decomposition
    of process performance data, 150–151
Analysis
    basic description of process, 36, 65–84
    of existing measurement activities,
        35–36
    of process behavior, 65, 221–231
    portion of improving processes, 191
    process capability, 179–186
Analytic studies, 67, 212–213, 221,
    223–227
Analytic tools, 54–64
Anomalous process behavior patterns
    assignable causes and, 162–163
    basic description of, 131–136
Archiving
    process performance data, 53
Arithmetic operations
    data assessment, 49
Assignable cause(s)
    anomalous patterns and, 163
    approaches to determining, 163–175
    bunching (grouping), 135
    cycles, 132
    detection tests, 80
    finding and correcting, 155, 157
    finding reasons for, 164–175
    generic summary of, 162
    grouping (bunching), 135
    hidden sources, 151–152
    "levels, rapid shifts in," 133–134
    mapping anomalous patterns to, 162
    mixtures, 134
    noncompliance and, 159–161
    signals and patterns, 158–162

    stratification, 135–136
    trends, 132–133
    variation, 68–71, 78
Attribute charts
    anomalous patterns and, 159
    interpreting process behavior, 159
Attribute(s)
    changes to process, 188–190
    common cause, 188–190
    data, 109–123
    list of process, 28–29
    process properties, 78
    selecting process, 25–26
Attributes data 78
    control charts for, 109–123
    data, 79
    XmR charts for, 120–123
Average (x-bar) and average range
    control limit equations, 217
Average (x-bar) and average standard
    deviation, 219
Average (x-bar) and median range, 218
Average (X-bar) charts
    interpreting process behavior, 158
Average charts (x-bar charts), 73–75, 78,
    80, 86–94
Average Range constants
    table of, 217
Average(s)
    computation of, 86
    standard deviation, 91

Bar charts. *See also* Analytic Tools, 55,
    61–62
Baseline process performance
    Onboard space shuttle example,
        172–175
Bias correction factors, 94–96, 216

243